UNSHRUNK

UNSHRUNK

A Story of
•• ● Psychiatric Treatment ● ••
Resistance

LAURA DELANO

VIKING

VIKING
An imprint of Penguin Random House LLC
1745 Broadway, New York, NY 10019
penguinrandomhouse.com

Set in Birka LT Pro
Designed by *Christina Nguyen*

LIBRARY OF CONGRESS CATALOGING-IN-PUBLICATION DATA
Names: Delano, Laura, 1983– author.
Title: Unshrunk: a story of psychiatric treatment resistance / Laura Delano.
Other titles: Story of psychiatric treatment resistance
Description: New York: Viking, [2025] | Includes bibliographical references.
Identifiers: LCCN 2024026603 (print) | LCCN 2024026604 (ebook) |
ISBN 9781984880482 (hardcover) | ISBN 9781984880499 (ebook)
Subjects: LCSH: Delano, Laura, 1983—Mental health. | People with
bipolar disorder—United States—Biography. | Mental illness—
Treatment—United States—History—20th century. | Mental
illness—Treatment—United States—History—21st century. |
Bipolar disorder—Treatment—United States
Classification: LCC RC516 .D445 2025 (print) | LCC RC516 (ebook) |
DDC 616.89/50092 [B]—dc23/eng/20240620
LC record available at https://lccn.loc.gov/2024026603
LC ebook record available at https://lccn.loc.gov/2024026604

Printed in the United States of America
1st Printing

Names and identifying characteristics of the people in this story have been changed,
except for those of the author's family and of one doctor.

The authorized representative in the EU for product safety and compliance
is Penguin Random House Ireland, Morrison Chambers, 32 Nassau Street,
Dublin D02 YH68, Ireland, https://eu-contact.penguin.ie.

*To Natalie, Fred, Rob, Nicholas,
Dylan, Rhiannon, and my countless other
brothers and sisters forever lost to
For Your Own Good.*

●

'Tis the tempestuous loveliness of terror;
For from the serpents gleams a brazen glare
Kindled by that inextricable error,
Which makes a thrilling vapour of the air
Become a [ ] and ever-shifting mirror
Of all the beauty and the terror there—
A woman's countenance, with serpent locks,
Gazing in death on heaven from those wet rocks.

—Percy Bysshe Shelley

●

"There is no way out," she said, but
she took one step forward.

—Ursula K. Le Guin

●

In women, blood collected in the
breasts indicates madness.

—Hippocrates

CONTENTS

PREFACE

My youth was shaped by the language of psychiatric diagnosis. Its meticulous symptom lists and tidy categories defined my teens and twenties and determined my future. I believed that my primary condition, bipolar disorder, was an incurable brain disease that would only worsen without medications, therapy, and the occasional stay on a psych ward. This belief was further reinforced each time I heard of the tragic destruction befalling someone who stopped her meds because she thought she could outsmart her disease. I embraced the promises of a psychopharmaceutical solution, welcoming the regimen of pills I ingested in the hope that they'd bring me stability, reliability, functionality. That they'd show me what it felt like to be happy or, at the very least, have some peace of mind. That they'd maybe, one day, even provide me with the chance to feel something close to normal.

I took all of this as objective fact; who was I to question any of it? I wasn't a doctor. I hadn't gone to graduate school to become an expert in brain biochemistry. I didn't know how to interpret scientific research or comprehend dense pharmacological information. Doctors made an oath to, first, do no harm, after all. If there was a better way to resolve my dysfunctional suffering, I surely would have heard about it. My parents had the financial means to get me top-notch care from some of the nation's best doctors and psychiatric hospitals, and so we dove right in, desperate for answers, eager to get me needed relief. We accepted the grave reality that came with a disease like bipolar disorder: the unpredictable ups and downs, the inability to take on too much stress or responsibility, the many impulsive mistakes and destructive behaviors I'd engage in during unmanageable episodes, the risk I'd kill myself. For fourteen years, I lived tethered to the belief that my brain was broken, and redesigned my entire life around the singular purpose of fixing it.

If you'd told me back then that I'd one day decide to face my agonizing emotions, twisted thoughts, and relief-seeking impulses without translating them into symptoms to be treated with prescribed pharmaceuticals, I'd have called you crazy. If you'd told me that I'd eventually decide to leave behind the idea that I had serious mental illness, the only framework for understanding my emotions and behaviors that had ever made any sense to me, I'd have been offended, convinced as I was that the only way for my pain to be properly acknowledged was through its medicalization. And if you'd handed me a memoir like this, I'd have glanced at the book jacket and handed it right back, outraged at the mere insinuation that my fourteen years of self-destructive madness might never have needed meds in the first place, or been symptoms of a brain disease at all.

The simplest way to put it is that I became a professional psychiatric patient between the ages of thirteen and twenty-seven. The best way to describe what happened next is that I decided to leave behind all the diagnoses, meds, and professionals and recover myself.

There is no "antimedication" or "antipsychiatry" moral to this story; to be clear, I am neither of these things. I know that many people feel helped by psychiatric drugs, especially when they're used in the short term. I find it counterproductive to orient myself "against" anything. In fact, there is much that I am *for* in the context of this labyrinthian ecosystem we clumsily call the mental health system. First and foremost, My Body, My Choice, and the right we each have for this choice to be fully, accurately, and therefore meaningfully informed. This book is a story about informed decision-making: what it takes to make a true choice regarding psychiatric diagnoses and drugs, the repercussions when you don't have the information necessary to do so, and what happens after you realize the choices you thought you'd been making were never really choices at all.

For a long time after I made the decision to leave behind my psychiatric diagnoses and drugs, I flailed and floundered, overwhelmed by raw emotion as I faced the menace of the unknown: *How will I explain my agonizing struggle, if not with the language of mental illness? What will I strive for, if not the right treatment? What will it mean for me if I can no longer explain away my hurtful behaviors as symptoms of a faulty brain?* I navigated the brutal aftermath of stopping psychiatric drugs in constant panic: *Can I really survive without my meds? What if it was a terrible decision to think I don't need them? What if I'll never be stable? What if I actually* do *have bipolar disorder and it gets far worse? What if those doctors were right and I can't manage on my own? What if I kill myself?* I was unsure of truth and delusion, right and wrong, and where I even belonged, but in the eye of that storm— at the culmination of this disintegration of self—I realized there was a force pushing me forward: curiosity. *If I don't actually have a chronic, serious mental illness that requires me to take meds for the rest of my life, what could my life become?*

It's been fourteen years since I last took a psychiatric drug or looked in the mirror and saw a list of psychiatric symptoms looking back—and not because I no longer experience intense emotional pain and paranoia and debilitating anxiety and unhelpful impulses, which I still very much do. Right now, were I to go through the *Diagnostic and Statistical Manual of Mental Disorders (DSM)*, psychiatry's diagnostic bible, I'd meet the criteria for several of its diagnoses. But here's the thing: I no longer view this textbook as a legitimate or relevant source of information about myself, nor do I have any use for the various diagnoses it would tell me I have. While a lot in my life has changed for the better as a direct result of healing my brain and body from psychopharmaceuticals, much of what happens in the space between my ears is as dark and messy as ever. (In some cases, more so.) When it comes to the inner workings of my mind, the primary difference is that I'm no longer afraid of what I find there.

I was once mentally ill, and now I'm not, and it wasn't because I was misdiagnosed. I wasn't improperly medicated or overmedicated. I haven't miraculously recovered from supposed brain diseases that some of the country's top psychiatrists told me I'd have for the rest of my life. In fact, I was properly diagnosed and medicated according to the American Psychiatric Association's standard of care. The reason I'm no longer mentally ill is that I made a decision to question the ideas about myself that I'd assumed were fact and discard what I learned was actually fiction. This book is a record of my psychiatric treatment, my resistance to that treatment, and what I've learned along the way about my pain. I decided to live beyond labels and categorical boxes and to reject the dominant role that the American mental health industry has come to play in shaping the way we make sense of what it means to be human. This book—these pages, this story, my story—is a record that has been unshrunk.

PART

I

The Mirror

It happened in front of the mirror as I brushed my teeth one Thursday evening. The year was 1996, and I was thirteen. Outside, the trees were thick and verdant, still weeks away from morphing into the polychromatic splendor of fall. Eighth grade had just begun, which meant goodbye to summer sports camps, mornings at the country club pool, beach days under the Maine sun. I was now faced with the upcoming season of national squash tournaments, schoolwork, and my new responsibilities as incoming middle school president, which included standing with our headmistress each Friday morning to lead assembly. My bones buzzed with this unfamiliar social power I possessed: elected leader, role model, student of character. I wasn't sure which feeling to trust in my gut, the thrill or the terror.

There I stood at the sink: thin arms, broad shoulders, lean, muscular legs covered with picked scabs and their purple consequences. My dirty-blond hair, chopped close to my chin, was flattened on my head from spending the evening in a baseball hat. I was aswim in my favorite T-shirt, the one that said "Hockey Is Life: The Rest Is Just Details." Over my underwear, I wore my favorite pair of boys' polka-dot boxer shorts.

What happened next as I watched myself in the mirror that night still feels close enough to describe like it's happening now: The edges of my vision start to blur. My arms become gangly foreign objects that seem to have sealed themselves to my shoulder sockets. My eyes lock straight ahead against my will, taking me down a narrowing pastel tunnel that morphs to gray and then black. All that's left is my visage in the glass. I stare, leaning closer over the sink, riveted by the sight of my face, my eyes. This face, these eyes. That girl's face and her eyes. A stranger now in front of me, someone I don't recognize. *Who is she?* For a brief moment, I'm curious.

And then: terror grabs my ankles, shooting up my legs, through my gut, up the sides of my throat to the back of my skull. I disintegrate into a million pieces, floating, fuzzy, disembodied in space, feet gone, nothing locking me to the earth, no legs, no arms, no belly, nothing: *I am nothing. I am nothing. I am nothing.*

There is only the tunnel through the dark to this stranger. Her brow is furrowed, her mouth agape, those blue eyes wide open with black bullets at their centers.

Why is she staring at me? I blink to see if this unfamiliar girl will go away, but she doesn't.

Eventually I notice that when I move my hand, she moves hers. When I turn my chin to the left, to the right, she goes right, then left. Somehow, I'm not sure how, I can see that we're connected. I struggle to make sense of what this means, to differentiate what's real from what isn't: *Okay, this glass is a mirror, this girl is my reflection, she is me, I am her.* But something feels fundamentally different. *Who am I? Who am I? Who am I?* The question loops on repeat until the words become meaningless sounds.

I am no longer the girl who loved to play board games against herself, or the one who created stacks of index cards on which she'd write facts about her favorite animals that she'd obsessively study until memorized. The one who swelled with pride each time she beat a boy on the tennis court, and who trained several times a week to get herself a top ten national squash ranking. The girl who looked forward to her afternoon ritual of grabbing a hunk of Cheddar cheese and a hard pretzel after practice before sitting down to do homework while listening to Billy Joel. I had no idea who that girl was anymore. All I knew was that she was someone else.

I left the bathroom in a daze, passing walls decorated with framed Christmas card photos of my two younger sisters and me in color co-ordination; a black-and-white picture of my twentysomething parents walking hand in hand in white lace and black tails down the aisle of a giant Manhattan church; an old photograph of my relative, Franklin Delano Roosevelt, aged ten or so, leaning on the net of the family's grass tennis court at their Hudson River estate alongside a dozen cousins and his grandfather; my father's collected oil paintings of beach scenes, his woodblock prints of old farmhouses.

Excruciating thoughts raced through my mind that night in bed as I tried to make sense of what had just happened: *I must not have a real self. My whole life's been fake. All those good grades and accomplishments and expectations I've been working for don't mean anything. It's all a performance—I'm just a fraud who's been tricking everyone into thinking I'm Laura, and I'm so good at it that I've even tricked myself. Is anything I've accomplished actually what I wanted? Do I actually care about the things I've always thought I care about? Have I just been brainwashed by them? Did they make me do it?*

I'd always taken the opinions of others as trusted signposts on the path to worthiness: a classmate's compliment on my painting, gratitude from a friend's parent as I cleared the dinner table, the smile of an elderly stranger after I held the door open for her. Absence of approval felt indistinguishable from blunt criticism, and it was the praise of adult authority figures that I most craved. By listening carefully to what I was told, following the rules, studying hard, practicing diligently, I would one day grow so saturated with external approval that it would no longer need to be the animating force of my life. Now this unfamiliar, nefarious *they* swirled in my mind, quickly becoming obvious as the cause of my newly discovered fraudulence. *They* were a dark force that was not to be trusted: my parents, my teachers, my school, the manicured hedges and bright smiles that characterized my affluent hometown. It seemed so clear now: *they* controlled me. *They* controlled all girls. *They convince us we have to look a certain way, talk a certain way, perform a certain way*, I thought. *We're just puppets.*

The only option I saw before me was to run away and make a fresh start. I'd move to Maine, where my grandmother lived in the 250-year-old farmhouse where she and Grampy had raised my father, aunt, and uncle. I'd spent every year looking forward to August, when my mother would drive my sisters and me up there for the month and my father would join us on weekends after work. I spent my days scouring tide pools for crabs, building drip castles with Mom out of muddy sand, reading books on the porch as I listened to peepers in the bog at dusk. I popped bubbly seaweed between my fingers as I watched Dad fish for striped bass along the rocky coast. He'd let me stand in front of him to have a turn casting, wrapping his arms around my shoulders to help me reel in the line when I was too small to do it alone, and when I grew big enough to manage the rod by myself, he'd stand back and take a swig from his sweaty can of Fresca as he watched. My legs were always decorated with mosquito bites, my feet splintered from barefoot trips through the old barn to find empty swallows' eggs. On overcast days, the low drone of a nearby foghorn added to the soundtrack of chugging lobster boat engines and occasional tugboat horns, these, the only sounds that reminded me there was a world out there that I was so afraid I'd never be good enough for.

In Maine, I could pretend life back home in Greenwich had never existed, and so I resolved to endure the next twenty-four hours until I could sit down with my parents and let them know I planned to leave it all behind.

The morning after the mirror, as I pulled on my polo shirt and buttoned my school kilt, I was flooded with a new understanding: The uniform was a costume. School, a performance.

Breakfast looked the same as always: My two sisters sitting next to me swinging their feet from rickety wooden stools at the kitchen table. Nina, three years younger than me, was a lover of Eloise books and an avid POG collector; Chase, six years my junior, already shared my obsessions with ice hockey and boys' clothes. The glass jar of whole milk that had been delivered by the milkman on the counter next to our Lucky Charms, Multi Grain Cheerios, and Müeslix boxes. Mom flipping through her worn leather organizer, scanning each page of flawless cursive writing that carefully mapped out our days as a cup of creamy coffee steamed next to her and she strummed the counter with manicured fingers.

I can picture myself sitting there, trying my best to participate, to feel authentic in my eating, my reading, my talking, my good posture, to not implode. But I'd fallen into the space between my ears and was pounding on the walls to get out.

A sea of hunter-green tartan overwhelmed me as I stood next to our headmistress at the front of the assembly hall an hour later.

Two hundred little bodies sat before us, elbows pushing into thighs, chins nestled into cupped hands, eyes locked on me. Mrs. Franklin's voice was dull and muffled, like she was coming out of a radio fifty feet away. I stared ahead and unfocused my eyes until the hall faded into a calming blur. And then reality clenched my neck. *I am actually up here onstage in front of everyone.* She'd been talking for a while, about what I wasn't sure. I looked down and noticed how clumsy my hands seemed, connected to these clunky arm things. I panicked that the back of my kilt was stuck in the waistband of my boxers, ran my palms beneath the loose pleats behind me as subtly as possible, and sighed relief as my fingertips traced the worn wool. I pictured strings coming up through my hands and arms and feet and legs, up from my head. I forced myself to take a deep breath, lift my chin, and set my shoulders back, wondering who was controlling me now.

Our living room was less a space we lived in and more one used for social rituals like the occasional cocktail party, a visit from the distant, elderly cousin of a grandparent, or the annual opening of Christmas stockings as Bing Crosby played on repeat. I don't know why my parents and I sat there the evening after that first assembly, but I remember how hard I prayed to a God I didn't believe in that I'd get what I was about to ask for.

I took a deep breath and told my parents the plan. "I can't be middle school president. I can't go to Greenwich Academy. I can't be here anymore. I want to go live with Grammy in Maine and start school there. Start over."

My mother cocked her head and looked at me like I was a crooked painting. "Laura, I don't understand. What happened? Where is this coming from?" My father sat quietly next to her.

I shook my head in frustration, my body suddenly tight. *No, no, no, it's not meant to go like this.* Screaming felt like the only expression intense enough to mirror what was happening inside me. I sensed where this was going, and it was nowhere good.

"Nothing happened! I just can't be here anymore. Please, I hate it here. Please just let me go!"

"Laura, you can't just move to Maine," my father said. "What about all your friends here? Your teachers? Your coaches? You can't just leave everything behind. You have a big year ahead of you. And you can't live with Grammy. That'd be too much to ask of her. Maine is a place for us to visit, not live."

I closed my eyes and shook my head vigorously, as if doing so might freeze the scene. "Please. *Please.* PLEASE let me go!" I pleaded, wringing my hands in front of me, overwhelmed by an urge to stomp my feet. If only I could make them understand why this was so important, but I couldn't tell them that I'd realized I was a fraud, that I didn't have a real self, that Maine was the only place that could save me. My parents were a part of the problem, after all.

"I hate you! I hate my life!" I screamed. "Fuck you!" My parents were shocked. I couldn't believe I'd uttered the word myself.

"What have we done? Why are you so angry?" My mother's eyes were tearing up and tinged with panic; I could feel her hurt. I paced the room, wanting to rip my hair out, whacking my sides with balled-up fists.

"I can't handle the pressure. Can't handle it. I can't handle it!" My screams escalated until it felt like my throat was ripping open. I coughed involuntarily, gasped for air, and then screamed again, and again, and again, as my parents sat there wide-eyed. I stormed out of the room, seeping a new, rancid rage. It was rage, I can see now, that seemed the best means of self-protection. Like a siren song, rage beckoned me: *Shoot me at them so they can't control you anymore. I'll keep you safe. I'll protect you.*

TWO

My First Therapist

Not long after that argument about Maine, my parents brought me to my first therapist. Her name was Emma, and they told me that she worked with families and would be helping us. She happened to live half a mile up the street, but the three of us drove to her home office on a weekend morning for our first session. As I stepped inside the waiting room, the force of shame was so heavy on my shoulders that I nearly collapsed in upon myself. I tightened up to keep from disappearing: shoulders to ears, arms locked, fists and jaw clenched, neck muscles contracted. I sat down and locked my gaze on the carpet until its hard patterns melted into softness. Bewildered by my parents selling me out like this, I was no longer willing to meet their eyes, nor able to.

Emma welcomed us into her office. Her voice had this warm, crackling-embers sound about it—I always think of Judi Dench when I recall her—and I was convinced it was the sound of everything wrong with the world. She had a short mop of white hair, wide hips beneath ankle-length pants, a soft stomach. The sight of her made me want to vomit. The instant her sparkling eyes made contact with mine and she smiled, I hated her.

I carry a faded snapshot of that first session in my mind: My parents, Emma, and I are sitting on chairs in a circle in her cozy office.

I'm hunched in my seat, arms crossed tightly over my chest, brow furrowed. To my left, my father is wearing a worn dress shirt tucked into old jeans; he has the body language of someone unselfconscious, relaxed but attentive. To Dad's left, my mother wears a cashmere sweater, cigarette-cut slacks, and needlepointed slip-on shoes; her arms, like mine, are crossed in front of her; she's taut and tense, mouth closed.

My most valuable artifact from that day is pure emotion, preserved in me, all these years later, like a prehistoric insect in amber: Shame radiating out from my face, despair surging within me. My throat closed, voice powerless. Panic in my chest as I felt all of their eyes home in on me like laser beams, penetrating my insides against my will.

Emma was only pretending to be kind and really wanted to control me, I felt, so I switched instantly into surveillance mode, scanning the room in self-protective sweeps, sure of what my mind was telling me: *They're lying when they say this lady is going to help all of us. I know they think I'm the problem, not them.*

My conviction would be reinforced in the coming days, when my mother would tell me I was to continue therapy with Emma, only moving ahead, I'd walk up the hill to see her by myself.

Not long after I started therapy, I drank alcohol for the first time. From the garage at a slumber party emerged a warm six-pack, this glistening beacon calling me toward rebellion. I watched the first can as it passed from hand to hand, *Yes no yes no, do it, you can't, do it, you can't* pinging about in my head. I knew that saying yes would mean the loss of something, but when I took that first sip, there was only an unfamiliar and comforting warmth in my gut.

None of us ever got anywhere close to drunk that year, but that wasn't the point. It was the meaning behind the act that mattered: breaking rules we'd been taught to never break, feeling the solidarity that arose from participating in the very things we were sure we'd never partake in. I'd duped myself by thinking that being good would help me feel worthy, but the night in the mirror had proved me wrong. Where else had I duped myself? What else had I been missing?

The quest to dismantle my moral framework continued through the summer. At mountain biking camp, I abandoned my yearslong dream of having my first kiss with Harris Fowler, the boy whose heart-covered initials I'd been decorating binders with since playing on rival ice hockey teams in fifth grade. Instead, one night, I found myself outside a tent kissing a boy I barely knew, giving away an experience I now believed I'd tricked myself into thinking should be special. I broke up with him a few days later and had kissed another boy by camp's end.

That August at tennis camp in Maine, I developed a fierce crush on a boy named Jake. One side of his head was buzzed, and the long wave of blond hair on the other was always carefully swept over the top. He was ruddy skinned, rosy cheeked. When we began catching each other's eyes over the picnic table at lunch and I felt a surge of excitement at the thought of being desired, I was sure I'd fallen for him.

One night at a friend's house, we drank beer and Jake led me through the dark to a trampoline. We lay down to look up at the clear night sky, and then he leaned over and began kissing me, deep, like he was trying to recover something he'd dropped at the bottom of my throat. I wondered if this was love. When he went to touch my butt, I let him. When he slipped his hands around my back to push up my training bra, I let him, too, despite the deep-down part of me calling out, *What are you doing? This isn't who you are.* The trampoline was taut and smooth beneath my palms; as he covered my stomach with his hands and mouth, I looked up at the stars and pictured myself far away.

As I lay in bed that night, I thought about how different I felt, how I'd left something behind that I couldn't exactly define. A new and wondrous thought dawned on me: *Maybe being bad will make everyone stop believing in you.*

Jake gave me a bunch of handpicked flowers the next week and called hours later to say he had something to tell me. I was staring out the window over the fields that made their way to the sea as I heard the words "I love you." It was fear I felt at first, and then disgust, and then numbness. How easy it was, I remarked to myself, to go from feeling so much to feeling nothing at all.

I sensed that even more freedom awaited me if I could only muster the courage to slack off in school that fall. Once ninth grade was under way, I disappointed myself by clicking right back into the pursuit of good grades, active class participation. At home, I quickly shed the facade, letting all the resentment I'd held in at school surge forth through the evening. Requests to help out with dishes or join the family at dinner made me lash out like a trapped animal. My perplexed mother couldn't understand what had happened to me, or how this seething menace of a daughter could possibly be the same one she was hearing such glowing reports about from teachers, coaches, and other parents: "She's such a leader." "She's so polite." "She's kind to everyone." "She did such a fantastic job as president last year."

In sessions with Emma, which continued against my will, I vented anger into the otherwise awkward silence: School was a scam! Being trapped at home every night was my idea of hell! I'm so mad, I could just punch a wall! And then the hour would be over, and Emma would gently escort me out into the dusk, and I'd walk home, disoriented and vulnerable.

For all my confusion, I was sure of one thing: I wasn't the problem. It was everyone around me who was, in my newly judgmental estimation, from the many classmates who didn't seem to realize that we were all puppets to my teachers for their ongoing compliments about my academic prowess and my squash coach for suggesting I add another weekly clinic to my calendar because he could see my potential as a top national contender. The biggest problem needing intervention, as I saw it, was my parents, who insisted that I stay at Greenwich Academy. It was clear to me that they had no plans to change themselves, which I took as further confirmation that they saw me as the only defective part of our family. To make matters worse, my mother requested that I not tell anyone I was in therapy. Who did she think she was, making me see this therapist I didn't want to see while also telling me I had to keep it a secret? I assumed she'd made this request because she was ashamed of me, unable to bear the thought of her friends hearing that Laura Delano, once this promising young role model, was actually a dysfunctional failure. It didn't occur to me that her fixation on maintaining a veneer of normalcy was actually fueled by her desire to insulate me from harm.

A group of us were at a friend's house for a sleepover one Saturday night that fall. Among us was my new friend, Rose, whose boyfriend, Pete, was staying at a house in the same gated community. Rose had a bad reputation among parents and teachers (I'd recently smoked my first cigarette with her). She was equal parts accomplished and rebellious, which gave her a miraculous aura of competency and chaos. She didn't seem to care what anyone thought about her but still got straight As. She had what I wanted: the ability to mock the game we were stuck playing while also winning it.

Rose begged me to go along with her to see Pete; I felt honored that she'd picked me as her companion. It was nearly eleven o'clock when we readied ourselves to walk the ten minutes it'd take to get there. We ignored our friends' protests that it was too late to go out, padded quietly down the stairs, and left them staring down at us nervously as we headed out the door.

Pete welcomed us in at the back door of John's house. We walked into a finished basement with a giant TV, sofa, pool table. I'd never met John before; he was a quiet sophomore who always seemed to be standing on his tiptoes behind his popular classmates at the all-boys school that sat across the street from our all-girls academy.

I remember the four of us played pool, drank beer. I remember Pete nuzzling Rose's neck, and how she told him girlishly to stop it. I remember John's eyes on my face as the television flickered on low in the background, and how I eventually looked back at him, held his gaze for two seconds, and then five, and then ten. I remember how the tipsier I got, the easier it felt to trick myself into thinking that maybe this was a guy I could like. With time, I got woozy. At one point, I lay down on the couch, looked sideways at the screen, savored how slow-motion life felt there, the way the air seemed to roll like waves of water.

When Rose and Pete eventually disappeared, John sat next to me. We didn't talk much as the television beamed on us. He asked if I wanted to go upstairs, and I said okay. I felt dizzy when I stood, the floor pulling at my left side, and he offered me his hand. He asked if he could carry me, and I nodded, wondering if it might be romantic. I felt so light in his arms as he took each step. I'd never been carried by a boy before.

He laid me down on a bed. Climbed on top of me. Began kissing me, me letting him. His hand pushed my shirt up, slowly at first, then faster, impatient, fumbling about with my bra strap. I was in and out of presence, participating while also a separate observer of the scene. The silent something deep in me that screamed *stop* was far less powerful than the need to feel wanted. The room was spinning, the pressure of his lips on mine, that tongue down my throat, the sound of his heavy breath, the weight of his torso, the heat off his skin.

I don't know how long we were on that bed. There was the feeling of being devoured, my confusion about whether this was a sensation to be excited about or terrified by, the strangeness in realizing I felt nothing.

At some point, John moved his hands down and went for the button of my pants. A voice in me, from where I didn't know, said, "Stop stop stop, please stop."

I pushed my palms against his chest. He sat back, out of breath, respectful of my request. I fixed my bra and shirt and steadied myself as best I could on my feet. Downstairs, as I waited for Rose to return, we said nothing to each other. I wasn't angry. I didn't feel violated. I was confused.

As we stumbled back to our friend's house, Rose jabbed my arm with her elbow. "So, John, huh?" She threw me a sideways smile before getting back to puffing her cigarette. I forced a giggle.

I'd actively participated in this encounter with John but couldn't shake the feeling that the girl back there had been someone else. Was I a slut now? I'd heard this word from mothers before, mine included, and knew it would be terrible to get called one. I thought about the likelihood of rumors spreading to my classmates, to their mothers, to *my* mother. I made a vow to pretend the experience with John had never happened and to never share a word of it with anyone else, but the image of that girl on her back on the bed, shirt pushed up, that square-headed boy with buzzed hair on top of her, panting: it was frozen on the backs of my eyelids.

"Please don't tell anyone, okay?"

Rose looked over with a playful smirk. "Maybe."

"Please, I'm serious, okay? Swear you won't tell anyone?" Sensing my growing panic, she promised.

The house was unlocked when we returned. We snuck quietly up the stairs.

"Oh my God, you're back!" someone whispered loudly. A friend's gaze zeroed in on me, followed by her voice. "Wait . . . what *is* that, Laura?"

The way she emphasized *is* made me wonder if I smelled bad. She walked toward me, hinging at the waist to peer closely at my neck. I froze.

"Laura . . . is that a . . . a hickey?"

I wasn't even sure what a hickey was. I pushed past the girls and locked myself in the bathroom. There were soft knocks, my name whispered urgently. Pinching my eyes shut, I braced myself for whatever I was about to see in the mirror. Two purply red circles the size of walnuts plastered across the side of my neck. Lips had been on me. Now everyone knew it.

In an instant, control of my life's narrative was ripped from my grasp. After a childhood fueled by an abiding commitment to honesty, I walked numbly to unlock the door and face their concerned looks. A response surged up in me, and out slurred a voice I didn't recognize. "Idunno whatchyour talkin'about."

I let my friends run with the story from there: I was totally blacked out, not partway blurry. At some point, "blacked out" morphed into "passed out," which I didn't correct. Ten minutes later, I was sitting clothed in the shower as water streamed down on me and I cried. I wasn't crying about what had happened with John, but my friends took the tears as a victim's reckoning with what had been done to me. They got me out of the shower and helped me change into my pajamas and they held me and comforted me until we all fell asleep. I let them do all of this, for how long it had been since I'd felt taken care of.

That Monday morning, the bruises taunted me in the mirror. I fiddled with the concealer I'd snatched surreptitiously from my mother's dressing table, dabbing at my neck desperately as layer after layer of cakey substance did nothing to hide the monstrous purple. A turtleneck would be my only option. I ran to my closet and slipped one on.

Later, in English class, there was a knock on the door. My teacher stepped out for a moment before returning and looking at me.

"Laura, you're needed in the office." I stood up and walked robotically down the hall to the office of the headmistress, where I was told that Danielle, the upper school counselor, would like to see me.

Danielle had gray-flecked hair cut close to her head. One of her ears was lined with gold studs. She wore Puma sneakers and casually cuffed pants and insisted on being called by her first name. You could reliably find at least two girls shooting the breeze with her between classes; focused as I was on compartmentalizing the humiliation I felt before the gaze of a therapist, I'd always reassured myself I'd never be one of them. It was hard enough to survive each session with Emma, who skillfully kept the focus on my anger and its destructive by-products: the screaming, pushing, threats of hitting, and cruel, hateful words. "How can we help you feel happier?" she'd ask. "How can we help you stop feeling so angry?" Murderous rage overtook me at her presumptuousness that she and I were a "we," which most certainly was not the case. The true "we," I knew, was Emma and my parents, who discussed the content of our sessions in phone calls. I knew that I had no power to free myself from these oppressive adults, and with my put-together performance at school already diffi-cult enough to maintain, I felt sure that I'd disintegrate if I showed even an ounce of that powerlessness to my teachers. I'd successfully convinced myself that the humiliating walks to and from each ses-sion with Emma were the tragic fate of some other girl, but now these two disparate realities seemed to be smacking hard into each other.

Danielle was sitting at her desk facing the open door when I ar-rived, and gave me an austere smile. "Hi, Laura. I'm Danielle." She gestured toward a chair. I walked in cautiously, smoothed out my kilt behind me, sat down.

"So, I wanted to invite you here in case there was anything you wanted to talk about."

I shook my head, willing my eyes to keep contact with hers.

"Laura, I get that you're not wanting to talk, so I'll just . . . Listen, I'll just come out with it. I heard some concerning rumors this morn-ing. I just wanted to check in with you, see if you're okay, see if there's anything you want to get off your mind."

There was a surge of rage, the urge to cry, and a tamping down of it all. *Who told on me?*

"Anything about the weekend you'd like to share? C'mon, Laura. Your friends are worried. People care about you."

"I'm fine."

"You know you can say anything in here. That's what I'm here for. What you share won't leave this office. You know that, right?"

I didn't trust her, but I knew I wouldn't get out of there unless I talked, and so I told her about John—not what actually happened but the story I'd let my friends believe.

Later that morning, I was called back to the headmistress's office. My mother was on her way to pick me up, the secretary said. *What does she mean, my mother's coming to pick me up?* And then it hit me: Danielle had betrayed my trust.

I was waiting outside a few minutes later when my mother's car pulled up. I slid into the passenger seat and buckled myself in, hugging my backpack and pressing my face into its creases. The corner of a binder pressed on my eye socket, and I kept it there, eyes closed, fantasizing about pushing it all the way through.

"Do I need to take you to the hospital?" Her voice wavered. We didn't look at each other. I shook my head silently. "Well, I'm taking you there."

"No, don't, Mom, please. I don't need to go there. I just want to go home." Unable to bear the silence, I added with a wince, "We didn't go that far."

"How could you let this happen?" She shook her head and smacked her hands on the steering wheel before pulling out with a jerk. I sank down into the leather, wishing she couldn't see me anymore, that the whole world would just forget I ever existed. I hated her for asking me this question, unable to recognize that her anger was a disguise for terror. I wished I had an answer for her as I stared out the window and said nothing.

THREE

Do You Know What Mania Is?

A winter evening my freshman year, just after coming home from squash practice. It had been varsity team photo shoot day, the ten of us girls posed in our white pleated skirts with hunter green trim, the collars of our white shirts mostly popped, faces flushed with sweat, painted with bright smiles. I went upstairs to the bathroom, locked the door behind me, turned the shower and sink on. My sisters were in their rooms; my mother, in the kitchen starting dinner; Dad, on the train home from Grand Central. I felt cold. Empty. I took the sweatband off my wrist and threw it in the hamper. Walked over to the shower, grabbed my razor, and returned to the sink. Ran water through the blades. Pulled out stuck hairs. Dried the razor off on my monogrammed hand towel. Pushed the blades up against my skin, next to the existing parallel scab lines on the underside of my wrist. I paused for a moment before slowly sliding right. The momentary pinch was followed by absence. The graceful dance of blood with gravity. I regarded the streams of red running down my skin with the cool detachment of an art critic. I held my arm under the water's steady flow, savoring its sting on the open slits of flesh, watching the rivulets of crimson disappear.

Over the months to come, I worked hard to find fault in just about everything my mother did. I was constantly yelling. I had chronic headaches because of how much I scowled. I occasionally resorted to pushing, even hitting, and sometimes chased down my younger sisters with a raised hand. I baffled myself with these behaviors but nonetheless felt at their mercy. I dreaded school each morning because I couldn't be sure who knew about John and who didn't. There were the paranoid ruminations on the long list of words I was sure flitted through people's heads at the sight of me: *Slut. Whore. Pathetic. Dirty. Disgusting. Trash. Ruined.* I yearned for weekends, when I'd begun to get drunk enough to trick myself, for just a little while, into thinking I had the capacity to feel good.

Emma eventually declared me too serious a case for therapy alone, informing my parents that I needed a more substantive intervention. "There's a wonderful psychiatrist in town," she said. "I think she'll be very helpful for Laura."

One day after school, my mother took me to meet Dr. Patel, my first psychiatrist. We pulled up to a small, white shingled house at the top of a short, steep driveway on a quiet cul-de-sac. Without saying anything, I opened the door, turned my back on her, and retreated into my coat before walking away. In the waiting room, my body thrummed with rage at her for leaving me there, even though she was the last person I wanted to be around.

Ten minutes after the hour, the doorknob clicked. I looked up, and there she was. In her midforties, the psychiatrist was strikingly beautiful. Her glossy shoulder-length dark brown hair framed even glossier green eyes. She wore an off-white crepe pantsuit. A small dog sat panting at her feet.

"You must be Laura. Welcome. I'm Dr. Anuja Patel. But you can call me Anuja. Please come with me."

Her outstretched arm beckoned me to a large sofa. I sent daggers at her back with my eyes as she walked across the room to a simple wooden chair. She picked up a notepad and pen, rested them on her lap, and crossed her hands delicately over them. Her dog curled itself comfortably on the floor between us, tucking its head between rust-colored paws. I hated the sight of it—and I loved dogs.

"So, I'd like to welcome you here, Laura. I'm a psychiatrist who works with children and adults."

I said nothing. She tilted her head and looked at me softly.

"So, Laura. Why do you think you're here?"

Looking down, I pushed my lips together and shrugged. "I dunno. Because my parents want me to be here?" I picked at my nails, scratched at the sofa fibers, anything to avoid meeting her eyes.

"Well, you see, Laura, they are very concerned about you. Very worried. It sounds like you've been having a tough time. Emma called to see if I can be of assistance to you and your family. You've been seeing Emma for some time now, is that right?"

I nodded, looking past her shoulder, out the window at the darkening sky behind naked trees. To my right, a floor-to-ceiling bookshelf with rows of tomes I assumed were about how to fix messed-up kids like me. Diplomas on the wall, these presentations of medical legitimacy that even my young mind could grasp meant authority.

I fought the impulse to stand up and flee, sensing that doing so would only get me in more trouble. Looking at the basket of toys sitting by Anuja's chair, I imagined a young child playing while her mother talked about her problems, wishing I could be that girl, so innocent.

"Why don't you tell me a little bit about what's been going on, Laura, what's been troubling you."

I replayed the Danielle debacle in my head, reminding myself that my words had the potential to destroy me; I would not make the same mistake this time. But as the session unfolded, and Anuja found ways to ask me the same questions over and over, approached from different angles, my resolve began to buckle. I eventually spewed everything out: how when I got sucked into a rage at home there was no stopping me, my screaming and cursing, the occasional hitting, the cutting with my razor, my night with John and the same story I'd let my friends believe about it, the drinking, the endless paranoid thoughts about people judging me and being repulsed by me, how hopeless I was. Anuja paid careful attention as I vented and fumed and rambled and shut myself up and started again and cried and got worked up and cursed and bounced my knee and cried some more and blew my nose and picked at a scab and rolled my eyes and stared off into space and sighed. The more I spoke, the more she asked. The more she asked, the more information I offered up against my will. *Why are you doing this?* I pleaded silently with myself. *Why can't you just shut up?*

"Laura, these emotions I'm seeing, and all this rage"—the word *rage* said with just a touch of emphasis, the *r* rolled softly like a cat's purr—"the things you're doing at home. The cutting. Hurting your mother. The sexual assault. This is all very concerning to hear."

I cringed at the term *sexual assault* as she continued. "It's normal to be angry or sad sometimes, but these behaviors, they aren't typical. Do you know what mania is, Laura?"

I shook my head.

"Well, many of these things you describe, they are signs of something we call mania."

Everything suddenly brighter, louder, harsher: Anuja's voice and face and pantsuit, the chair and rug and bookshelves, my inflamed cuticles, the scratchy wool of my kilt. Emma never used a word like this to describe me.

"Mania is a symptom of a disease called bipolar disorder. It used to be called manic depression. Maybe you've heard of that?"

What I wanted to say was *Yes, I have, and FUCK YOU.*

"Based on everything you've shared today, and what I've learned from Emma and your parents, it's clear to me that you're suffering from this illness. Has anyone ever told you this before?"

No one ever had. I'd heard the word *bipolar* before, but never once in relation to me. All I knew was that it meant "really crazy."

She went on to tell me that mania in children typically manifests as intense anger and irritability, impulsivity, outbursts, rapid changes in mood. And on the flip side, my self-harm, isolating behaviors, and hopelessness were signs of depression. Put together, these symptoms were clearly consistent with a diagnosis of bipolar disorder, for which there was no cure. I'd have this disease for the rest of my life.

I shook my head in disagreement.

"I know this is a lot to take in. Try to understand, with therapy and proper medications, you can live a very good, manageable life."

"Nope." I stared at her defiantly for a second before looking away. While I may have been confused about who I was, I knew clear as day that this was a false proclamation. "No way."

She continued like she hadn't heard me. "I'm going to write you a prescription for some medicines that will help you. They'll make your emotions more stable. You'll have fewer rages. They should help you feel happier. You want to feel happier, Laura, don't you?"

I was an ashamed, bewildered fourteen-year-old girl overwhelmed by painful emotion. I didn't understand who I was or where I belonged. *Of course I want to be happy*, I wished I could say. But not this way, not with pills doled out by some doctor. I knew I could never again articulate to an adult the true depths of my pain, that doing so would only lead to further betrayal. I was in a battle to protect myself. Opening up would be tantamount to defeat. I said nothing. Anuja kept talking.

"One is Depakote, a new medication that's shown great promise in helping to balance out ups and downs, and the other you've probably heard of before, Prozac, which will help with your depression." I sat in shock as she wrote out scripts for the mood stabilizer and antidepressant. She ripped them cleanly off the pad, leaned over, and handed them to me. I stared in disbelief at the incoherent scribbles. "Please have your mother call me tomorrow so we can set up another appointment for next week. I think seeing each other weekly will be very helpful. That's all for tonight." She stood up with a smile and put out her arm, hand upturned, fingers toward the door.

I floated down the hall with that fluffy dog behind me, through the waiting room and out the door into the cold, darkening air, down the long steps to the street, where my mother waited in the car, engine running. I was unsure of what had just happened, knowing only that I had these two sheets of paper in my pocket and that Anuja had stolen something unspeakable from me.

I slipped into the passenger seat with my head hung low.

"How was it?"

"Fine," I mumbled, handing my mother the two prescriptions. "I'm meant to take these."

"Oh." She looked down at them for a moment, betraying no emotion. "I'll take those to the pharmacy in the morning."

All these years later, I can only hypothesize that my mother's neutral expression was a panicked attempt to suppress shock: never once in our family had the topic of psychiatric medications come up, nor had I ever heard of any relatives or friends taking them; I imagine my mother had never entertained the possibility that one of her children would one day be in need of such drastic intervention. Betrayed and alone as I then felt, though, I mistook her blank expression as a mask over what I assumed was actually triumph. My cruel parents and these awful shrinks, as I saw it, had won.

FOUR

Ask Your Doctor If Depakote and Prozac Are Right for You(r Child)

There were a number of important facts about Depakote and Prozac that I didn't know when Anuja prescribed them to me, things that would have been impossible for me to have uncovered, young as I was and with the internet just budding. This was 1997, and at that point, neither drug had been approved by the U.S. Food and Drug Administration (FDA) for psychiatric use in children. Prozac didn't gain this approval until the early aughts; as of 2024, Depakote still doesn't have it. In fact, if you look at the official drug label for Depakote—not the patient pamphlet you're handed at the pharmacy but the complete fifty-seven-page label on the FDA website—it states that only one trial was conducted on 150 children to determine the psychiatric efficacy of Depakote and that such efficacy "was not established."

Anuja was prescribing these drugs to me off label—meaning for a use or to a specific population that has not been determined by the FDA to be safe or effective. (It is legal for medical professionals to prescribe drugs off label to their patients, and, at least in the psychiatric context, this is not uncommon.) Depakote was approved in

1995 for the treatment of mania in adults based on two trials that each lasted three weeks. In one trial, patients were put into either a placebo or a Depakote group; in the other, a placebo, a Depakote, or a lithium group. Before patients were started on their respective trial drugs, psychiatrists scored them using subjective rating scales that included measures like how fast they seemed to be speaking, how distractible they appeared, and how well groomed they seemed. At the end of three weeks, the scores were calculated again and compared with the previous ones. Averaging the two studies, in the opinions of the assessing researchers, 59 percent of the Depakote-taking patients showed at least a 30 percent reduction in symptom score compared with about 28 percent of their placebo-taking counterparts. (For reference, on the sixty-point Young Mania Rating Scale, which was used in the first trial, your score would vary by eight points if you appeared "hostile" or "uncooperative" on one day compared with appearing to have no irritability three weeks later; similarly, appearing to have "pressured" speech on one day while appearing to have "no increase" in the rate or amount of your speech three weeks later would change your score by eight points. Together, that sixteen-point difference would be enough to declare you've had a nearly 30 percent reduction in your symptoms.) This was the sole basis upon which Depakote was determined to be an effective treatment for acute mania in adults, though the label still says, more than two decades later, that "the safety and effectiveness of Depakote for long-term use in mania, i.e., more than 3 weeks, has not been systematically evaluated in controlled clinical trials."

A close look at the scientific literature underpinning the FDA's approval of Prozac and other selective serotonin reuptake inhibitor (SSRI) antidepressants reveals that the trials were typically of similar design to the two conducted on Depakote, in that they mostly lasted only a few weeks and determined outcomes based on subjective, clinician-administered rating scales. The most used assessment tool is the fifty-two-point Hamilton Rating Scale for Depression, or HAM-D, which was originally developed in 1960 by a British psychiatrist looking for a convenient way to track the effects of drug treatment. It has since been standardized by various entities, including pharmaceutical companies themselves. For example, in the Glaxo Wellcome (now GlaxoSmithKline) version of HAM-D, a clinician asks his patient to rank a list of symptoms such as "depressed mood (sadness, hopeless, helpless, worthless)," guilt, insomnia, agitation, and anxiety on a number scale between 0 and 2 or 0 and 4. The total number of points is added up. If a patient scores between 8 and 13, she is diagnosed with mild depression; 14 and 18, moderate depression; 19 and 22, severe depression; more than 23, very severe depression. (For reference, a six-point difference can be obtained solely by reporting changes in sleep; four points is the difference between having no agitation and biting your nails.)

Any clinically significant efficacy that SSRI drugs showed in trials submitted to the FDA was about the same as that of the inactive placebos against which they were compared. (Clinical significance essentially means that whatever change a person feels after starting a treatment could be said to be *meaningful*: something she can measurably see or feel; something practically relevant to her in her life; something tangible, impactful.) And these outcomes, according to Irving Kirsch, associate director of the Program in Placebo Studies at Harvard Medical School, occurred even with the vast majority of these trials starting with what's called a placebo run-in phase, in which all patients begin on the placebo and, after a week or two, "are reassessed, and anyone who has improved substantially is excluded from the trial." In a 2012 *60 Minutes* segment called "Treating Depression: Is There a Placebo Effect?" Kirsch says the difference between the efficacy of antidepressants and that of a placebo is, for most people, "very, very small, and in half the studies, non-existent." He explains that this finding was based on multiple meta-analyses he conducted with colleagues on antidepressant efficacy (a meta-analysis combines and analyzes data from multiple studies on a particular subject). The first, published in 1998, caused such an uproar among those who claimed antidepressants had well-established benefits that Kirsch decided to conduct a broader meta-analysis in 2002. This looked at both published and unpublished antidepressant studies, the latter of which had to be obtained through the Freedom of Information Act, because, as Kirsch put it, "[pharmaceutical companies] took the more successful studies, they published most of them, they took their unsuccessful studies, and they didn't publish them." The 2002 study drew the same conclusions about antidepressants—an especially significant outcome, according to Kirsch, because "the data in the FDA files were the basis upon which the medications were approved. In that sense they have a privileged status. If there was anything wrong with those trials, the medications should not have been approved in the first place."

This second meta-analysis garnered a new wave of criticism that claimed Kirsch and his coauthors had analyzed only the data from clinical trials in which participants had minor symptoms of depression, so the results shouldn't be taken seriously. In response, Kirsch led a *third* meta-analysis in 2008, in which closer attention was paid to the severity of participants' symptoms at the start of the trial. "For all but one sample, baseline HRSD [Hamilton Rating Scale for Depression] scores were in the very severe range according to criteria proposed by the American Psychiatric Association (APA) and adopted by NICE [the UK's National Institute for Health and Care Excellence]," Kirsch and his coauthors explained, clarifying that the sole outlier trial looked at participants on fluoxetine (the generic version of Prozac) who fell into either the "very serious" or the "moderate" range.

"Even among those patients, the drug-placebo difference was below the level of clinical significance." While Kirsch acknowledged that patients classified at the most severe end of the spectrum of depressed symptoms had a slightly larger, clinically significant difference in benefit from taking a drug rather than taking a placebo—on average, 4.36 points higher than placebo on the 52-point HAM-D scale—he proposed that part of the reason for this benefit was a phenomenon known as "broken blinding." While a double blind trial is set up so that neither the researcher nor the participant knows who is on a drug and who is on the placebo, participants are informed at the outset of the possible adverse effects of the trial's drug; those who are assigned to the drug group often figure this out relatively quickly, as they begin to experience the adverse effects they've been told about, thus breaking their blind.

In August 2022, Kirsch published yet another comprehensive analysis of antidepressant effectiveness in *The British Medical Journal* alongside coauthors from Johns Hopkins University, the Cleveland Clinic, and the FDA's Center for Drug Evaluation and Research (the lead author on the study is the FDA's deputy director for safety in the Division of Psychiatry). This analysis looked at the data of more than 73,000 individual participants in 232 randomized, double-blind, placebo-controlled trials of antidepressants submitted to the FDA by pharmaceutical companies between 1979 and 2016. The 2022 analysis corroborates what Kirsch found in all the previous meta-analyses: there is no overall clinically significant difference in performance between drug and placebo, with antidepressants outperforming placebos, on average, by less than two points on the 52-point HAM-D rating scale. Similar to the 2008 meta-analysis, a small percentage of participants—15 percent—appeared to receive greater benefit from the drug than from the placebo, but there was no way to predict who would benefit. According to the results, there was no pattern in the severity of symptoms and outcomes, and Kirsch again proposed that the breaking-blind phenomenon was likely a significant factor affecting the positive outcomes of this subgroup.

When I called Anuja in 2013 to request my medical records, she told me that she'd destroyed them (in Connecticut, doctors are required to keep patients' medical records for only seven years). She also said that she didn't recall ever diagnosing me with bipolar disorder, even though clinical notes I've obtained from the psychiatrist I saw after her, when I was eighteen, confirm that I had a history of bipolar disorder and had previously been on Depakote and Prozac. Today, Depakote remains one of the drugs most widely prescribed to children for "mood stabilizing" purposes, in spite of the fact that there is no evidence that it is safe or effective to do so.

While it's legal for doctors to prescribe off label, it is illegal for pharmaceutical companies to market drugs for off-label purposes. In 2012, Abbott Laboratories pleaded guilty and was forced to pay $1.5 billion in fines, forfeiture, and civil settlements for criminal and civil violations that included promoting Depakote for unapproved uses and illegally marketing it to elderly and pediatric patients between 1998 and 2008. That same year, GlaxoSmithKline pleaded guilty to criminal and civil charges that included the illegal marketing of Paxil and Wellbutrin to teenagers; its $3 billion settlement remains the biggest for any health care fraud case in U.S. history.

In the 1990s, pediatric psychopharmacologist Joseph Biederman, who, until his death in early 2023, was a prominent Harvard Medical School professor and leading researcher at Massachusetts General Hospital, began to author articles about what he considered a common and often undiagnosed psychiatric population: bipolar children. Symptoms of bipolar disorder, he and his coauthors proclaimed, look different in kids from how they do in adults. "One major source of diagnostic confusion in childhood mania is the potential for variable expression of symptoms at different developmental stages," they explain in an article published in October 1997, around the time I first met Anuja. "Unlike adult bipolar patients, manic children are seldom characterized by euphoric mood. The most common mood disturbance in manic children is irritability, with 'affective storms,' or prolonged and aggressive temper outbursts." Between 1994 and 2003, there would be a fortyfold increase in the diagnosis of bipolar disorder in children.

In 2008, a decade after Anuja first prescribed me that bipolar medication regimen, Senator Charles Grassley began an investigation into hidden financial relationships between pharmaceutical companies and physicians. He would uncover that Joseph Biederman and two of his MGH colleagues had received in excess of $4.2 million from various pharmaceutical companies between 2000 and 2007 but had "made it seem that they had received only 'a couple of hundred thousand dollars.'" One of Biederman's most lucrative relationships was with Johnson & Johnson, which manufactures the antipsychotic Risperdal (I would take this drug briefly as a young adult myself). Internal emails revealed that Biederman had "approached Janssen [which is owned by Johnson & Johnson] multiple times to propose the creation of a Janssen-MGH center for C&A [child and adolescent] Bipolar disorders. The rationale of this center is to generate and disseminate data supporting the use of risperidone in this patient population." The center ended up getting funded by the "Risperdal Brand team" to the tune of $500,000 in 2002 alone.

I've thought a lot about possible reasons why my parents didn't challenge my bipolar diagnosis or the idea that I'd need to be on psychiatric drugs for the rest of my life. Anuja was a psychiatrist with years of education and training; my parents had no medical background. She had extensive experience helping suffering teenagers; they had never been through it before. I imagine they thought it would have been irresponsible to question her judgment, as they'd always been full of faith in the medical profession, heading straight to the doctor anytime one of us was unwell. By the time I was three, I'd been on antibiotics half a dozen times for chronic ear infections (I don't think the importance of a healthy gut microbiome was on many people's radars in the mid-1980s). I have more memories of my pediatrician's waiting room—its crinkled *Highlights* magazines, colorful bead maze propped on a side table, and pastel green patient pamphlets—than I have of almost any other indoor space in my youth. I had my first surgical procedure in first grade: tubes put in my ears and the removal of my adenoids (it seems clear to me, in retrospect, that these were signals of inflammation in my body as opposed to pathologies to be surgically intervened upon). Afterward, to my delight, I received a stack of hand-drawn get-well cards from my thirty classmates. In fourth grade, when I tore knee ligaments during tennis practice, neither my parents nor I batted an eye when the orthopedic surgeon prescribed me four two-hundred-milligram ibuprofen tablets per day for the next two months. In fact, I remember feeling proud for needing so many pills, each one a symbol compounding the depth of my pain in the eyes of my parents, my friends, my coaches.

I'd learned by then that being physically ill was a way to feel seen, to feel special. I was still a few years away from feeling the very same way about being mentally ill.

FIVE

Be Worthy of Your Heritage

A few weeks after the first appointment with Anuja, my mother handed me my nightly medications at the dining room table. "Here you go," she said. "You can take these with your milk."

As I took the pills, a part of me wanted to collapse into her arms, for her to hold me, comfort me, rock me, for her to tell me all of this had been a big mistake and we should just wipe the slate clean and start fresh. Another part of me wanted to kill her. Fueled by wrathful thoughts, I believed that the purpose of these pills was to hijack my mind, to possess me—that they symbolized my unacceptableness as a daughter and a girl. I brought the dose to my mouth, the stick of gelatin on tongue a visceral reminder of the war my parents had waged against me. I swallowed the capsules down with a slug of whole milk.

My mother sat down, forcing a smile. She sighed, tucked a loose strand of hair behind her ear, and stabbed repeatedly at a floret of broccoli covered in melted Velveeta cheese.

"So, how was your day, girls?" Her cheery voice told me my real mother remained hidden. Pushing food around my plate while Nina and Chase responded, I readied myself to spew anger before storming off to my room, slamming the door, and claiming my aloneness. Thinking about how I hated them all left me with the fleeting but fulfilling sense that I was winning. I turned to rage whenever I needed to feel powerful, whenever I wasn't emptied out and feeling nothing at all.

My mother began to leave my nightly meds in my bedroom for me to take on my own. She had no reason to suspect I wouldn't; after all, I'd never actually told anyone how much I hated the pills, how humiliated I felt each time I took them, how beholden to my parents and to Anuja they made me feel.

I was doing homework when she knocked. "Come in," I said. The latch clicked open, and there she was, pills in one hand, a glass of water in the other.

"I'll take them in a second," I muttered without looking over. My mother put them at the edge of the desk and slowly backed away, as if anticipating I might attack at any moment. She clicked the door closed behind her.

I waited a few minutes before beginning the nightly face-off with these inanimate chemicals. Sometimes I'd hide the pills in my closet inside a jewelry box, careful to restack my string bracelets and dELiA*s necklaces over them. I also liked to send them to a worse fate by smushing them up in my hand with hot water and washing them down the drain. Other times the fear that I'd get caught in a lie about whether I'd been taking my meds would outweigh my desire for autonomy. *Change me into whatever it is they want me to be, whoever the fuck she even is.*

Anytime I took the meds, indignation lit me up like a fluorescent sign. All other emotions—sadness, loneliness, shame, grief—were drowned out. My nerve endings seemed to abandon one another, retreating into themselves like snails in shells. I was never sure whether this was caused by the meds or my body's best effort at protecting me from them. The compounding consequences of each daily dose left me feeling ever further from myself.

Homework finished. Pills taken. It was time. I tucked my chair in, walked across my room, and pushed the window up. I climbed onto the pink plaid upholstered window seat and swung my legs over the sill, out into the cool night air. The slate patio tiles awaited me thirty feet below. I closed my eyes, gripped the sill tight, and leaned forward into the dark. I pictured myself falling through the air, smacking the ground, twisted and crumpled into a mess of dead, neck broken, body bent unnaturally, found in the morning by Mom walking the dog. I thought about my funeral a week later, buried before a crowd of shocked classmates and parents wondering what had happened to Laura Delano. Time froze and all fell away save this exquisite awareness that it could all be over in a matter of seconds. I had the power to do this. They could never take it from me.

I survived the rest of ninth grade by reassuring myself I'd found a reliable escape from my troubles: boarding school. My last glimmer of hope.

Going back generations on both sides of my family, children had been shipped off to preparatory boarding institutions in Switzerland, Massachusetts, New York, and Connecticut, sometimes as young as eight. For years, my parents had brought up the idea of my going away for high school. I knew they'd sign off on it. A foolproof solution.

I kept my grades up, fueled less by a desire to excel than by the fear of what it would mean for me if I didn't. I did well enough in squash tournaments to keep my national ranking in the top ten. I acted in a play and sang a cappella. On paper, I had it all together. Behind my mind's closed doors, I was completely broken apart.

On Friday nights, I slept over at the houses of friends whose parents seemed to have forgotten they had children. I relished this freedom; my mother, for all our conflict, had always stayed a part of the day-to-day happenings of our lives. On weekend evenings, my friends and I roamed curfewless in the cars of older boys, chain-smoking cigarettes out back-seat windows as we blasted music and tricked ourselves into thinking we were blissful. Our fake IDs got us plenty of beer, which we carried to finished basements and pool houses for drinking games on Ping-Pong tables.

At home, I spent most of my time alone in my bedroom with the door shut. When I was forced to interact with my parents and sisters, I cursed and screamed and slammed doors. My sisters were scared of me and left me to myself. My mother didn't know what to do with me, the live wire that I was, and we revolved around each other in continual polarization. I secretly took razor to skin whenever the chaos in me grew too much to bear, patting the bloody wound dry with the gentle care I was otherwise unable to afford myself, careful to hide my scabs beneath bracelets, sweatbands, and long sleeves. The hidden pile of antidepressants and mood stabilizers slowly grew in my jewelry case. I suffered through weekly therapy sessions with Anuja, knowing that she was speaking to my parents afterward. Knowing I had no right to privacy left me convinced there was no one in the world I could trust, not even myself—after all, look at the mess I'd gotten into. The windowsill at night remained a soothing reminder of my one untouchable power.

I applied and was accepted to three boarding schools. Two of them had seen many of my family members through their doors, and the third, Deerfield Academy, had no connection whatsoever to any relatives. I chose Deerfield, determined to arrive as a blank slate and construct a new identity. Once I got there, I was sure I'd feel reborn.

I arrived on Deerfield's campus a week before school started to participate in varsity field hockey tryouts. Out of SUVs and luxury sedans slipped the tanned legs of teenagers back from island summers. Shaggy mops of hair tossed confidently to the side. Popped collars, Nantucket red pants, pastel floral prints on short skirts. Canvas duffel bags and athletic equipment slung over shoulders. The air seemed charged with possibility.

The next morning, Deerfield's colorful historic homes were lit up by September sun. Across the street from my sophomore dormitory, the four white columns of the redbrick main school building stood straight and tall. "Be worthy of your heritage" was our school motto. I had no idea what it meant to be worthy of anything, but I held on to hope that maybe, now that I was far away from my family and Anuja and John and Greenwich Academy and everyone who knew the fraudulent me, this school would help me figure it out.

I savored how unfamiliar it all was: the thin mattress, the beige walls, the worn institutional carpet on the hallway just beyond my heavy, fireproof door. In the Colonial Revival dormitory that I'd now call home, toilets flushed every few minutes through the wall. Doors slammed constantly. Voices trickled through cracks. My body felt so still here, so quiet. I wondered if I'd finally found the peace I'd been looking for.

No matter that going to boarding school was a common, even expected practice for high-achieving teenagers from Greenwich, or that a New England prep school was arguably not just a continuation of the same set of high expectations that I'd felt so trapped by back home but an amplification of them. None of this crossed my mind as I slapped the snooze button, savoring the fact that I'd finally succeeded in running away.

I didn't have a clear picture of who I might become at Deerfield, but I certainly knew that I would no longer be bipolar. I was determined to ignore the razor scars on my skin, to forget about my bedroom windowsill. Now that I was away from my family, I felt confident that I would never again lose myself in a rage. As for the night with John? No one here would ever know about it. It didn't matter that my prescription bottles had traveled with me; I'd already tucked them away at the back of my desk drawer. I resolved to ignore Anuja's request that I see a therapist on campus until I could meet with her when I was next home. Lucky for me, my parents never asked me whether I was taking my meds or seeing a counselor; perhaps the newfound geographical space between us freed them from the urgency of their fears. I would never step foot in the campus health center, because I was *not* mentally ill. The diagnosis had been an insulting injustice, but it was behind me now.

Before tryouts began, I told myself that making the varsity field hockey team didn't matter and decided to slack off as an experiment to prove it. I smoked cigarettes at night without caring if other players smelled the smoke on my clothes at dinner. I sat out on sprints because my knees were a little sore. I slouched my shoulders after missing a shot instead of firing myself up to try harder the next time. When the roster was posted and I saw that I'd succeeded—I'd been placed on the junior varsity team instead—I panicked. What had I done? I tried to muffle my regret by reassuring myself that I was simply getting sucked back into the pressure-cooker culture I'd left behind at home.

Over the months to come, I worked hard—so hard, bless that young me—to continue my revolt against the story that told me my personal worth was a measure of how well I performed. Instead of taking Advanced Placement Physics, I signed up for astronomy because I heard it was easy. I checked out in Latin class, flirting with boys instead. I let Jack Fanner run his hand up my skirt under the large mahogany table during English. I skipped the dorm activities that were meant to help solidify friendships on our floor. Once, I even snuck out my first-floor window in the middle of the night to smoke in a nearby abandoned barn before sprinting between the security guard's golf cart rounds to the boys' dorm next door, where I sat around eating chips with five guys before climbing back out the window and heading to my room.

But no matter how hard I tried to shed the vestiges of the girl I'd been, I never stopped feeling like a fraud. By springtime, I had given up on the bad-girl charade and stopped breaking rules. I became expert at finding the most hidden spots to smoke and, afterward, carefully washed my fingers to rid them of any smell. I studied diligently. My grades shot back up. The varsity tennis coach was impressed by how hard I was working in the number two slot behind our senior captain. I was more aware than ever of the meaninglessness of it all but couldn't, for the life of me, figure out how to stop the performance.

• ● •

Two years later, in late 2000, after a squash match one Saturday afternoon during the winter of senior year, I was dropped off at the train station to head into New York City. A classmate had invited thirty of us to join him at the Delmonico Hotel, where he'd booked the Beatles' suite. The ceiling was made of wobbly mirrors, and gold records and photographs covered the walls.

At the start of the night, a few of us locked ourselves in a room and gathered in a circle. Someone distributed water bottles as pills of ecstasy were ceremoniously doled out and swallowed with long sips. We made a pact not to tell anyone what we were up to—it would be more fun that way. We unlocked the door and slipped back out, one by one, to the party.

I spent the night gliding over city streets with a friend, talking into the early hours of the morning about how the linear unfolding of time was an illusion, that there was only the present, that everything that ever was or would be was actually happening right now. At some point, it dawned on me that my nose and eyes and ears and mouth and skin were the sole architects of my reality: the stimuli surrounding me—the squash courts and classrooms, the textbooks and letters on a page, the uniforms, the properly set tables and napkins in laps and *pleases* and *thank yous*—felt important to me only because I perceived them. What would it be like, and who would I be, if I had no sensory perceptions at all—not in a coma but fully awake and without sight, sound, smell, taste, touch? Would that be what it took to finally liberate myself? To feel like I wasn't programmed by all that controlled me?

I considered that up until this moment, my mind had been trapped inside a tiny box that I'd never before noticed because of its invisible walls. Ecstasy had stained those walls so that I could see them—and see, as well, that there was no lid: I could rise up over the edges of this box and expand endlessly beyond them. The chains of expectation that I'd assumed for so long had me in an existential snare—the striving to succeed, to accomplish, to perform—suddenly seemed laughably illusory and ephemeral. I was, I always had been, free!

The next day, I rode the train from Grand Central to make my way back to school, staring numbly out the window as the dank cavern of the underground tunnel crept by. The train car smelled of engine oil and body odor and perfume and urine and cleaning solution. I hadn't slept or eaten in what felt like forever, and my feet were blistered from miles of walking. My hazy brain was throbbing, the previous night's strike of clarity long gone. (It would be many years before I'd come to deeply appreciate the boundary-rupturing effects that this and other psychedelic experiences in my late teens had on my consciousness, which have lasted to this day.) What had felt like my first authentic escape from fraudulence, I could see now, had actually been a synthetic, ecstasy-induced mirage. I was returning to the robotic performance of successful student-athlete, made all the more imprisoning by the fact that just a few weeks before, I'd been accepted early to Harvard University. I hoped I'd got it all wrong and that once I got to college, I wouldn't feel broken anymore.

SIX

The Debutante

C'mon, Adam. Do it! Burn me!"

I was at a party a few weeks after the start of my freshman fall at Harvard University, surrounded by a circle of thick-necked hockey players.

Adam shook his head and snorted in disbelief. "No way, Delano! I'm not fucking doing that, not happening."

"Why not? Are you scared?"

One of Adam's teammates said, "Ooh-ho, A.G., you gonna take that?"

Ramped up by liquor and cocaine, I took it a step further. "I don't think you can handle it. I think you might be a pussy." A surge of belligerent power coursed up in me; I felt alive, fearless.

"No, that's not it—"

"Psshaw, no way, man, you're afraid!" I interrupted.

"I'm not, I'm fuckin' not, Delano, I just don't wanna hurt you." He was drunk—I could see it in the way he swayed, ever so slightly—and I could tell I had him. He'd give in.

"I just told you it won't hurt. I'm serious—I've trained myself. Look, just do it. I need you to do it." I put my right hand out, palm down. The raised pile of scars from an August night when I'd last used my skin as an ashtray was an angry shade of scarlet. I savored how riveted the hockey players were by this unfolding scene.

Adam stood frozen a foot away. "Fucking do it!" I yelled at him. He jerked his head back as if hit by a gust of wind, then put his hands up in surrender.

"Okay, okay, if you say so . . ." He trailed off, taking the cigarette out of his mouth. He pinched it at the filter and moved it down over the top of my hand before pausing. "Are you sure?"

"Yup. Do it." I smiled as I stared deep into his eyes. "And I want you to hold it there, too." He looked terribly uncomfortable, which only fueled my defiant conviction that I was more powerful than him, than all of these guys. *They have no idea what my mind is capable of.*

He sighed and moved in. There was a sizzling sound, the rancid smell of burning flesh. The soundtrack of *Holy shit*s as the guys watched my skin melt. The wince on Adam's face as I pushed my hand up into his cigarette and told him to keep it there. The satisfying pulse of power shooting up my arm and into my body, tricking me into believing I had full control over my mind, my brain, myself.

My first semester at Harvard, that fall of 2001, can best be described as a willful lurch toward self-annihilation. I drank frequently because it felt like the only reliable way to forget that matriculating at an elite college hadn't fixed me and now here I was, with no more promising landmarks ahead to bank on as the solution to my pain. I spent many nights walking the Cambridge streets aimlessly with a friend as we discussed postmodern philosophy and its presupposition that nothing is real, everything a social construct. On weekends, I sought out ephemeral happiness with each cocaine snort, just one more line, one more. I slacked off at squash practice, frequently hungover and riddled with colds and sore throats. My teammates knew I smoked a pack and a half of cigarettes a day, and I didn't care.

At Deerfield, I'd seen homework, tests, and papers as challenges that were relatively easy to overcome. At Harvard, an obfuscating lens slipped over my eyes, muddling my perceptions and turning otherwise straightforward academic information into a murky morass that felt impossible to wade through. I couldn't assemble my cognitive capacities enough to write a coherent response paper, let alone a lengthy, formulated essay. I struggled to absorb what was being said in lectures, so I began to skip them. It felt easier to avoid the agony of not simply incomprehension but *de*comprehension, as though my brain had actually unraveled its once delicately interwoven networks of cognition.

And then there were the young men. I quickly developed a modus operandi that would beset three hapless male souls by winter: (1) Get intoxicated with this guy who seems to be interested in you. (2) Embark on an epic philosophical conversation about the meaning and meaninglessness of life that will leave you sure you've found your soulmate. (3) Hook up. (4) Weeks later, when you realize that no matter how hard you try, you can't muster desire for this person, cut ties with him quickly—and do not, no matter what, explain why. It's best to disappear.

I spent many nights in Harvard Square sitting alone by the subway entrance, where I liked to hide in a hooded sweatshirt, write poetry, listen to Radiohead, chain-smoke. I always left an open pack next to me to attract runaways and bums seeking nicotine, finding comfort in these fleeting connections with strangers who seemed as lost as I was. I often looked behind me at the Harvard gates and wondered how I'd ever been so foolish as to think I belonged there.

And then Christmas came, and I had to face the fact that it was time to put on my wedding gown.

I stared into her eyes. *Are they blue or gray?* I'd heard people call them both before, and it had been a long time since I looked closely. She came up a little while ago from the beauty salon on the first floor of the Waldorf-Astoria Hotel in New York City and now stood before me: hair washed, dried, brushed, pinned back, sprayed, firm instructions from the stylist to not touch, no matter what. She put her hand on top of her head, hesitated, and pushed down slightly, just enough to feel the hardened crust begin to give.

I suddenly remembered that those eyes were mine. That I was standing in front of a full-length mirror. That it was my body zipped up into the bodice of this fancy wedding dress, a sumptuous display of white satin billowing to the ground like rolling, snowy hills. That I was about to "come out," as they say, to society as a debutante—something women in my family had done for generations (a 1930s headline in *The New York Times*, for example, announced that my teenage grandmother was being feted at a party in honor of her forthcoming debutante season). This debut was something I felt I had no say in; I knew that my refusal would mean facing the disappointment of family elders. I glanced down at my hands, turning them over, stretching my fingers apart and curling them back in, one by one. *What an odd-looking thing the human hand is.*

Bright white light blinded me as we emerged from behind the lush velvet curtain and stepped onto the ballroom stage: Ben, my best friend from Deerfield and escort for the evening, in a black swallowtail coat and white gloves; me in my wedding dress with white gloves up past my elbows. I was clenching my leg muscles to keep from tottering in the two-inch heels I'd never worn before. I rested the underside of my forearm on top of his, kept my shoulders down, and held my back straight, just as I had been taught in rehearsal. We walked slowly toward the light, unable to see the hundreds of people seated at round tables below us in the ballroom, sipping whiskey on the rocks and goblets of red wine. Through his gritted smile, Ben asked how I was doing. Aware of all the eyes and cameras on us, I muttered,

"Okay." The flutes of champagne I'd just chugged backstage certainly helped.

A mellifluous voice through a loudspeaker spoke my full name, then my escort's, which meant it was time to take my curtsy. I looked to Ben, who nodded slightly, then stepped my right foot away from him, keeping my hand atop his. I straightened my left leg out in his direction, and then swept it counterclockwise in a half circle until the top of my left foot touched the floor behind my right. I bent my knees and plunged into a deep curtsy, my left knee just a couple of inches above the floor, my gown a fluffy cloud around me. Dropping my chin, I tilted the top of my head toward the audience. And then I lifted my gaze, looked straight into the glaring light, told my thighs to clench and stand me back up. There was applause. Ben guided me in a circle to show the back of my dress to the crowd. We walked out of the spotlight.

After the rest of the debutantes were presented to the audience, our escorts paraded us around in circles and figure eights, the endless, measured applause like droning TV static. "You know, you're 'grade A' quality meat, Delano," Ben whispered playfully in my ear as we walked. "You're ready for high society!"

I wondered if this was the punch line to the colossal practical joke that was my life, a joke everyone was in on but me. The literal stage, my costume, my performance: if only I could explain it all away as mere caricature.

I spent the night downing drink after drink to fuel the mingling and dancing and cheek-kissing performance expected of me. When I snuck off every thirty minutes for a cigarette, I carefully removed a glove and bent at the waist to make sure not to ash on myself. At one point in the evening, after hearing about a bowl of cocaine in a friend's hotel suite, I took off my heels and sprinted to the elevator through the entire first floor of the hotel, past the display windows and Christmas decorations and crowds of tourists in the lobby.

The next night, I had to do it all over again, this time at the Plaza Hotel. This debutante ball required me to have a second male escort alongside Ben, and our audience was much smaller. We had to start the evening in the entry hall, where the debs and escorts stood in line as two hundred guests, one by one, shook each of our hands. I ached from head to toe but did my best to imitate grace and hold the piercing gaze of so many strangers.

My memories from the rest of the night are blurry: There is the sloppy mess of tears down my cheeks mixed with fear that I'd get makeup stains on my dress. There is sweet, gentle Thomas—my Harvard classmate and one of those unlucky guys from the fall—guiding me through the crowds, out the hotel's main entrance, down the steps, and safely into a cab. I remember looking out the back window at him as I drove away, his arms hanging awkwardly at his sides, his tuxedoed body getting smaller in the distance, the confusion on his face fading into the night. A few minutes later, I politely asked the cab driver to pull over so that I could vomit on the sidewalk.

When I awoke the next morning in my grandmother's guest room on the Upper East Side of Manhattan, I felt emptier than ever before. I stumbled to the bathroom and looked at the smeared mascara, the bags under my eyes, the knotted, sticky hair. There was the acidic aftertaste of vomit in my mouth. My throat and nose, raw from cocaine.

Back in the bedroom, I sat down and began to rock back and forth on the edge of the bed, head in hands, fingers pushing in hard at my temples. *There has to be something wrong with me, there has to be, there's no reason I should be feeling this way, something is wrong with me, what is wrong with me, what is wrong with me, WHAT IS WRONG WITH ME?* A deep, low wail started up from my core and I let it out, and rocked, and took in breath, and wailed, and wanted to die so badly, so damn badly. *I just need to be dead, I can't do this, I can't do this, please please please I can't do this.* My parents ran in at the sounds. They stood panicked before me.

For the first time in as long as I could remember, I looked them dead in the eyes as I said, "Please, I need help."

The next day, when we were back in Greenwich, my parents scheduled a consultation with a local psychiatrist named Dr. Anderson. The outrage I'd felt four years earlier when they'd taken me to Anuja was gone; now I yearned for someone to tell me what was wrong with me and what to do to fix it. In the session, I poured out everything that had unfolded through the fall to this goateed stranger: the drugs, the alcohol, the guys, the cocaine, the sleepless nights, the cigarette burns, the loneliness, the despair, the growing absence of hope. I told him I'd been diagnosed with bipolar disorder in the ninth grade by Anuja Patel but had refused to accept it, and now I was wondering, Could she have been right? He listened carefully, taking notes. At the end of the hour, he whipped out his prescription pad and wrote me two-week prescriptions for Depakote, the mood stabilizer that Anuja had put me on years earlier, and Seroquel, an antipsychotic. These, he said, would tide me over until I had an ongoing prescriber in place near school. He'd be contacting a Harvard Medical School–affiliated colleague to ask for a recommendation.

I began both meds without hesitating, desperate for relief. Gone was the conviction that these were chemical agents hijacking my bloodstream. I was ready to view them as gentle, healing balms.

Dr. Anderson soon followed up with the name of a young doctor who his colleague thought would be a good fit: Paul Bachman, MD, PhD. He was expecting a call from me, Dr. Anderson said, so that we could schedule an appointment for right after I was back at school. I nodded and asked where this new psychiatrist's office was.

"Have you heard of McLean Hospital?"

PART

II

SEVEN

Asylum for the Insane

Before McLean was McLean Hospital, it was the Asylum for the Insane. A true asylum, after all, is a place of refuge, and hospital administrators in the early 1800s had been inspired by a new therapeutic model in England called moral treatment. Developed by Quakers, it emphasized conversation, nourishing food, manual work, and cultivating a sense of family. Asylums were built in bucolic landscapes and medical interventions generally rejected. "We . . . profess to do little more than assist Nature, in the performance of her own cure," explained Samuel Tuke, an English Quaker and one of the model's earliest proponents. By 1895, when it left Boston's crowded outskirts to rebuild itself atop a sprawling hilltop of woods and fields two towns over, the McLean Asylum had already been rechristened McLean Hospital—this change, a harbinger of its medicalized future.

When state-run facilities opened in the nineteenth century to take on patients who couldn't afford their own care, McLean quickly became the go-to place for the most well-to-do families of Boston to send their mad, inconvenient, unacceptable, or otherwise struggling loved ones. These patients' elite status was "reinforced in comforting ways," according to historian of psychiatry Jack D. Pressman. "Nurses and attendants were instructed to refer to patients by their proper names, exhibiting as much deference as possible, while physicians approached them 'as equals and companions.'" There was a working farm on the grounds that, until World War II, provided most of the food for both the patients and the hospital's doctors, nurses, and janitors and their respective families, who all lived on the grounds. The nurses had their own softball team. Patients put on musical concerts, watched movies, and enjoyed afternoon tea; they could ride horses, play tennis, visit the art studio. There was even a bowling alley, which fellow patients and I would spend many unsuccessful hours trying to find while exploring the hospital grounds. Many patients stayed for months or years; some, the rest of their lives. In the words of Pressman, "If it had been your fate to go insane in mid-twentieth century America, there was likely no better place to end up than at McLean Hospital. . . . Admittance to McLean meant that your family was willing and able to spend considerable sums on your behalf, perhaps indefinitely."

Because of its low staff-to-patient ratio, McLean managed to mostly stay true to its reputation as a retreat in the first half of the twentieth century, avoiding the custodial warehouse fate that befell many bigger but understaffed public institutions. Yet the reality of what happened within McLean's walls was not always idyllic. Well-to-do clientele enjoyed lavish comforts and freedoms, but less privileged or more difficult patients were sometimes carted off to the campus edges, out of sight and earshot, where nudity, visible urine and feces, and screams were not uncommon sights and sounds and uncooperative patients might find themselves physically restrained and isolated or, as an alternative, assaulted with freezing water from a fire hose in the hydrotherapy room.

At that time, while psychoanalytic and psychodynamic therapies were growing in popularity and the tenets of moral treatment continued to undergird much of private institutional care, the psychiatric profession as a whole was also in hot pursuit of groundbreaking physical cures. (These included pulling teeth, inducing malarial fevers via infected rat bites, and injecting horse blood.) McLean administrators were initially wary of using medical interventions on patients in whom there was no proof of medical pathology but eventually gave in to the pressure they felt from employees and competitors. Beginning in the 1930s, McLean doctors deliberately induced comas in patients by injecting them with insulin; the standard protocol for insulin coma therapy, as it was called, was up to sixty comas—six days on, one day off—over the course of two months. (The hospital's recipient list for this treatment would include Sylvia Plath and John Forbes Nash Jr.) Causing seizures by injecting high doses of Metrazol, a circulatory and respiratory stimulant, was another available treatment at McLean for a time; adverse effects included vertebral fractures, pulmonary tuberculosis, and myocardial damage.

The hospital eventually replaced these treatments with electroshock, today called electroconvulsive therapy (ECT), which required staff to hold or tie patients down, fully awake, to prevent their limbs from breaking due to the violent seizures that would knock them unconscious. (A primary difference between electroshock in the 1940s and today is that anesthesia is now used, which increases a patient's seizure threshold, which means higher volts of electricity.)* And when

---

* A lengthy side note: In 1976, when federal regulation of medical devices first began, ECT, which was already in use, was allowed to remain on the market without having to go through the new, more stringent approval requirements, and given the highest FDA risk category, class III, meaning its devices present "a potential, unreasonable risk of illness or injury" (https://www.fda.gov/medical-devices/device-approvals-denials-and-clearances/pma-approvals). At the time, doctors were allowed to continue administering ECT because the FDA declared it would soon be requesting that device manufacturers submit a premarket approval (PMA) application proving safety and efficacy of class III devices; as of 2018, more than forty years later, the FDA had yet to make such a request. That year, a California lawsuit against an ECT manufacturer proved that its devices caused brain injury. The company was required to update its disclosure accordingly and added, on its website, "ECT may result in anterograde or retrograde amnesia. Such post-treatment amnesia typically

Walter Freeman went on tour with his revolutionary lobotomy procedure, which involved driving an ice pick–like tool up through the eye socket with a mallet and then wiggling it around to sever the connection between the frontal lobe and the thalamus, McLean jumped on the bandwagon. Between 1938 and 1954, its doctors performed the procedure on eighty patients, 82.5 percent of them women. In 1947 alone, McLean lobotomized around 8 percent of its patients. These procedures were considered signs of great medical progress. António Egas Moniz was even awarded the Nobel Prize for developing the prefrontal leucotomy, a cousin of Freeman's transorbital lobotomy.

Though many assume that electroshock and psychosurgery have been relegated to psychiatry's dark archives, it's estimated that about a million people a year receive ECT around the world, 100,000 of them in the United States. (In 2016, McLean proudly declared that it was providing nearly 10,000 ECT treatments annually, making it "one of the largest ECT centers in the country.") Procedures similar to (if far less crudely done than) the lobotomy and leucotomy continue to this day; disguised by euphemisms like *neuroablative technique, psychiatric neurosurgery,* or *stereotactic radiosurgery,* they are primarily offered as a last-resort intervention to people with diagnoses of obsessive-compulsive disorder (OCD) or depression who have not been helped by first-line psychiatric treatments. "We only perform the surgery on patients who are being completely refractory to all forms of conventional therapy," explained Harvard Medical School associate professor and Massachusetts General Hospital (MGH) attending neurosurgeon G. Rees Cosgrove during a session at the Pres-

dissipates over time; however, incomplete recovery is possible. In rare cases, patients may experience permanent memory loss or permanent brain damage" (https://web.archive .org/web/20230321005854/http://www.thymatron.com:80/catalog_cautions.asp). Two months later, despite those four decades of absent patient safety data, the FDA decided to downgrade ECT as a treatment for catatonia or a "severe major depressive episode" from class III to class II, which removed the PMA requirement altogether.

ident's Council on Bioethics in Washington, D.C., in 2004. "So you must look at this as a salvage operation or a palliative procedure, and it's only performed on patients who have actually exhausted all forms of modern psychopharmacology and pharmacotherapies. Typically this means . . . they've had three trials of modern SSRIs with up to maximum tolerated doses augmented with either lithium or Wellbutrin or clonazepam, any of those things." Besides MGH, other U.S. hospitals offering psychosurgery include, but are not limited to, Brigham and Women's Hospital in Boston, Butler and Rhode Island hospitals in Providence, and Columbia University Irving Medical Center in New York City. The target of these procedures, roughly speaking, is the limbic system, the part of the human brain responsible for functions like emotion and behavior regulation, motivation and reward seeking, and memory. In the wake of ice picks and eight-inch leucotome instruments, neurosurgeons now opt for more understated methods of brain tissue destruction, or "therapeutic lesioning," using CT and MRI imaging to guide them. Certain procedures require the drilling of one or more holes, each roughly the diameter of a pencil eraser, into the patient's skull, at which point an "ablating" instrument is inserted to commence burning—depending on the procedure, this might be a laser-transmitting fiber-optic cable or a ten-millimeter exposed-tip electrode that's placed on the brain and heated to 85 degrees Celsius (185 degrees Fahrenheit) for a minute and a half.

All these years later, nothing has changed insofar as the scientific justification for these procedures is concerned: the literature explaining the neurobiological logic behind psychosurgery is still peppered with waffly, imprecise phrases like "is thought to be associated with" or "is assumed to be" or "is thought to play a role in," and so forth. As the authors of a 2023 review of psychosurgery for OCD acknowledge, "there are notable obstacles faced by both patients and medical practitioners when considering neuroablation, including a lack of comprehensive understanding of its mechanisms, doubtful efficacy, occasional serious adverse effects, and prejudges [*sic*] from history."

Insofar as ECT is concerned, outcomes are arguably poor—so poor, in fact, that the standard practice, for decades, has been to put people on antidepressants (or a combination of antidepressants and something else) immediately following the procedure to mitigate the high likelihood of relapse, and sometimes even offer ongoing "maintenance" ECT. In 2001, to better understand which "continuation pharmacotherapy" had the best outcomes following electroshock, a team of researchers led by Columbia University professor Harold A. Sackeim—a longtime proponent of ECT who owns a patent on "focal electrically administered seizure therapy" (FEAST) and has received decades of funding from a long list of device manufacturers and pharmaceutical companies—conducted a large randomized controlled trial. In this trial, researchers took a group of recently electroshocked patients whom they'd deemed "remitted" according to subjective, clinician-rated scales and split them into three groups—one of which was put on nortriptyline (a tricyclic antidepressant), another on nortriptyline and lithium, and the third on a placebo. They followed the groups for six months to see which had the best outcomes. "Our study indicates that without active treatment, virtually all remitted patients relapse within 6 months of stopping ECT," Sackeim and his coauthors concluded. (The two medicated groups didn't fare so well themselves in that time period: 60 percent relapsed on the antidepressant and 39 percent on the combination.) A 2013 meta-analysis titled "Relapse Following Successful Electroconvulsive Therapy for Major Depression" confirms these poor outcomes, noting that even patients who continued with ECT relapsed at a rate of 37.2 percent within six months.

Despite its reputation as a go-to treatment for depressed people for whom medications haven't worked, ECT lacks a reliable evidence base for safety and efficacy. Only eleven placebo-controlled trials, averaging thirty-seven patients per trial, have ever been conducted on ECT in the entire history of the procedure, with the most recent one in 1985 (in the UK) and the last one in the United States back in 1963. "Five of these studies found no difference between the two groups at the end of treatment, four found ECT produced better outcomes for some patients, and two produced mixed results, including one where psychiatrists' ratings produced a difference, but the ratings of nurses and patients did not," writes University of East London professor John Read. "In the 80 years since the first ECT no studies have found any evidence that ECT is better than placebo beyond the end of treatment. Nevertheless, all five meta-analyses relying on these studies have somehow concluded that ECT is more effective than placebo despite the studies' multiple failings." In 2019, Read and fellow researchers set out to assess both the quality of these meta-analyses and the scientific rigor and legitimacy of the eleven SECT trials they analyzed (the *S* in SECT stands for *sham*, meaning that the "placebo" arm was put under anesthesia but not actually given shock treatment during the trial). After carefully rating the quality of those eleven trials on a scale that assessed factors like randomization, blinding, data transparency, design quality, and rater reporting, the researchers concluded:

> The quality of most SECT-ECT studies is so poor that the meta-analyses were wrong to conclude anything about efficacy, either during or beyond the treatment period. There is no evidence that ECT is effective for its target demographic— older women, or its target diagnostic group—severely depressed people, or for suicidal people, people who have unsuccessfully tried other treatments first, involuntary patients, or children and adolescents. Given the high risk of permanent memory loss and the small mortality risk, this longstanding failure to determine whether or not ECT works means that its use should be

immediately suspended until a series of well designed, randomized, placebo-controlled studies have investigated whether there really are any significant benefits against which the proven significant risks can be weighed.

Insofar as ECT's safety is concerned, a 2019 systematic review and meta-analysis published in *Anesthesiology* found that "major adverse cardiac events and death after ECT are infrequent and occur in about one in 50 patients." (I'm not exactly sure what is "infrequent" about a one in fifty chance that you'll die or have a heart attack from receiving a treatment.) Anterograde and retrograde memory issues—in other words, losing the ability to form new memories and losing the ability to recall old ones—are common. According to a 2003 systematic review, at least a third of patients report significant post-ECT memory loss, warranting the authors to conclude, "Although clinical trials concluded that electroconvulsive therapy is an effective treatment, measures of efficacy did not take into account all the factors that may lead patients to perceive it as beneficial or otherwise." Even ECT proponent Harold A. Sackeim acknowledges that "virtually all patients experience some degree of persistent and, likely, permanent retrograde amnesia." He then goes on, however, to claim that the lasting memory issues that people report experiencing are actually their "ongoing psychopathology" but that "for understandable reasons the profession has not emphasized this phenomenon. . . . It is uncomfortable for the field to be perceived as 'blaming the victim,' and attributing memory complaints to unresolved psychiatric disturbance, even if true."

In its 1955 Midcentury Survey on Medical Research, the American Foundation Joint Commission on Mental Illness and Health remarked, "Some critics would ask of psychiatry simply better use of traditional scientific methods, on the ground that, after all, 'what exists exists in some quantity and can be measured.'" It went on to state that the psychiatric profession was "regarded by some medical educators as not a scientific or teachable discipline and as thus having no proper place in the medical school curriculum." One prominent Columbia University neurology professor at the time described psychiatry as "an odd mixture" of various unrelated fields plus "various drug assaults on the personality, mental hygiene, philosophical speculation." Critical assessments like these catalyzed many midtwentieth-century psychiatrists to work hard to shed any vestige of moral treatment and redefine themselves as legitimate medical authorities. When I peruse old compilations of symposia that I've managed to track down from the early days of biological psychiatry, as the mostly American and British collective of newly biochemically oriented psychiatrists then renamed themselves, I see exuberant, ambitious confidence woven through the mildewy pages. "Things obviously were possible, even with local [X-ray] equipment, and we were off," recounted Joel Elkes, considered a psychopharmacology trailblazer, about that time. "I was moving away from somebody else's field, and entering a field that somehow mysteriously pulled me—the nervous system; albeit by way of creeping up the myelin sheath!" To Elkes and his colleagues, their growing arsenal of biochemical technologies would soon enable them to crack the code of human suffering and madness. In "our own new science," he declared at the inaugural International Neurochemical Symposium of 1954, "it would seem we are as attracted to substance as we are to symbol; we are as interested in behavior as we are aware of the subtleties of subjective experience. There is here no conflict between understanding the way things are, and the way people are, between the pursuit of science and the giving of service. Where else does one find a field as rich and powerful as ours?"

This commitment to seeking explanations and cures under a microscope catalyzed a new zeitgeist within psychiatry. As one founding biological psychiatrist put it, this created the "important climate of acceptance for the concept that mental illness might be biochemically determined and consequently reversed with drugs." Note "might be"—for this zeitgeist was rooted in a belief lacking in actual evidence: that mental and emotional suffering arises from a biochemically defective brain in need of a biochemical cure. McLean Hospital was at the heart of this biological revolution in psychiatry, setting up research laboratories starting in the 1940s. Financially speaking, the pursuit of biological explanations and solutions wasn't exactly a path to riches: in 1983, the year I was born, McLean nearly sold itself to the biggest international for-profit health care conglomerate, and almost two decades later (a few years before I became a patient there), it initiated a complex, lengthy process of selling off land. McLean was floundering in debt, and its board concluded this was the best way to save it. The era of moral treatment had kept the hospital's coffers full, with wealthy families of patients doling out exorbitant sums to keep their loved ones in its care, sometimes for many years. But when the psychiatric profession began diligent efforts to redefine emotional pain and mania and psychosis as medical conditions requiring medical treatment—what's called the medical model of mental illness—such extravagant hospital stays were no longer considered necessary.

These efforts had been prompted, in part, by the accidental discovery of psychiatry's inaugural drug, chlorpromazine, an antihistamine that was being tested as an anesthetic potentiator. Researchers saw the apathy-inducing, tranquilizing effects it had on lab animals and realized there was a huge, untapped market for humans. According to French psychiatrist Pierre Deniker, who, together with a colleague, is often credited with bringing chlorpromazine to the field of psychiatry in 1952, "after initial trials, specialists were particularly impressed by the potent sedative activity of the drug. . . . This was the real beginning of research on drugs that would soon increase in number and would be referred to as 'tranquilizers.'" The other name coined back then for these major tranquilizer drugs (which are today called antipsychotics) was *neuroleptic*: in Greek, literally, "the seizing of the nerve." "It was found that neuroleptics could experimentally reproduce almost all symptoms of lethargic encephalitis," Deniker explains. "In fact, it would be possible to cause true encephalitis epidemics with the new drugs." (Encephalitis is a serious, potentially life-threatening inflammatory brain condition typically caused by an infection or autoimmune response.) Deniker goes on to say that the drugs they were developing as psychiatric treatments were "precisely those that cause 'therapeutic diseases' of CNS [central nervous system] regulatory mechanisms" and that "better results are sometimes obtained when marked neurological syndromes are systematically induced."

Chlorpromazine was introduced to Canada in 1953 by Montreal-based psychiatrist Heinz Lehmann, who touted the drug as a possible "pharmacological substitute for lobotomy," and soon thereafter to the United States by biological psychiatrist Frank Ayd. Neuroleptics spread rapidly inside American psychiatric hospitals in part because of their promotion as chemical lobotomies—the same subduing effects as the ice pick procedure, only without need of such a crude tool. "The most noticeable effect of the drugs," the Joint Commission on Mental Illness and Health would remark in its 1961 report, "is to reduce the hospital ward noise level. . . . In the surprising, pleasant effects they produce on patient-staff relationships, the drugs might be described as moral treatment in pill form."

This shift to the medical model was fueled further by the rise of the managed care industry, which took off with the 1973 passage of the Health Maintenance Organization Act, in which the U.S.

government empowered various managed care entities, among them health maintenance organizations and preferred provider organizations, to implement strategies aimed at controlling health-related costs. (Whether this has been a successful enterprise is another matter; a 2021 Commonwealth Fund study of eleven high-income countries found that the United States not only spends far more on health care as a percentage of gross domestic product than any of the ten other countries—nearly 17 percent of GDP in 2019—but also has, by far, the worst health outcomes.) Among their strategies, managed care organizations incentivized doctors to use cheaper interventions and hospitals to discharge their inpatients as swiftly as possible. These new incentives prompted McLean and other psychiatric institutions to shift patients' inpatient hospitalizations from slow-paced retreat experiences to rapid, sterile, psychopharmacological ones: medicate a patient immediately to get her "stabilized," and focus on getting her back out the door. By January 2002, when I first set foot on McLean's grounds, five to fifteen days was the average length of stay on one of its wards.

• ● •

I was completely unaware of McLean's financial woes when I walked up its winding, tree-lined path for the first time that winter of my freshman year, in early 2002. I paid no attention to the sagging, abandoned outbuildings, crumbling brick, and cracked walkways, nor did I notice the jarring contrast between the newly developed condos on the hospital's sold-off land and its elegant Tudor structures at the crest of the hill. I was focused, instead, on the hospital's historical legacy, its clinical prestige—and on Sylvia Plath, Anne Sexton, Susanna Kaysen. I felt proud to be joining these women as a patient on this hallowed psychiatric ground.

Within the giant subterranean landscape of the hospital, as I looked for Dr. Bachman's office, I traversed the very underground tunnels that I pictured Plath, Sexton, and Kaysen walking, looking up at the same steam pipes on the ceiling, tracing my fingers along the same plaster walls I imagined they'd touched. I eventually located the office beyond a creaky, rusted door. In the waiting area, humming white-noise machines sat on the floor. Acrylic display cases held promotional flyers for medication trials.

I took a seat, smiling and making small talk with my fellow waiting patients before ripping off a hangnail and sucking at the blood on my finger. I wondered where I'd start with this new doctor; what would he need to know to figure out what was wrong with me and how to fix it? I heard muffled movement behind his door before a woman in a peacoat slipped out. Dr. Bachman looked around the waiting area. His brown hair was curly and cut tight to his head, and he wore wire-rimmed glasses, a fitted suit, and an understated tie, which he adjusted. I guessed he was in his late thirties. I caught his attention with a subtle wave.

"Laura?" There was a gentleness about him that put me right at ease. I nodded. "I'll just be a few minutes." I nodded again. He backed away and clicked the door closed.

Ten minutes after the hour, Dr. Bachman reemerged with a smile. "Please come in." He gestured to an upholstered chair. I noticed works of poetry, philosophy, literature, sociology, and anthropology on his bookshelves, an array of diplomas on his wall. His PhD was in philosophy, which sparked my interest. I made a mental note to be sure to bring up my obsession with postmodernism.

When I think of that first session, I see Dr. Bachman sitting across from me, legs crossed, elbow on knee, chin nestled in palm. I hear him acknowledging my suffering as he inserts validating sounds and remarks. I see him skillfully gather up my spoken bits and pieces—the impulsivity and reckless behaviors, the substance abuse, the sleeplessness, the racing thoughts, the loneliness, the isolation, the dysfunction in school, the expansive thoughts, the suicidal fantasies—and put them back together in a clear articulation of who I am: bipolar. This would be the diagnosis I believed I had when I left his office at the end of that appointment.

But here's the thing: many years later, when I called Dr. Bachman to request my medical records (which he quickly obliged me, unlike most of my former psychiatrists), I looked at his intake of me and saw "Mood disorder NOS. R/O bipolar II disorder." *NOS* stands for "not otherwise specified," psychiatrist talk for "I don't know exactly what this is but it's something." *R/O* stands for "rule out," which means that he wanted to observe me before determining whether to diagnose me as bipolar. It appears the only psychiatric diagnosis he officially gave me that day, according to his records, was one he never told me about: borderline personality disorder.

Dr. Bachman wrote me new prescriptions to continue the bipolar regimen of mood stabilizer and antipsychotic that had been started by Dr. Anderson, and we made plans for me to call him the following week. Despite the diagnostic ambiguity captured in his notes, he'd said enough to me, in that inaugural session, to help me feel newly refined by clinical definition. *If only you'd listened to Anuja back in ninth grade*, I remember thinking as I left his office. *All the pain never had to have happened if you'd just accepted at the outset that you had bipolar disorder.* But the past was the past. I had this brilliant new doctor who'd right my ship. It was all going to be okay now, for I was finally ready, after far too long, to embrace being sick.

I crossed the dank tunnel, made my way up the crumbling stairs, and burst eagerly through the heavy metal door to face the bright January sun. Everything was sharper—the trunks of courtyard trees, the bricks, the sky, the air itself. I grinned uncontrollably, swinging my arms as I let gravity pull me down the hospital's hill. I couldn't wait to see what the meds would do for me—how they'd settle me down, balance me out, help me feel more productive. I pulled out my phone to share the good news.

"Dad, hey, it's Laura."

"Hi. What's going on?"

"I'm just leaving McLean," I said. "I saw Dr. Bachman, you know, the psychiatrist Dr. Anderson connected me with?" I went on to tell him how good I felt, that the appointment went great, that I was already feeling so much more optimism about my future. "Dad, he figured out what's been going on."

"What did he say?"

"Well, you remember Anuja?"

"Of course. She was quite helpful." I grimaced at that word, *helpful*, assuming that the benefit to which he referred did not have to do with me as much as it did him and my mother, with whom Anuja had shared regular updates about my therapy sessions during my ninth-grade year. I let it slide.

"She'd given me a bipolar diagnosis all the way back in ninth grade. Not sure if you remember that. Anyway, I explained everything that's been going on to Dr. Bachman and I told him about my history with Anuja, and he thinks she accurately diagnosed me back then. Basically, that I've had bipolar disorder this whole time and because I haven't been getting treatment it's gotten worse."

"Okay—"

"And I mean, shit, Dad, I'm so mad at myself. If only I'd listened, maybe I never would have gotten here—"

"That's neither here nor there, Laura," my father jumped in. "I'm so happy to hear the news. What does he say the next step is?"

"I'm going to see him regularly—it's pretty easy, I just come out on the bus. And the meds I'm on should kick in over the next few weeks."

"Sounds like a good plan. Have him send me the bill, okay? If he needs to talk to me about payment, just give him my number."

"I will, Dad. Thanks so much. I love you."

"I love you too, Laura. Everything's going to be okay."

My father had said this to me countless times over the years, and while I appreciated his efforts, I'd always quietly dismissed the reassurances. Now, for the first time, as I touched the folded prescriptions in my pocket, I actually believed him.

Of my medical records that I've been able to obtain, the notes from Dr. Bachman have, by far, been the most detailed and informative. In early February, two weeks after we began therapy together, I reported that I was having insomnia. He added a sleep aid, Ambien, to the mix, writing, "She requests 60 minute sessions bc she feels that she has so much to talk about. I agreed to this for the time being given her enthusiasm, expansive material to discuss, and good response so far to extended sessions. We will meet approx. 2x/week."

Through those early months of 2002, I pursued full actualization of this new life of mental illness with the same zeal for success that had once gotten me excellent report cards, high SAT scores, and top national squash rankings. I relished the relief that came from accepting my diagnosis, sure now that the desperate search for answers to why I was in so much pain was over. I didn't need to berate myself anymore for being a fuckup, because I *wasn't* actually a fuckup. I *wasn't* bad, or lazy, or a failure: I was sick. And with the diagnosis came clear next steps that would lead me to feeling better: call up the pharmacy every month for a refill, take my daily doses as prescribed, and keep in good contact with Dr. Bachman. I knew I could do this.

This surge of motivation carried over into the rest of my life. There was my quick adoption of the routines and temperament that I imagined a high-functioning Harvard student should have: No alcohol or drugs. Inflexible academic rigor. An air of seriousness in all matters. No patience for wasted time. I dove into my schoolwork, savoring the pleasure of reading and taking notes and outlining papers for hours at Café Algiers while I chain-smoked, downed black coffee, and listened to Elliott Smith, Nick Drake, Björk, and other artists whose music felt appropriately cerebral. Interactions with other people came to feel like the squandering of my newly rediscovered solitude, so I avoided going back to the dorm until just before bedtime. My grades shot up. My sense of confidence in my capacities did too. I actively participated in my discussion classes, sometimes shocked by the clarity with which words now seemed to glide from my mouth. Dr. Bachman wrote around this time, "She continues to do extremely well in all areas." I started to contemplate whether being bipolar was actually something I should be proud of. Could it mean that my brain, now pharmaceutically treated, might exist on some kind of higher neurological order than those around me?

I diligently took the mood stabilizer and antipsychotic. Though the Ambien had initially been written as a PRN—"pro re nata," a Latin phrase used by doctors to mean "as needed"—I was needing it every night before long. Anytime I tried to skip a dose, the insomnia returned with a vengeance, which I assumed was my untreated mental illness. I did not consider the possibility that this was, in fact, a sign of "therapeutic disease," as psychiatrist Pierre Deniker had put it so straightforwardly a half century earlier—a biochemical signal that something far more concerning was going on.

EIGHT

Ambien

Since the late 1990s, the FDA has provided the general public with an online database that allows anyone to look up materials such as FDA staff reviews of clinical trials, correspondence between drug companies and the FDA, and summaries of drug approval documents.* While incomplete and heavily redacted, each package contains a trove of information about pharmaceutical drugs—information that would be highly beneficial for anyone to read prior to starting a new prescription.

I never thought to dig up the FDA approval package for Ambien prior to starting it because I had no idea that such a resource even existed. Had I educated myself about the drug, which was approved in 1992, I would have gotten a clear picture of what, exactly, the three trials submitted to the FDA by Lorex Pharmaceuticals (which was eventually acquired by what today is Sanofi) showed about Ambien's effectiveness. (Of note, Lorex actually included forty-one trials in its NDA [New Drug Application], but the FDA decided to factor only three "definitive" trials into its decision, along with four trials it considered "supportive," and to shelve the remaining thirty-four due to "(1) insufficient data for review . . . and/or (2) substantial flaws in

---

* As of 2024, you can find this database here: fda.gov/drugsatfda.

the design or conduct of studies.") The first trial split 462 participants with completely normal sleep function into six groups, one of which was put on a placebo and the rest of which on varying dosages of Ambien. They were followed for one night, under the presumption that they would have difficulties because they were sleeping in a laboratory for the first time. Sleep latency (SL) (how long it takes to fall asleep; usually this is determined objectively using electrodes and sensors that track things like brain activity, heart rate, and breathing) was measured; those taking Ambien fell asleep about ten minutes faster than those on a placebo. The number of awakenings was measured; those on Ambien woke up, on average, five times in the night instead of about seven, as with the placebo group. Sleep efficiency (SE) of those on Ambien was measured at 91.7 percent, compared with 87.8 percent of placebo takers (SE is a ratio of the total time asleep to time spent in bed; according to a 2016 paper in the *Journal of Clinical Sleep Medicine*, the peer-reviewed journal of the American Academy of Sleep Medicine, when people are doing sleep therapy, the goal is to get them to 85–89 percent SE).

The second and third trials, which were much smaller, started out by putting patients on a placebo without telling them—this is called a single-blind run-in phase, and it's a strategy often implemented by drug companies to improve outcomes of a drug by screening and then removing anyone who responds positively to a placebo prior to starting a trial—and the remaining participants were then split into active drug and placebo groups. They were followed for thirty-five and thirty-one days, respectively. At the end of the second trial, patients on Ambien were falling asleep around ten to twenty minutes faster than prior to being put on the drug and about twenty minutes faster than the placebo group (whose time to fall asleep hadn't changed). Ambien takers' sleep efficiency scores were 87.9 and 87.3 at the end of the trial, compared with 80.7 in the placebo group (all groups, it should be noted, started with at least 80 percent, not far from the 85–89 percent range recommended in that sleep medicine journal article). The Ambien group generally had *more* awakenings per night than those on the placebo. Researchers in the third trial acknowledged that "there was no statistically significant difference between active drug groups and placebo beyond 2 weeks of treatment, except for sleep latency," and in the case of this specific trial, they had omitted any objective sleep-related measures—one can only speculate as to why—and left as the only measure of efficacy the subjective opinions of the patients regarding how well they thought they slept.

And had I read the section in which the FDA provides required warning text for the patient package insert, I would have seen the following:

> Sleep medicines can cause dependence, especially when these medicines are used regularly for longer than a few weeks or at high doses. . . . When people develop dependence, they may have difficulty stopping the sleep medicine. If the medicine is suddenly stopped, the body is not able to function normally and unpleasant symptoms (see "Withdrawal") may occur. They may find they have to keep taking the medicine either at the prescribed dose or at increasing doses just to avoid withdrawal symptoms.

When I began Ambien in early 2002, the sleeping pill industry was just starting to boom. Between 2001 and 2005, prescriptions ballooned by 55 percent, to 45.5 million per year. By 2005, Sanofi-Aventis was making $2.1 billion per year on Ambien sales alone, and I'd been taking it every night, as prescribed, for years, completely unaware that it had never been approved for long-term use or that it was dependence-forming. I can't be sure what Dr. Bachman knew about the drug. I don't recall him ever bringing up concerns about renewing my monthly prescription.

Accompanying my worsened sleep issues in the wake of starting Ambien was a concerning array of newly amplified emotions. I was started on Prozac "to help ameliorate anxiety, tearfulness, obsessive + compulsive approach to food, etc.," wrote Dr. Bachman. A week later, I shared with him that I was newly jittery. He suggested I cut back on caffeine.

At some point that spring, after developing a skin rash, I was switched from Prozac to Effexor, another antidepressant, and then switched back to Prozac when the rash didn't subside. Therapy, Dr. Bachman recorded, focused on "finding a middle ground between roles of rebellion-conformity, partying-studying, etc." We analyzed my dreams, some of which, half a year after the September 11 attacks, involved bombs, missiles, and dead bodies. Dr. Bachman began to mention issues with "body image" and "eating habits" more frequently in his notes, and he encouraged me to call him between appointments if I was having "particular difficulty in this regard." On the whole, however, he started most of his notes with statements like "Pt. continues to feel well." I was always sure to share enough details about my progress to make Dr. Bachman proud of me.

In April 2002, Dr. Bachman noted that I had stopped my mood stabilizer after running out of refills. "Since diagnosis of bipolar I or II disorder is uncertain (borderline personality traits, along with substance use is a more likely diagnosis)," he wrote, "for now she will remain off VPA [valproic acid, the generic version of Depakote] and I will observe her clinical progress carefully."

Through the rest of freshman year, I saw Dr. Bachman twice a week and took my meds diligently. As my Prozac dose slowly crept up, I simultaneously developed an agitating, compelling urge for control.

The compulsion grew so demanding that I began to focus it on the closest available target: my body. (I'd had a bout of what would have been diagnosed as anorexia or "eating disorder not otherwise speci-fied" in high school, so it was easy to slip back into the old, familiar practice of pruning away at my physical self.) I tracked the loose stomach skin I could pull at, the extra meat on my arms and shoul-ders, the flesh on my inner thighs. These were all, now, redundancies to be gotten rid of. Never before a runner, I began jogging along the Charles River, making silent bets to go an additional quarter mile each day "or else you'll die," I'd tell myself. I systematically omitted entire food groups that newly threatened me until I was eating solely fat- and sugar-free items sequestered behind thick plastic packaging listing unpronounceable, lengthy ingredient lists.

That summer, I went on a six-week cross-country road trip with Catrin, my best friend from Deerfield. Though I intended to speak regularly with Dr. Bachman, I never followed up after our first phone appointment to schedule the next one. In spite of the breathtaking sights around us, I obsessively focused my attention every day on running many miles and religiously taking my meds, which were stored for easy access in a quilted Dopp kit next to my pillow. I pan-icked when our travels took us to places that didn't afford me access to what I'd decided I was allowed to eat, shuddering at the thought of slipping from my diligent daily routine just once. I grew increasingly irritable, quick to pounce at Catrin when she suggested itinerary plans that threatened the integrity of my dietary regimen. We lis-tened to dozens of hours of Harry Potter audiobooks to distract from the tension I'd created between us. My flesh dissipated, my cheeks grew concave, my eyes hollowed out. By the trip's end, my clothes were falling off me. I returned home convinced I was more on top of my life than ever before.

I couldn't have known at the time that SSRI drugs like Prozac would soon be linked to abrupt behavior and personality changes similar to what I'd begun to experience. In 2004, two years after our road trip, the FDA issued a required warning for all SSRI antidepressant drug labels, part of which said:

> Patients, their families, and their caregivers should be encouraged to be alert to the emergence of anxiety, agitation, panic attacks, insomnia, irritability, hostility, aggressiveness, impulsivity, akathisia (psychomotor restlessness), hypomania, mania, other unusual changes in behavior, worsening of depression, and suicidal ideation, especially early during antidepressant treatment and when the dose is adjusted up or down.

When I moved into my sophomore dorm the next fall, I avoided the student dining hall and instead stocked up on packages of dehydrated vegetables, fat-free processed meats, mustard, and jars of pickles. I hid anything that didn't need refrigeration in the back of my closet, convinced that one of my roommates might steal it. I drank excessive amounts of diet soda and black coffee and kept a diary tracking each day's progress: *4 pieces of dried mango; 1 cup of nonfat cottage cheese; 5 slices of fat-free turkey breast; 7 pickles. 1 hour on elliptical and 4-mile run. 1,500 calories burned.* My roommates, who frequently tried to hide the scale due to their concerns about my shrinking frame, increasingly annoyed me. Dr. Bachman upped my Prozac dose, noting, "She is feeling a little 'guilty' and 'weird' about a sense of 'arrogance' and desire to be alone and introspective more this semester. We agreed that overall this is part of her growth, development of self and ego boundaries, etc."

It was only a matter of time before my irritation with others grew to include Dr. Bachman. I'd successfully excised nearly all social interaction; why not cut out therapy as well? After all, I hadn't talked to him once all summer, during which time I'd managed to get my life into impeccable order. I began to cancel sessions. Eventually, I stopped scheduling them at all. I spent the rest of the fall and early winter in a frenzied fervor of self-obsession, sporadically dabbling in alcohol and having fleeting dalliances with guys when I felt especially terrible about myself.

The next time I contacted Dr. Bachman was in late January, by email:

1/22/03 7:33am

hey dr. bachman–

i've been doing really well with respect to squash and studies the past couple months. i've been really good about remaining healthy, still not smoking cigarettes, drinking much, or anything else. all in all, i feel great on the outside. i really miss talking to you, though, because i've sort of gotten back to that state where i have a lot of thoughts about stuff no one else would really understand besides you. . . . i'm still living a psycho extreme life, with my eating, following my schedules, and i've basically lost all ability to socialize. . . . i'm having serious guy-issues, and am actually worried that i'll never be able to get married because i have such a problem with letting anyone else into my life. literally, i love being by myself. i'm obsessed with it, and can't get enough of it. if i could go through the day not talking to anyone, i would. . . .

anyway, i wanted to send you an e-mail to apologize for being so bad about keeping in touch. i sort of went into my own little world the past two months, and found that i had no time to step out of my intense schedule of squash, studying, and going to sleep early. i guess i got cocky too and thought that i'd be ok not talking to anyone for a while. well, i was wrong. i've found that all the stuff is building up again. . . . i just wanted to let you know that, if you can fit me in, i'd love to come back to see you. i'm pretty desperate. i've transformed into a machine, and my closest friends have said the same thing. it's so weird . . . anyway, just e-mail me back when you read this and tell me what you think about starting to see eachother [sic] in february. I hope you've been doing really well, and i can't wait to be in touch!

~laura

"I've transformed into a machine." This remark is particularly striking to me. At nineteen, I was so close to thinking critically about what was happening to me. I had a clear understanding that I wasn't *feeling*. Wasn't *connected*. Wasn't *present in myself*. I'd morphed from a raw, suffering, lost young woman at boarding school into a detached, self-absorbed, empathyless machine. I must have known there was something wrong with this; otherwise I wouldn't have mentioned it to Dr. Bachman and called myself "desperate." Yet in the wake of this disintegration, I sounded intrigued, at best, by the strange curiosity I'd become. In the text of my email, I see no desire to actually change myself.

Dr. Bachman wrote a kind reply, and we resumed therapy. In notes from our next meeting, he wrote, "Pt. expressed some concern that she had ignored or hurt me by not being in touch over last few months. I reassured her that I missed her but was not angry at her, and she expressed relief that we could reinitiate our work together." Still new to psychiatric patienthood, I hadn't figured out that a professional sitting across from me was not a friend I could hurt but a stranger paid to listen to my pain. Shielding me even further from this realization was the fact that Dr. Bachman's weekly bills—paid for out of pocket, and hundreds of dollars a pop—were being sent directly to my father.

My insomnia issues continued to worsen, so Dr. Bachman increased my nightly Ambien dose. Soon after, I began to fall asleep in class. Deep sleep. The kind you can't pull yourself out of. I tried every method I could think of to stay awake—chugging coffee, prying my eyes open, pinching myself—but nothing worked. Reliably, within ten minutes of the start of a lecture, I'd get swallowed up by a sedation so intense that it felt like I'd been given a horse tranquilizer.

I brought the problem to Dr. Bachman and was relieved to hear he had an answer: antinarcoleptic medication. (He said nothing about how daytime drowsiness had been one of the most commonly reported adverse effects in the clinical studies that got Ambien its FDA approval.) In his notes, he wrote, "Due to decreased attention/concentration/focus in class (and falling asleep there easily), will add Provigil, 100mg 6AM."

I thanked him profusely. After getting back to Harvard Square, I made a beeline for the pharmacy.

NINE

Provigil

P rovigil's effect on me was immediate and astounding: I was suddenly alert through the day, full of energy, mentally sharp. "She
had a very good week and feels the Provigil has been helpful," Dr.
Bachman wrote. "Mood, energy, attention and concentration all are
notably improved. Sleep is good." I could now take crisp, thorough
notes during class with ease. Reading seventy pages in one sitting before diving in to write a five-page response paper felt like a walk in the
park. I was convinced that Dr. Bachman had saved me, and I silently
thanked the cashew-sized pills each time I fingered them in my palm.

What I didn't know, and wouldn't for many years, was that Provigil is essentially a potent form of speed.

Similar to cocaine and methamphetamine, Provigil acts, in part, by
inhibiting the reuptake of dopamine, thus artificially increasing dopamine levels in the human body. It was approved by the FDA in
1998 as effective in "improv[ing] wakefulness in patients with excessive daytime sleepiness associated with narcolepsy," based on two
nine-week efficacy studies, both of which showed that narcoleptic
patients on Provigil, on average, stayed awake for two to three minutes longer than they'd been able to prior to starting the drug. In the
one study that tracked patients' total sleep time, those taking Provigil gained, on average, about one to two extra minutes of time spent

awake over those on the placebo. (I, on the other hand, reliably gained about one to two extra *hours* of time spent feverishly highlighting my "History of Science 175: Madness and Medicine" sourcebook until it looked like a full-on Easter basket of fluorescent Tetris blocks.) Among the significant percentage of adverse events reported by patients on Provigil during those trials, the most frequent were physical issues like headache, nausea, and diarrhea, along with nervous system issues like nervousness, insomnia, and anxiety.

For all my excitement about this new medication, its positive effects were short-lived; I soon began to fall asleep again in class. Dr. Bachman increased my dose to 200 mg per day. I felt back on track, better than ever, and began waking up early to get to hot yoga every morning at six o'clock. After class, I'd hit the campus gym, where I used pseudonyms on the equipment sign-up sheet to evade the thirty-minute limit, reserving two and a half hours' worth of my favorite elliptical machine. Afterward, as I fought faintness with each step while making my way to the mat to stretch, I savored the sight of my dwindling visage in the mirror: the protruding collarbones, scrawny legs, shrunken breasts. This disappearance felt like the sign of my arrival. (While Dr. Bachman makes clear in his notes that he was aware of my progressing eating issues and body image problems, he never diagnosed me with an eating disorder or referred me to a specialist.) At some point, I discovered that antipsychotics are notorious for causing weight gain. I stopped mine—Seroquel—immediately, fearful of impeding my weight loss efforts. This was the only adverse drug effect I cared about.

By the end of the squash season, I was spending approximately six hours a day exercising. One might think such an excessive routine would have led to collapse, but the fact of the matter, which speaks, in my estimation, to the resilience of the human body—and likely to taking growing daily doses of prescribed speed—is that I played the best squash of my life that year, reaching the fourth slot on our ladder and helping our team win the Ivy League Championships and secure second place in the nationals. I could run court sprints faster than almost all my teammates, and, ramped up on adrenaline, I'd loudly announce at the end of practice that I was staying late to do more sprints, and would anyone like to join me? Sometimes our number one player took me up on the offer; usually, everyone politely declined and headed off to dinner. At various points throughout these two-hundred-milligram Provigil days, I felt painful twists in my chest, and when at rest, my heart pounded hard, seeming to frequently skip beats; I ignored this, along with the new, chronic headaches and terrible constipation. I disregarded the stares from the women who worked at my favorite Vietnamese restaurant, where I frequently came in sweaty squash attire to imbibe two giant bowls of vegetable broth with steamed vegetables. I interpreted the instant irritation I felt toward anyone interfering with my daily routine as a justified response to their ignorance of my body's needs. By any clinician paying close attention, I'd have been declared manic. In my estimation, I was doing better than ever.

• • •

Laura Delano

5/1/03 60-min psychotherapy—

Obsessionality with restriction of calories and compulsive exercising discussed. Relation of these sxs to her self-critical tendencies also explored. She worries that she is too complicated and "pathetic" for others (esp. men) to handle. . . . Increase Prozac to 60mg.

F/U on 5/8 at 3:00

5/8/03 Appt cancelled by pt and rescheduled for 5/15. Then rescheduled for 5/21/03

—*From Dr. Bachman's notes*

The increase in my Prozac dose didn't make me happy, but by that point, the pursuit of happiness wasn't even on my radar. In May 2003, I came back to the dorm from an appointment with Dr. Bachman to find my roommates waiting for me with solemn faces. After watching me deteriorate for months, they'd organized an intervention.

"We can't watch you doing this to yourself anymore, Lo," my closest friend and bunk bed partner, Beth, pleaded. "Please, you need help. You have an eating disorder. We want to help you!"

"Noooo way," I said, shaking my head as I forced my way past them to the bedroom. "No fucking way!"

Beth tried to catch me in the hallway. "Lo, we love you! I can see how much you're struggling!"

"Fuck. You."

The next day, I packed up all my things and drove to my parents' house in Greenwich. There were no more classes on campus anyway, just papers to finish. I left a voicemail for Dr. Bachman saying I'd gone home unexpectedly and would be in touch about a next appointment. Just as the previous summer, I never followed up.

A few weeks later, an impacted wisdom tooth required me to get an emergency extraction. I was told to avoid solid food for several days and rest. The disruption to my exercise and eating routine was devastating, but without a choice, I agreed to my mother's offer to make me fat-free milkshakes while I recovered. "You have to use skim milk only, and fat-free chocolate frozen yogurt. Promise?" I'd insisted, to which she'd agreed, knowing that saying anything else would have meant a blowup.

After the surgery, I was sprawled on my parents' couch, examining the opacity of a half-empty milkshake in a panic. Was this beverage actually free of fat? I'd been so hungry that I'd chugged it right away, but partway through, an overwhelming richness on my tongue got me suspicious. It tasted a little too good to be true.

"Mom?" I called. She came up from the basement and stood before me, cautious from my tone. I put the TV on mute. "Is it possible you didn't use skim milk when you made this?"

She paused for a moment. "Well, your father—"

I interrupted her with a dramatic "Ugh" as she continued, "Laura, listen, there wasn't any skim left. Dad must've finished it this morning. I used whole milk instead. I really didn't think it would be a problem—"

"Mom!" I roared, the volume of my voice startling me. "You promised you'd only use skim! Why didn't you just tell me there wasn't any more? I could've gone and gotten some!"

"Laura, please, c'mon, settle down—"

"Settle down? Do you have any idea what you've done?"

"Now, really, is it that big of a deal? One time?"

I stood up from the sofa quickly, suddenly dizzy, and stormed up the stairs. I considered rushing to the bathroom to make myself vomit but was too afraid. (There were two things I told myself I'd never do, no matter what: *Never make yourself puke on purpose, and never try heroin.*)

My mother, of course, didn't know what she'd done. No rational person could have. After my long, slow slip into my exercise and food obsessions, I was, you could say, a bit out of touch. To any outside observer—to me, today—this scene of me on my parents' couch yelling at my mother for not making me a fat-free milkshake is cringeworthy.

But what I felt at the time—and I remember this clear as day—was unadulterated terror: *I've lost control. I've ruined everything. It's all over.*

One chug of full-fat milkshake was enough to make me throw out all my hard-and-fast rules: I stopped tracking my daily routines. I became a human vacuum cleaner, regularly eating all the ice cream in my parents' freezer, or making a trough of oatmeal covered in cream and butter and sugar, or devouring multiple pieces of buttery toast with jam followed by a half block of Cheddar cheese. The gorging had me frequently in so much physical pain that I'd need to un-button my pants and lie curled up in a ball for fear I'd rupture my stomach. At night, I drank excessive numbers of beers during excessive numbers of drinking games with old friends from home, then ate excessive amounts of cheesy fries and burritos during late-night trips to our favorite hole-in-the-wall restaurant. By the end of summer, I'd gained twenty pounds—weight that left me looking perfectly healthy to everyone else, which to me meant entirely unacceptable.

The rapidity with which I'd lost control of my body led me to lose faith, in turn, in the Prozac, Provigil, and Ambien. Despite this, I continued them. I didn't reach out to schedule an appointment with Dr. Bachman until right before I was supposed to move back to Cambridge—this time into an off-campus apartment with a woman from my squash team, as I'd decided to separate from my roommates after their intervention.

In his notes, Dr. Bachman wrote,

Pt has spent most of summer with family in Maine and in CT. She has been very out of sorts lately with worsening eating d/o sxs (frequent bingeing followed by excessive exercise; no ac-tual purging, laxative or diuretic use). No SI/HI [suicidal idea-tion/homicidal ideation], mania, or psychosis. . . . She discussed

her discomfort with sexual relations with men; she generally
feels like she is being "raped" during consensual intercourse, as
though the man is no longer relating to her as a person but is
just using her "animalistically" for his own needs.

This is the last of Dr. Bachman's medical notes. Given his meticulous documentation of our appointments and calls, I can only assume it was our last appointment as well.

Promptly after moving into my new apartment, I began a nightly ritual of walking two blocks to the market, buying a gallon of whole milk and two boxes of cereal, walking back, taking my night meds, climbing into bed to wait for the loopy disinhibition to kick in—this usually took about twenty-three minutes after taking Ambien—and inhaling the entirety of my purchase before picking up my journal to draw twisted, dark drawings and write disturbing poems that I had no memory of by morning. The only reason I knew any of this the next day was the evidence: empty cereal boxes, spilled milk in the bed, and an open journal.

Two years later, in March 2006, a class action lawsuit involving around five hundred plaintiffs would be filed against Sanofi-Aventis, claiming that the company failed to properly warn people about the possible risk of sleep bingeing and sleepwalking on Ambien. One of the plaintiffs, a fifty-five-year old woman, reported that while asleep, she ate "raw eggs, uncooked yellow rice, cans of vegetables, loaves of bread, bags of chips and bags of candy" and awoke an hour later, vomiting; another plaintiff recounted a sleep-driving incident that led to getting arrested; one plaintiff was sexually assaulted by a neighbor after letting him into her home while sleepwalking. While the judge ruled in favor of Sanofi-Aventis, which never had to pay damages to the plaintiffs, the FDA required the company to add or strengthen multiple warnings and precautions to the drug's label in 2007, among them:

> A variety of abnormal thinking and behavior changes have been reported to occur in association with the use of sedative/ hypnotics. Some of these changes may be characterized by decreased inhibition (e.g. aggressiveness and extroversion that seemed out of character), similar to effects produced by alcohol and other CNS depressants. Visual and auditory hallucinations have been reported as well as behavioral changes such as bizarre behavior, agitation and depersonalization.

As the nightly blackout eating escapades continued, I drew two conclusions: I was at the mercy of another very serious mental illness—binge eating disorder—and I needed help.

For all the kindness Dr. Bachman had shown me, I'd lost the confidence I'd once had in him to help. Our therapy sessions hadn't touched my self-destructive bipolar behaviors, and the meds had done nothing to remediate my symptoms. I needed eating disorder specialists. They were my only chance at getting my life back under control.

I looked up a well-known inpatient eating disorder clinic in Connecticut and called to inquire about admission, not caring that this would mean dropping out of school. I felt immediate relief as I imagined sneaking off to a hospital where staff would control how much I ate, give me whatever therapy I needed, and put me on better meds. They asked me a list of questions on the phone, and after I shared my height and weight, they told me that I didn't meet the criteria for inpatient admission because my numbers weren't "critical." The devastation! Did they not understand the depth of my anguish, how out of control my eating had become? Did they not see that I needed to be locked away from the convenience store? From my kitchen? From myself?

I was told to contact an outpatient eating disorder clinic just outside Harvard Square. Disappointed but unsure of where else to turn, I gave them a call, explained my situation, and set up an intake appointment.

"I think you'll do great in our evening intensive outpatient program," Lina Farnetti, the head psychiatrist, told me a few days later. "This will also allow you to stay in school. You don't want to have to drop out in the middle of the semester, do you? And lose all the work you've put in?" She sounded so far away.

"You'll be assigned to work with a psychopharmacologist who specializes in eating disorders," Lina continued, "and you and I will do therapy. We'll get you set up with a nutritionist, and you'll come here each weekday evening for group and, most importantly, community dinner. Each patient brings her own food, and everyone eats together."

I yearned for some kind of translation device that could take everything I'd been through since the milkshake and implant it in this psychiatrist's mind to help her better understand my situation. I signed the waivers and requested that Dr. Bachman send his records to my new psychiatrist.

Initial Evaluation Report—Cambridge Eating Disorder Center

HPI: . . . [Patient] says she is "obsessed with analyzing" people, and is unable to have a conversation without trying mentally to take the other person apart. She is also obsessed with "having intense conversations with strangers." This has something of the effect of a drug for her: she uses it to improve her mood. The patient has been seeing Dr. Paul Bachman at McLean 2x/week for the past 9 months. She is requesting a change at this time in order to consolidate her treatment . . . and also because she finds it difficult to talk with a man about some personal issues.

MSE: The patient is an alert, oriented young woman who makes good eye contact, is cooperative with the interview. There is some psychomotor agitation. Speech is somewhat rapid, slightly pressured. Mood is variable, depending on eating/drinking patterns. Affect is full range, appropriate. TP [thought process] linear. No SI/HI. Denies PI [paranoid ideation], delusions of persecution or grandeur. However, she does feel that "people don't really know me."

ASSESSMENT: The patient is a 20-year-old college junior who presents with a variety of symptoms, most of which are long-standing. She has had episodes of depression as well as apparent episodes of hypomania. Her pattern is consistent with a diagnosis of rapid-cycling bipolar disorder. This diagnosis is also consistent with the patient's impulsive behaviors, including self-injury and substance abuse. She has also had symptoms of OCD and now has obsessive thought patterns (e.g., analyzing). Her eating disorder seems to be exacerbated by her compulsive tendencies. The treatment regimen should be multifaceted, to address both psychological, psychopharmacological and substance abuse issues.

DIAGNOSIS: *

Axis I: Bipolar II Disorder with Rapid Cycling; Alcohol Abuse, r/o Dependence; Marijuana Abuse; Bulimia Nervosa, non-purging type; r/o OCD

---

* The American Psychiatric Association introduced a multiaxial system in the third edition of its *Diagnostic and Statistical Manual of Mental Disorders* so that diagnosing clinicians could "ensure that certain information that may be of value in planning treatment and

Axis II: deferred

Axis III: h/o [history of] amenorrhea

Axis IV: school, family stressors

Axis V: 55

PLAN:

1. *Begin treatment with Lithium [sic] for mood stabilization. Patient needs to obtain labs including BUN, Creatinine, TSH prior to starting drug.*

2. *Continue Prozac 60mg for now; continue other meds.*

3. *Continue individual psychotherapy with Dr. Farnetti.*

4. *Continue nutritional counseling.*

5. *Refer patient for substance abuse treatment, either on- or off-campus.*

6. *Patient is to begin an outpatient evening group at the CEDC.*

7. *Consider family meeting for psychoeducation around patient's illness.*

8. *Follow-up in 2 weeks after obtaining labs.*

---

predicting outcome for each person is recorded on each of five axes." (See page xxv in the *DSM-III-R* [1987].) This multiaxial system was removed two editions later, in the *DSM-5*. The APA's definition of each axis, according to the *DSM-III-R*, was as follows: Axis I: Clinical Syndromes; Axis II: Developmental Disorders or Personality Disorders; Axis III: Physical Disorders and Conditions, Axis IV: Severity of Psychosocial Stressors; Axis V: Global Assessment of Functioning (GAF). In the revised fourth edition of the *DSM*, the APA explained that the purpose of its hundred-point GAF scale was for "reporting the clinician's judgment of the individual's overall level of functioning." The clinician was to select one of ten ten-point ranges, with 1–9 denoting "persistent danger of severely hurting self or others (e.g., recurrent violence) OR persistent inability to maintain minimal personal hygiene OR serious suicidal act with clear expectation of death," and 91–100 indicative of "superior functioning in a wide range of activities, life's problems never seem to get out of hand, is sought out by others because of his or her many positive qualities. No symptoms." (See pages 32 and 34 of the *DSM-IV-TR* [2000].)

Outward Bound

I attended eating disorder treatment faithfully that fall in spite of my limited optimism. How could a few measly hours of group therapy and meals each night do anything for me? The way I saw it, the only feasible solution to my completely out-of-control eating disorder was to strip away my freedoms—to literally lock me away from the endless opportunity to gorge myself. Every time I walked down Massachusetts Avenue to join the broad spectrum of fellow patients in the evening—young and old, some skeletal, others extremely rotund, all of us women—I dreaded the walk back to my independence, for it meant having to endure another day at the mercy of my all-powerful "Ed," as we liked to call our respective eating disorders.

I decided to cut back on my involvement with the squash team, which had become too much to manage alongside the program. I was "tired of team camadarie [sic]," according to my medical records. "Feels 0 support for struggle and problems." I was so uncomfortable in my swollen body, anyway, that training felt like psychological torture. (Though I was still taking Provigil, it had long ago stopped speeding me up.) I attended weekly therapy with Lina, who, unlike Dr. Bachman, wasn't interested in discussing my upbringing or the broader socioeconomic context of my life. Instead, as we sat across from each other every week—Lina with her bob of dark-blond hair and dark-stained eyebrows, always in a conservative blazer and well-tailored pants or calf-length skirt, me with my greasy sheen of showerlessness and my baggy, stained sweat suit—she focused on the frequency and intensity of my symptoms, asking with a detached, journalistic air about each binge-eating episode I'd had since our last appointment: What was happening when I first felt the urge? What efforts, if any, did I make to shut it down? How long did it take before I gave in to my impulses? What did I feel while I was downing that box of Lucky Charms? I saw no point to Lina's questions, which seemed premised on the notion that my thoughts, drives, and behaviors were simply wild animals in need of proper taming; what I wanted was to get a pharmaceutical machine gun and blow their heads off. And so I held on to faith that it would be my new psychopharmacologist, Dr. Mankey, who would save me, as long as I stuck around long enough for her to find an effective drug regimen during our once-monthly fifteen-minute sessions. Of the multiple meds I was on at the time (Provigil, Prozac, Ambien, and, briefly, Lithobid, a brand-name version of lithium, which I quickly discontinued after learning it could cause weight gain), she claimed it would be an especially high dose of Prozac that could be my game changer. She increased my daily prescription to 80 mg (the maximum recommended dose is 60 mg), noting, "(1) ↑ Prozac to 80mg, targeting obs./comp. activity; (2) consider Topomax [*sic*], Lamictal." When I reported that my daytime sedation was continuing to worsen, she doubled my Provigil dose to 400 mg (the recommended daily dose for people diagnosed with narcolepsy is 200 mg), noting to herself to "consider alt. stimulants." The only change I felt was more of the same: more bingeing, more despair, more self-imposed isolation, more shame.

Late one evening months later, in early January 2004, I sent a two-thousand-word email to Dr. Bachman, describing how I had no friends, as socializing felt "just too energy-consuming." "i feel so miserable and pathetic all the time," I went on, "that i wouldn't even think about letting another person into my life, let alone take on the responsibility of me becoming a part of theirs." I shared how unmotivated and incapable I felt academically. "right now," I said, "i'm meant to be writing a research proposal that is due tomorrow; i haven't even started doing it, and it will probably take about 9 hours to do. this upcoming month will be horribly challenging, with about 80 pages of papers due, two exams, and a shitload of research for my thesis. i'm not very excited, and the sad thing is, i can say right now with confidence that i'm at the edge of a cliff and am about to plummet downwards, and i don't even care."

"dr. mankey has upped the Prozac to 80mg," I went on, "and i just feel numb and dead. atleast [*sic*] it's better than feeling the intense sharp pain in my head i used to feel."

I continued, "with regards to my thoughts—well, suicide has become a daily topic of conversation i have with myself. the sad thing is, i hate how i think about it all the time but i can't stop the thoughts from coming into my head. i plan out ways, think about how peaceful it would be if my mind didn't exist, you know, i'm sure it's typical suicidal thoughts. there have been a few times that have been such close calls, i can honestly say that the only thing that keeps me from doing it is my guilt complex with my family and how horribly they'd feel."

I closed by sharing the following with him:

> i know i've been so awful at communicating, but it's just been so hard to get out of bed everyday [*sic*], even, that to think about talking to anyone outside of my own self and the group would be too stressful. i lie in bed for hours at a time staring at the wall and wishing so much that I could be "normal," capable of functioning in the world, and content with living in my

body and with my racing thoughts all the time. i really don't want to kill myself on those days when i have glimmers of hope for recovery, but those days get lesser and lesser by the week and i'm starting to think there's no point anymore in even trying. . . . all i ever want to do is lie in my bed, cuddle with my dog, and read books from writers whose minds I can relate to. that's all i ever want to do. thanks for taking the time to read my letter, and i hope you'll write back soon.

~laura

Dr. Bachman wrote back a supportive reply, saying that I'd "been courageous in standing up to the difficulties" and that he'd be happy to start meeting with me again if that felt helpful, an offer I never took him up on.

A couple of weeks later, I was up late, unable to sleep, even with the Ambien. My Dopp kit of pills kept beckoning me from its perch on the bedpost. *Just swallow us. We're here for you, Laura, we're the only ones here for you. Doesn't your mind want some quiet, once and for all?* There were two weeks left until the semester was over, and though I'd resolved to make it through, I wasn't sure I could. All those skipped lectures, the excuse-laden emails to my graduate teaching assistants, the in-person meetings where I had to tell them about my bipolar disorder and my eating disorder and how bad this depressive episode was and that I was trying my best, I really was, I was taking meds and going to therapy, but I just couldn't manage, couldn't handle it all. They'd been so understanding, but where had their accommodations gotten me? Nothing had changed. I saw no light at the end of the tunnel.

Fuck it. I reached over and grabbed the bag, unzipped it, took the numerous pill bottles out. I shook them to feel their weight. Paused for a moment.

No, no, no, Laura, nonono, you can't do this. Without letting myself think too long, I picked up my phone and dialed home, cringing as I thought about disturbing my parents' sleep.

"Hello?" my father answered.

"Dad." My voice was shaking.

"Laura, is everything okay?"

"I, I, I just, I don't think I can do it, Dad, it's too hard, I can't handle it—"

"Slow down, Laura. Has something happened?"

"I wanna die, Dad. I can't stop thinking about killing myself. I can't do this, I can't do this, I can't do this!"

I heard him adjusting the chair in his dressing room, the creak as he sat down, Mom's concerned voice in the background asking what was going on.

"Just slow down. Everything's going to be okay. I mean it, Laura, okay? We're going to figure this out."

"How, Dad? How? I'm doing everything I can, I'm taking my meds, I saw Dr. Bachman, I went to the eating disorder center, they upped my doses and added more meds, and nothing's working, Dad, nothing's working, I keep getting worse, I can't handle anything!"

"Slow down, Laura. Take a deep breath. I need you to, okay? Do it for me."

I rested the Dopp kit on the comforter beside me. Closing my eyes, I focused on getting air back into my lungs.

"Listen, we're going to come up with a plan, okay?"

"I can't do it anymore, Dad."

"You said last week that you can make it the rest of the semester. Do you think you need to drop out now? If you do, that's okay. We'll call the school tomorrow and pull you out."

I thought it over. "Okay, I think I can do it, Dad. I, I, I think I can."

"That's great. And remember, if that changes, that's okay too. So, what do you need right now to help you get to sleep? We can begin putting a plan together in the morning."

"I dunno, I took my sleeping pill a while ago and it isn't working. I guess I could take another one."

"If that's okay to do, maybe you should go ahead and do that."

I opened up the Ambien bottle and swallowed another pill.

The next morning, I awoke groggy to the ringing of my cell phone. It was my father, letting me know he was outside my apartment. He'd left Greenwich at 4:00 a.m. so that he'd be in Cambridge by the time I woke up.

We spent the morning talking through a game plan with my mother on the phone. They helped me map out which assignments I still had due and how long I'd need to spend on each of my three lengthy final papers. We talked through different options for me during the months I'd be off from school. Dad said, "You know, that Outward Bound trip I took when I was sixteen changed my life, it really did. Maybe we should sign you up for one."

I'd heard many stories over the years from my father about his time on that three-week outdoor adventure program. I especially remembered his three day-long "solo trip," which he spent fasting, entirely alone. Instantly, I pictured myself out in the wilderness, not a gallon of milk or box of cereal or convenience store in sight. I'd hike and run and eat next to nothing as my mounds of flesh dissipated!

"I think you're right, Dad. Let's find out what the longest, hardest trip is, and sign me up."

A month later, I was on my way to El Paso, Texas, for the most challenging course that Outward Bound offered: a three-month semester program of hiking and canoeing in Texas, Mexico, and Minnesota.

I'd double-checked to make sure I had everything I needed from the packing list, which did *not* include any of my meds. None of them were helping me, anyway, so I figured there was no point in taking them any longer. I had no understanding of what stopping Prozac, Provigil, and Ambien so abruptly would do to me.

In the early morning hours on the first night of the trip, I lay wide awake under a flimsy tarp in Redford, Texas, population ninety. A downpour of rain had soaked through my sleeping bag two hours earlier as my mind thrashed about in a sea of all-consuming horror. What had I been I thinking, believing I could make it without my meds? Why had I ever thought it made sense to leave my illnesses untreated?

Over the next three months, we hiked dry desert and belayed rock faces in Big Bend National Park. We spent weeks canoeing the white waters of the Rio Grande. We drove to Chihuahua, Mexico, took long, bumpy bus rides, walked for two days through tiny villages, and hiked past lone adobe houses on steep cliffs until we were deep in Copper Canyon. We drove north to Minnesota, where we spent six weeks hiking through snow and slush, pushing our canoes across vast, mostly frozen lakes, and portaging for miles with fifty pounds of gear on our backs and upside-down canoes perched on our shoulders. Through all of this, debilitating insomnia rocked me. There was a constant ache in my joints, a daily headache, and terrible constipation. My body's fight-or-flight response to any and all stressors was magnified beyond all recognition. I had worse-than-ever cravings for sugar and no sense of satiation, and, to my dismay, huge bags of trail mix and pots of cheesy rice seemed always at my fingertips. My mind vacillated between fixating on paranoid thoughts about what my fellow Outward Bounders thought of me and drowning in despair. Any leftover energy was spent pretending otherwise. I assumed this was my baseline state of untreated mental illness. It was hard to accept that this was all my future held for me if I continued without my meds.

The truth—which I was in the dark about and would be for many years to come—was otherwise: This wasn't life with untreated mental illness. This was the agonizing aftermath of coming off psychiatric drugs cold turkey.

I made it through the trip that spring. I even made it through the summer—more than six months without my meds. But by the end of August, it was clear to me that if I went back to school, I would kill myself.

My parents were watching television when I came down to tell them the news. "Mom? Dad? Can I talk to you?"

My father pressed Mute. My mother set down her magazine.

"What's going on? How's packing going?"

"I'm, I'm mostly packed, but—I don't know how to say this—I just can't, I can't go back to school. I know if I go back there I won't make it. I'm telling you, I can't do it. I won't be safe with myself. I'll die—I'm afraid I'll kill myself. I can't handle it, I can't handle any of it. There's just no way . . ."

My tears escalated into uncontrollable sobs. My mother stood up and took me in her arms.

We settled on the one last option we saw before us: I would check myself into a psychiatric ward. There was a private hospital close by that happened to be one of the best in the country. Mom would drive me there the next day.

PART

III

ELEVEN

The Haven

·

I stayed mostly silent during the twenty-minute ride to the psychiatric hospital as my mother nervously offered up reassurances that everything would be okay. Staring out the window, I was hoping, but not believing, that she was right.

NewYork-Presbyterian sat hidden behind thick woods on a high hill overlooking the Westchester Mall; sitting at the stoplight on the busy street below, you'd never guess a mental institution was just overhead. Originally called the Bloomingdale Insane Asylum, then the Payne Whitney Psychiatric Clinic, until it finally became NYP, the hospital was founded in the early nineteenth century in Manhattan. Like McLean, it catered primarily to wealthy patients, while poorer ones were sent to the public New York City Lunatic Asylum located on Roosevelt Island. NYP opened up its second campus in White Plains, New York, at the end of the nineteenth century on 235 acres of farmland that had been carefully landscaped by Frederick Law Olmsted, who also helped to select McLean Hospital's hilltop campus in Belmont and designed New York City's Central Park. There were flower gardens, a diverse array of trees, lush woods, and orchards. The hospital even had its own golf course, tennis courts, and gymnasium, and until the 1920s, patients maintained a farm on the grounds. Like McLean, this institutional design had been inspired by the pastoral model of moral treatment. Also like McLean, NewYork-Presbyterian eventually cut ties with that model in order to rebrand itself as a strictly medical enterprise.

We parked in the visitor lot. I grabbed my overnight bag with my sweat suit, baggy T-shirts, books, toiletries, and journal and trudged up the steps of the admissions building. We waited for an hour until someone said they were ready to evaluate me. In an exam room, I undressed, put on a gown, and sat on a table as a nurse poked and prodded me and measured my blood pressure, heart rate, weight, and height. She asked me a series of questions about my physical health; I shared about the chronic headaches, the many months of insomnia, the aching joints, the bowel movements the size of deer pellets. I informed her that I had bipolar disorder and binge eating disorder, but I'd been off my meds for about half a year. After the exam was done, the nurse moved me to a small room with big windows looking out onto the overcast day. A psychologist came in and sat across from me with a stack of papers. She asked me questions as she took diligent notes. I noticed she was wearing gray Hush Puppies and pantyhose.

"On a scale of one to ten, how would you rate your depression?"

"Ten."

"How long have you been feeling this low for?"

"It's been especially bad since January. I had to take the spring semester off from school."

"Where do you go to school?"

I paused, as I always did when asked this. "Uhh, I go to Harvard."

"Wow, you must be smart," she said. I tried not to cringe. I always felt undeserving of such praise.

Eventually we got to the magic word: *suicide*. She asked if I'd had any thoughts of harming myself or someone else. I nodded, sharing that the idea of killing myself had been on my mind a lot recently. She didn't need much more information after that: the *S*-word is a one-way ticket in the land of medical liability. They had a particular unit, the Haven, that would be just the right fit for me. It was the hospital's highest-end ward, complete with its own desktop computer, chef, and daily menu.

"Why don't you go back to the waiting room and join your mother. It might be a little while before they're ready for you. In the meantime, I'm assuming you brought a bag? We'll need to have a look at that before you're admitted to the unit."

Admitted to the unit. Never could I have pictured this as my future. When my bag was returned a few minutes later, a string from my hooded sweatshirt had been removed. I felt satisfied by this, trusting that they understood how serious this was—that someone finally, truly understood.

The door clicked closed behind me, and there I was, twenty-one, looking down my first inpatient hall. It was long and wide, had turquoise paneling, bright white walls lined with mass-produced floral prints. There were vinyl-cushioned chairs and love seats and hospital signage bolted behind scratched-up acrylic. A giant whiteboard displayed the day's schedule of groups along with a list of first names, each followed by the number 1, 2, or 3. I'd soon learn that these designated each patient's "privilege level" on the unit.

Bland institutional carpeting led to a giant Plexiglas window that started at waist height and went all the way to the ceiling. Behind it was the nurses' station, where I was told I could keep the wire of my phone charger ("Just to help keep you safe, Laura"). It would also be where I'd head each morning and evening for meds.

"Now let's get you settled into your room, okay? Come with me," said Bev, the woman who'd met me at the door. She wore her graying, dark hair pulled back in a ponytail. Bright-colored glasses were perched halfway down her nose. The smooth resonance of her voice did wonders to soothe me. I was actually excited to be there.

My room was farthest from the nurses' station, right near the entrance to the ward. I had a single bed and was pleased to discover that inside the armoire, bolted to a shelf, sat my very own television. There was one locked window with reinforced glass thick enough to blur what lay beyond. I had my own bathroom, complete with a toilet, a shower, and a mirror made of polished metal. A small bar of soap enclosed in plastic sat at the edge of the sink. All in all, the place was far cozier than I could have hoped for.

"Okay, now we've gotta do a body scan," Bev said. "You'll need to take off your shirt and pants so that I can see if you have any scars or wounds or anything else that might be important for us to know about."

"Uh—"

"It's standard for everyone coming in. We want to make sure we can stay on top of any injuries folks have while they're here."

"Okay, I see . . ."

"You can leave your bra and panties on, but socks, pants, and top will have to come off." As she said this, she gently pulled the door closed. I sucked in my stomach as I pulled off my shirt and covered my belly and chest with my arms. I slipped out of my pants. "Have you hurt yourself before?"

"I have, actually." I was pleased at this opportunity to mark myself as especially sick, and did my best to keep my tone somber.

"How recent? Do you have any scabs or scars?"

"I do have some scars. I haven't done it for a while. The last time was, like, a year or two ago, I think?" I was disappointed that I didn't have anything more recent. I showed her the different mounds of keloid scar on my hand, and the underside of my wrist, where white razor lines were barely visible. Bev gently touched my skin in each place, then pulled out a page from her folder with the outlines of a generic body. She circled the right hand and left forearm and scribbled a few notes.

"Anywhere else?" I shook my head. "Okay, I'm just gonna take a closer look." She walked my circumference, bending down to look at my toes, scanning up my legs and thighs, the rest of my arms, my back, my belly. I stayed stiff, fighting the urge to cover myself up. I wondered how disgusted she was with my body. I couldn't wait to climb into my sweat suit.

"We are all set. I'll leave you to it to get settled in. When you're ready, why don't you come down to the nurses' station and we'll show you around. Dinner will be at six. Oh, that reminds me"—she paused as she pulled out another piece of paper from her folder and handed it to me with a pen—"I'll need you to circle what you want."

I looked down at the dinner menu: salmon, chicken, penne with vegetables. Rice pilaf, potato, french fries. Broccoli, carrots, salad.

"You mean, I can pick any of these?"

"Yup, Chef really goes above and beyond. He'll be around tomorrow if there are any dietary concerns you need to share with him."

"Wow, okay." I circled salmon, broccoli, carrots. Now that I was under the care of this place, it already felt easier to nourish myself.

"Welcome to the Haven, Laura. Don't you worry, we're gonna help you."

I sat by myself at dinner that night. A multitude of crude drawings that I presumed were done by patients had been taped on a window, reminiscent of a kindergarten classroom.

A young man with buzzed hair, facial scruff, and tanned skin sat hunched in his chair at a nearby table. He wore a fitted white T-shirt, tight sweatpants, and fancy, spotless sneakers and was sandwiched between his parents, who had brought what looked like homemade chicken and vegetables. They were doing their best to engage him with updates, prompting him with questions about what he'd been up to. He mostly stared at the table, chin dropped, sometimes offering up one-word answers. Every so often, at the encouragement of his mother, he'd move some food around on his plate. It was a strange sight to witness, this man who looked like someone you might bump into at a nightclub, now ghostly and slumped, so absent and deflated.

After visiting hours ended that evening, I crossed paths with him in the dining room. In a strong Long Island accent, he introduced himself as Phil. I asked him how long he'd been on the unit.

"Don't know exactly, somewhere around two months," he said, though it sounded more like *Dunno zackly, s'mer roun two mons.* His hands were trembling. I didn't yet understand that slurred speech and shaky hands are telltale effects of antipsychotic drugs and lithium.

"Two months? Jeez, that's a long time. They told me the average stay was, like, a week?"

He shrugged. "They say I'm not getting better. I guess I'm bipolar." His ambivalence about the diagnosis struck me as odd. Why hadn't he embraced it, like I had?

"Hey, me too. Small world. If you don't mind me asking, how did you end up here?"

"A girl."

"What do you mean?"

"My girlfriend—was going to marry her. Found out she was cheating. Lost my shit."

Phil went on to tell me how he got drunk after discovering her betrayal and then impulsively decided to drive to the nearest suspension bridge, where he pulled his car over, got out, and began to climb up to the top of one of the cables to jump off.

"I have a lot of pride, y'know? I just cracked, couldn't handle thinking about her fucking some other guy."

He described what it was like seeing all those passing cars below; how, after watching the scene grow colorful with flashing lights, he thought about how nice it would be to have one final cigarette before he ended it all. When he went to grab for the pack in his pocket, he realized it was back in his car.

"I needed that last cigarette," Phil said. "Wanted it really bad." He decided to climb back down to get it, where he was apprehended by police and turned over to paramedics. Eventually, he'd been admitted to the Haven.

"That's intense, Phil. I'm so sorry about your girlfriend," I said.

"Before this whole mess I was doing great, y'know. I had my own gym and everything was good with my girl. I was happy. None of this bipolar shit. And now I'm here. All happened so fast."

"You mean you hadn't had mental illness before you found out about your girlfriend?"

"Nope. Some anger issues, maybe, but that's it. All these shrinks have me on a whole bunch of meds for it. ECT too now, because apparently the meds aren't working. That's why I'm still here."

"ECT? Really?" I knew nothing about electroconvulsive therapy beyond what I'd seen in *One Flew over the Cuckoo's Nest*. I wondered whether I'd ever be considered a serious enough case for it.

"Yup, they said I need it for the depression. I'm fuckin' miserable. Not sure it's doing anything beyond frying my brain. Can't remember shit."

"Well, it's good you're here. And again, I'm really so sorry to hear about everything you've been through."

There was a knock on my door that night as I lay in bed thinking about Phil. "Come in?" I said hesitantly. A man with a clipboard peeked his head in and shone a flashlight on my face. I winced in the harsh light.

"Just doing checks. While you're at level one, we'll do them every fifteen minutes."

I said okay and returned to my thoughts as he pulled the door gently closed and left me back in the dark.

TWELVE

Panopticon

After about six months of spinning out without my medications, I was eager to comply with my new regimen: Lamictal, a mood stabilizer; Lexapro, an antidepressant; and Seroquel, the same antipsychotic I'd been put on just before meeting Dr. Bachman. I told myself I'd never again make such a grave mistake as to think I could manage without meds.

Within a couple of days, I progressed from privilege level 1 to 2, which meant I was no longer on fifteen-minute checks and could go out for supervised walks with other patients. That first afternoon of my upgrade, Bev gathered level 2s and 3s by the announcement board. We obediently followed her in single file as she unlocked the unit door and led us down the stairs and outside. Smokers instantly lit up. I took in a long breath. It was my first time getting fresh air since I'd been there, and I was struck less by how refreshing it smelled and more by the fact that I hadn't noticed I'd been missing it. Our slow-moving pack walked over a massive sprawl of well-maintained fields behind the hospital buildings—this, I realized, was the blurry green I could barely see through my thick window—as we followed Bev to an old basketball court near some outbuildings in various stages of disrepair. A few patients picked up a ball and started shooting hoops. I sat off on my own and read, making sure to position myself far enough away that I wouldn't feel obligated to speak to anyone but close enough so as not to worry Bev that I might abscond.

The late summer sun felt good on my face. I closed my eyes and soaked in the peaceful surroundings as a foreign sense of idyll overtook me. I could get used to living in a place like this, where people took care of me twenty-four hours a day, a chef cooked my meals, and I had my own private room. If viewed from a bird's eye, we looked like a group of friends out for a walk and picnic at a picturesque retreat. No one could have guessed we were mental patients on privilege levels 2 and 3 out for our daily supervised constitutional.

It was easy to settle into the days of simple sameness on the ward: After breakfast, we lined up for morning meds, holding our wrists out one by one so that the nurse could double-check our ID bands before handing us miniature plastic cups of pills along with paper cups of water. (We had to take our meds right there to ensure we didn't tongue or toss them, though just the thought of such defiance sent a chill up my spine.) Afterward, most of us got a refill of decaf coffee before wandering back to our respective rooms, where I imbibed my daily *SpongeBob SquarePants* from bed and alternated between napping, attempting to read, and eating my stockpile of unripe oranges from the dining room. Eventually we were beckoned back for the first group of the day—topics included "Anxiety Management," "Family Issues," and "Coping Strategies"—and while I much preferred the notion of staying in bed, I never ignored whichever cheery staff person arrived at my door to encourage my participation. I couldn't risk being perceived as lazy about my care, of course, and wanted them to know that I was taking my illness far more seriously than ever before. There was the daily meeting with the case manager and the ten-minute check-in with the prescriber, who barely looked up to make eye contact as he ran down the list of questions: Sleep? Appetite? Mood? Thoughts of hurting yourself or others? Though most of us tried to disappear to our rooms every chance we got, mental health workers were on us like hawks, coaxing us into playing board games or drawing pictures with them as they gently encouraged us to rest, relax, we were being taken care of now, no need to worry about all that lay out there in our day-to-day realities: The responsibilities, conflicts, challenges, expectations. The guilt about the past. The terror about the future.

A couple of years before that hospital stay, while reading Michel Foucault's *Discipline and Punish: The Birth of the Prison* for a medical anthropology class, I'd learned about an eighteenth-century architectural model for a prison called the panopticon, designed by Jeremy Bentham. In the layout, an observation tower is placed at the center of a strategically lit circular room lined with individual prison cells (if you picture a wheel, the hub would be the watchtower, and the cells would run along the inside of the rim). The design ensured that guards could see each prisoner at any time and that prisoners would be aware that they could be watched at any moment, while never knowing when. The theory was that this would make prisoners behave properly at all times, which in turn would make things easier for the guards. Compared with the previous dungeon model of imprisonment, "full lighting and the eye of a supervisor capture better than darkness, which ultimately protected," Foucault explained. "Visibility is a trap."

Though none of the dozens of wards that I have stayed on, worked on, or visited friends on since that first hospitalization in 2004 were designed exactly like the panopticon, they evoke a similar climate of surveillance. No one points this out to you when you're admitted, but if you're focused on being a good patient, as I was, you quickly sense it. It's like those times when you're compelled to turn around without knowing why, and then you catch someone's eyes on you. But all the time. Every second. Even when you're sleeping.

When I think back to that stay on the Haven, I remember how reassured I was by the never-ending possibility of being watched. Knowing that I was under supervision—or could be at any moment— meant that I was safe from myself. Not all patients are this passive; many of my friends who have been hospitalized in various institutions around the world, for example, are baffled when I describe my compliant history, as they were always proud to actively defy the clinicians tasked with treating them. Sometimes this meant having to sacrifice their bodily autonomy and endure degrading consequences, like getting put into four-point restraints (in which a person's arms and legs are each secured to a bed with straps), having their pants and underwear pulled down, and receiving an unwanted injection of a potent tranquilizer into an exposed butt cheek. On a locked ward, this so-called treatment is sometimes done inside an isolation room—otherwise called solitary confinement—where friends of mine have reported being left restrained and alone for hours, sometimes a whole afternoon, to urinate on themselves while swallowed up in what Canadian ex-patient and academic Erick Fabris poignantly calls the "tranquil prison" of forced antipsychotic injections. I, on the other hand, thrived under endless psychiatric observation. A lifelong people pleaser accustomed to striving for perfection within any monitored setting in which I found myself—squash court, classroom, stage, or otherwise—I now pursued top-level patient performance. I was eager to listen to whatever the staff suggested, take whatever meds the unit psychiatrist wanted to prescribe, complete all the worksheets handed out in groups. I instinctually knew that the better I behaved on the ward, the better I'd be treated, and the better I was treated, the better I could feel about myself. I've seen this pattern in so many people I've met on psych wards over the years. Compliance comes to be the sole thing we rely on to orient us on a path forward, to give us purpose, to help us feel good about ourselves.

One day, as I attempted a word search puzzle in the dining room, I heard shouts. A few patients and I peeked our heads out the door and saw several staff running down the hall in the direction of Phil's room. I thought back to the med window after breakfast, when Phil had asked to use a razor to shave; he'd been given one and told to return it immediately after finishing. Someone came around the corner and told us all to go to our rooms. My hunch that Phil had slit his wrists wasn't confirmed until dinnertime, when he came in with a thick white bandage on one of his arms.

Phil was taken off the unit for an ECT session early the next morning. (This is standard timing for the procedure, as an empty stomach is necessary to ensure the anesthetized patient doesn't choke on vomit during the seizures a doctor induces by firing up to several hundred volts of electricity into his brain.) After breakfast, as I read in a chair by the nurses' station, there was the click of the locked door opening at the end of the hall. I watched as Phil was pushed onto the ward in a wheelchair. This was my first time seeing him return from electroshock; he was wrapped up tightly in blankets, slumped over in the chair, open eyes vacant, his chin at his chest, jaw slack, a giant strand of drool hanging from his lips. He was awake but clearly not there. As he was wheeled by me, I said, "Hey, Phil," but he gave no indication that he heard me. I wanted to cry—knew, somehow, that this was something to cry about—but couldn't.

About a week in, my case manager told me, to my great dismay, that I was soon to be discharged to an intensive outpatient program. This made no sense to me. While the break from real life had been a temporary reprieve, no one had really *done* anything besides start me on a regimen of Lamictal, Lexapro, and Seroquel, which I couldn't be sure was even helping me. Wasn't the point of going inpatient to have doctors make a dent in resolving whatever was going wrong inside me so that I would start to get better? I knew that any relief I felt had been rooted entirely in the knowledge that I was safe from myself behind these locked doors, and now they were expecting me to go back to the same world under the same circumstances as before. I did not feel ready for this.

I said goodbye to Phil and the other patients, and my mother drove me home. For many weeks, I returned to NYP each morning for day treatment, spending my evenings watching television and doing jigsaw puzzles. Eventually I was told that the time had come to cut back on groups and find part-time work, and so I got in touch with an old squash coach and began coaching middle school students at Greenwich Academy a few afternoons a week. I felt like a fraud standing on court with all these girls I'd once been like—girls with endless promise and possibility before them, girls who seemed happy, hopeful. (Convinced of my terminal uniqueness, I never considered the likelihood that at least some of them were masking their innermost struggles just as I had at their age.) After lessons, when parents asked what they should be doing to get their daughters into Harvard, I stammered out my best attempts at an answer: good SAT scores, good grades, leadership accomplishments, volunteer experiences, athletic or artistic accomplishments. I felt queasy every time I had to speak like I was some role model to emulate, and feared I might slip up and be seen for what I truly was: a mentally ill fuckup fresh off the psych ward.

THIRTEEN

Medical Nemesis

By wintertime, in spite of all the therapy and meds, not much had changed. I felt empty and lost and couldn't shake the ominous sense that I was deluding myself if I thought there was a way out of this. I knew that if I didn't return to Harvard for the upcoming semester, I'd likely never go back—nearly a whole year had passed—and so I forced myself to reenroll in classes. I talked with my old roommates about everything that had happened between us following their eating disorder intervention, we resolved to make a fresh start, and I moved back in with them.

I began to see a new psychiatrist named Dr. Julia Weinberg—Weinberg, for short, as I always referred to her by her last name to my family. She and her psychiatrist husband lived in a giant shingled house on a quiet dead-end lane near Harvard Square. They had high-ceilinged offices next to each other over their stand-alone two-car garage. Weinberg and I saw each other two to three times a week. Appointments usually happened in the early morning, when I'd arrive on my bicycle with a travel mug of coffee, let myself in through the unlocked door at the side of her garage, head up the stairs, and plop myself down on the oversize sofa. The sense of safety that reliably found me in those quiet waiting minutes was something I felt nowhere else.

Weinberg was around fifty and had a son, a daughter, and a springer spaniel. She'd gone to an Ivy League college and started out as a professional artist before changing course and returning to the Ivy League for medical school. Her tight curls of brown hair were usually gathered up into an elegant twist clipped at the back of her head, and she wore bright red lipstick, cashmere sweaters, tailored slacks. Some mornings, she'd mindlessly flick a loose stiletto pump on and off her heel as she sat with casually crossed legs; others, she'd take her pumps off and tuck her pedicured toes beneath her. She had a sumptuously upholstered analyst's couch in the corner that I never once lay on, and psychoanalytic texts in her floor-to-ceiling book-shelf next to art history books. Weinberg was quick-witted and in-sightful, sophisticated and articulate, the kind of psychiatrist who left stacks of old *New Yorker*s for patients on the side table in her waiting room. I instantly respected and admired her.

She always arrived ten minutes late. I can still hear the suction sound as she pushed the downstairs door open with her hip, one manicured hand gripping her giant coffee mug, the other holding the morning papers under her arm; the soft pad of shoes up carpeted steps and the calm "Good morning" as she rounded the corner; the click as she flicked on the white-noise machine with her foot, a sea-like sound suddenly infusing the waiting area. I savored feeling like an obedient child each time she entered her office and I stood up to silently follow her.

That safety I felt with Weinberg touched a primal unmet need for protection that I wasn't conscious of. We spent our sessions discuss-ing my schoolwork, my mother, my father, my sisters, my room-mates, my teammates, whichever unfortunate young man happened to be on my radar. I confessed to her all my foibles and fuckups: the latest conflict with a family member, the drunken sex I'd had with a guy I barely knew from the lacrosse team before I puked all over his couch and fled without cleaning up, the night I humiliated myself at the bar by yelling false accusations at the friends I was out with that they were whispering insults about me, the threesome I'd had with my graduate student teaching assistant and his wife, whom I'd never met before, simply because he'd asked me to—and how I'd had to obliterate myself with alcohol beforehand so as not to feel used. I came out of hiding with Weinberg, elaborating upon these disgraceful blunders without fear of rejection or even as much as a judgmental response. (Whether Weinberg was actually privately judging me I couldn't let myself think too long about.) I never worried she'd try to coerce me into doing things differently; even when she brought up the observation, say, that excessive drinking seemed to be linked to interpersonal problems, it was with careful curiosity and absent agenda. My life had grown so lonely and small that a psychiatrist was the only person I trusted.

I sometimes wonder if talk therapy has become a source of absolution in the way that weekly confessional has historically been for many churchgoers—and whether, over the previous five decades in which Americans have come to identify less and less with organized religion, therapists have become proxies for priests. In my case, because therapy was usually with the same doctor prescribing me my meds, my faith was even more compelling. The doctor handing me my prescription note, the soporific piano on the pharmacy hold line, the crunch of stapled bag passed over the register, the squeeze and twist of the white cap, the soft weight of pills in palm, the bitterness of chemicals dissolving on tongue: all of this, my sacrament.

By the time I met Weinberg, I assumed the purpose of therapy was to keep one's shrink up to speed on any symptoms and the issues they were causing, which required me, in turn, to maintain a long list of them. Therapy was also my only reliable, if fleeting, source of self-forgiveness: I craved the weekly reminder that I was doing the best I could, that I wasn't fundamentally slutty, or selfish, or entitled, or evil—that because of how sick I was, none of what I did was my fault. I don't recall any therapist ever holding me accountable for my actions, or calling bullshit on my justifications, or challenging me to take even a little bit of responsibility for myself. (Had one of them, I probably would have gotten offended and found a replacement, which would have benefited neither of us.)

As Weinberg would write many years later, in retrospective summary notes she compiled for me about my treatment:

> *Laura made it clear that she hoped to avoid rehospitalization and the agreed upon frequency of sessions was used as essential means of providing a therapeutic relationship that could function as a vehicle to manage her suicidal tendencies, control the regressive tendencies secondary to affective symptoms and provide active support to persevere with her academic life and work towards graduation in Spring 2006. I made it clear that she had 24 hour access to me through the use of my cell phone.*

Manage and *control*: these terms, to me, evoke a state of immobilization, a holding pattern of sorts. Weinberg accurately captures my understanding at the time of the purpose of my therapy.

To be clear, I don't believe that my therapists were bad or incompetent. I have many therapist friends today who work with their patients in radically different ways from what I experienced, and I know many people who've found therapeutic modalities that have helped them transform their lives. I just wasn't one of them. None of the talking, talking, talking I did with so many shrinks over so many years led to progress. With hindsight, I see that a long list of complex factors had converged, by the time I was eighteen, to create a perfect storm that made all the therapy I had to follow inevitably unhelpful, even disabling. First, I didn't know what it looked or felt like to be fully open with others about my flaws and mistakes—and not only that, but subsequently understood and accepted, as well. I was desperate to be recognized, validated, forgiven, and when I finally found this in therapy, I couldn't get enough of it.

Second, my therapists and I operated under the assumption that my emotional and mental difficulties were symptoms of an incurable brain disease for which medication was my first-line treatment, which led me to logically conclude that therapy was at best an enjoyable exercise in connection and conversation and at worst entirely futile. Because I'd been told, and come to believe, the primary cause of my problems was medical, the solution needed to be medical as well: taking this malfunctioning organ in my skull to be tinkered with and maintained by a trained physician. I would have been insulted at the idea of sitting down over a cup of tea with someone who'd been through her own struggles as an alternative to therapy or meds. And I would have scoffed at the proposition that the objective of living is not the absence of pain but the embrace of it—that suffering might not always be a problem to be solved. The years I spent inside the medicalized industry of psychiatric care—what I like to think of as my "psychiatrized" era—had taught me that I lacked the power to endure my struggles on my own, or solely with the help of friends and family. I don't think my doctors considered these possibilities either; with the best of intentions, they saw themselves and their treatments as necessary to my survival. The philosopher and social critic Ivan Illich describes this nemesis of modern, industrialized medicine as "the negative feedback of a social organization that set out to improve and equalize the opportunity for each man to cope in autonomy and ended by destroying it." The more I suffered, the more medical treatments I was convinced I needed, but the more treatments I received, the more I suffered. As I became increasingly reliant on doctors and their therapeutic interventions—and they, increasingly reliant on me as their devoted consumer—I was shrinking down the chance that I would ever gain sovereignty over myself.

Finally, layered on top of the "I have incurable mental illness" narrative was another immobilizing story of self I had internalized, perhaps as a means of bearing the guilt and shame that otherwise felt unbearable: "My upbringing fucked me up." Both had me pinned as a helpless victim of circumstance, because it wasn't just bipolar disorder that I was at the mercy of but also my family and its repressed WASP heritage and my tony hometown of Greenwich and its extreme set of successful social standards. I blamed my Boston Brahmin background for the pressures and expectations I felt so heavy on my shoulders, convincing myself that any relief on order was to be found far, far away from home, and I embraced Weinberg as a surrogate parent who wouldn't take my dysfunction as a statement of who she was or what kind of guardian she'd been. The more I depended on her, the further I removed myself from the most fundamental source of support free from profit motive: the family, however wounded and flawed its members always are.

I came home from school in the summer of 2005 and things rapidly deteriorated. I was earning marginal income through sporadic squash coaching and had limited contact with Weinberg. Despite taking my meds religiously, I began to feel occupied by my thoughts, as though they were external forces that had taken me hostage, obsessively looping in endless circles about the meaninglessness of existence, the absurdity of the human condition, and how it really didn't matter whether or not I stayed alive. In retrospect, I think my fixation on postmodernism played a large role in this. Deconstructing everything had become an inescapable mental compulsion: Nothing felt real. Powerful forces seemed to be everywhere, trying to control me. Besides Weinberg, there was no one to rely on, least of all myself. I dismantled the content of every conversation, the motivation behind every action I took, the nature of each belief I carried, the very words in the thoughts I was having about the socially constructed nature of my thoughts. I was simultaneously observer and observed, and it was exhausting. I stopped sleeping much at night.

When I got back to campus in the fall for senior year, resumed therapy with Weinberg, and brought her up to speed, she was concerned by my deterioration. I had rejoined the squash team and, with the season under way, had stopped drinking and using any drugs—the team captains required each of us to abide by a one-month "dry period" each season—and hoped this might help me feel more grounded. It didn't. Eventually, Weinberg grew worried enough about my mental state that she asked me to see her mentor for a psychopharmacology consultation, explaining that he might have some insights about how to optimize my medication regimen. Albert Feingold was a prominent Harvard Medical School professor who was considered by many to be one of the premier psychopharmacologists in the country. I eagerly took the subway to his office in Newton, ready to tell him everything, to take whatever he had on offer.

FOURTEEN

The Motions of Living

November 21, 2005

Dear Julia:

I saw Laura Delano in consultation on 11/21/05. As you described, she is a 22 year old single Harvard senior with bipolar disorder. Her current medications include lamotrigine 237.5mg, Lexapro 10mg, and clonazepam 1.5mg. She takes birth control pills as well. She does not smoke, drink, use drugs and is in good physical health. She drinks a considerable amount of caffeinated beverages (which I advised her not to do).

Since age 13, Ms. Delano has been in psychotherapy and treated for mood disorders. As a teenager she was medication noncompliant, cut herself frequently, was depressed, anorexic, exercised compulsively, and was a high user of street drugs. As a freshman in college in 2001, she was depressed, and excessively used cocaine. The winter of 2001 she started outpatient treatment with Paul Bachman at McLean and stopped alcohol and cocaine use, but continued marijuana, and developed an eating disorder. She withdrew from individuals and a social life. By 2002 her eating disorder was worse as was her depression. She was taking Prozac 40mg, Provigil 400mg, and Ambien. She abused Provigil. She describes herself as being very thin, successful academically but not socializing. By the fall of 2003 she had enrolled in [an eating disorders program]. Lithium was added to her Ambien and Provigil which was not clearly helpful. She states that she was highly suicidal, nialistic [sic], and felt "decontructionist . . . nothing is real."

By January 2004 she was planning to overdose, and discontinued all medications abruptly. A three month sojourn with Outward Bound was not helpful as she continued severely depressed and bingeing. In the summer of 2004 she was unable to work and finally by the fall of 2004 she was hospitalized for two weeks. . . . ("This was the lowest point"). . . .

At present Ms. Delano is hypomanic. She admits to being hypersexual and having racing thoughts. There is pressure of speech and a marked decline in sleep. Indeed, her sleep cycle is disregulated [sic] with long afternoon naps and then staying awake until 4AM. She states "I don't feel grounded . . . I am floating." There are elements of eratomania [sic] and in the past apparently there was risky sexual behavior although not at present. She states that she is euphoric at night but not irritable. . . .

It is clear that Ms. Delano has had excellent treatment and has made significant improvement. Her current sleep disregulation [sic], however, puts her at great risk for becoming significantly hypomanic and, as you have noted, she is becoming hypomanic now. I suggest the following:

1. *Continue lamotrigine and continue slowly increasing the dose.*

2. *Continue Lexapro 10mg and clonazepam 1.5mg.*

3. *Add very low dose Seroquel. If this is too sedating, then switch to Neurontin hs. The doses of Neurontin can be substantial (e.g. 300–2000mg/d).*

I hope this information is useful to you.

Warm Regards,
Albert Feingold

Weinberg followed Dr. Feingold's advice with careful precision, and I began taking Seroquel again, though only on an "as needed" basis, as I was worried about weight gain. Through the rest of senior year, I played steady squash and maintained good grades—fueled, I believe, by a desperate desire to cling to something, anything, that helped me feel competent—but I retained nothing that I learned. I finished my thesis, which explored the ways that psychopharmaceutical medications shape a mentally ill person's sense of self—all these years later, I remain fascinated by how simultaneously close and far I was from having a robust critique of these drugs—and couldn't muster the will to edit it before submission. When it came time to graduate in the late spring of 2006, I skipped the ceremony, feeling nothing about the fact that I'd actually made it through college. My brain felt so mushy that leaving my dorm for the last time was like emerging from a college-length blackout. I moved into an apartment in Boston without any job prospects. My parents covered my living expenses, tempering their fears and frustrations by reassuring themselves that I was simply in a transitional rut that Weinberg, soon enough, would help to pull me out of.

• ● •

In a graduate-level medical anthropology class during my final semester at Harvard, I'd met a psychiatrist named Phillip who worked at Massachusetts General Hospital and was doing a fellowship in cross-cultural psychiatry. After bumbling around aimlessly in Boston for part of the summer, I found the motivation to reach out to him about job opportunities. He offered me an unpaid research assistant position at the hospital to get my foot in the door.

I was photographed and printed an ID badge at MGH's security desk. Phillip told me to use it to swipe myself onto a specific locked psychiatric unit on the eleventh floor each workday, walk into the nurses' station, and look through the files of each newly admitted patient to find potential candidates for a study he was running on first-episode psychosis. The criterion was that the patient had to have been diagnosed for the first time with some kind of psychotic condition, or the possibility of one, upon admission. If I found a candidate, I'd notify Phillip and his co-researcher, and we'd approach the patient to ask about participating in the study. I was responsible for recording and transcribing all interviews.

I knew that if I looked honestly at myself, I couldn't stomach what an impostor I was, this mentally ill person pretending to be a research assistant who studied mentally ill people. On weekday mornings, I'd drag myself out of bed, tie my greasy hair back in a bun, and slip into work clothes, all while avoiding the mirror. I'd walk the mile and a half to the hospital, always sure to wear my ID badge in some highly visible place. I saw it as an emblem I could hide behind, hoping that passersby would instantly recognize the iconic hospital acronym and assume I was a doctor. I passed young mothers pushing strollers, businessmen on phones with briefcases, college students in headphones, dog walkers with packs of dogs. All of it baffled me.

Trapped endlessly in self-derogation, I'd compare myself with these strangers and wonder what horrible things they were thinking about me, not once recognizing that perhaps I wasn't the center of everyone's universe in the way that I and my mental illness were to me.

Now that I was working at the intersection of medicine and academia, I told myself that maybe I should try to become a psychiatrist-anthropologist. I told Phillip about my plan, and he invited me to attend morning rounds so that I could learn more about the inner workings of a psychiatric ward. I took diligent notes as psychiatrists discussed which patients might be good candidates for specific drug trials they were conducting on the ward (there were several), whom they were considering for a course of ECT (the majority seemed to be women, which makes sense; historically, around 70 percent of electroshock recipients have been women), which patients were the most disruptive, and who seemed especially "attention seeking," which I quickly pieced together was a coded way of saying "has borderline personality disorder" (again, most seemed to be women). As I silently observed the rolled eyes, laughter, and collegial commiseration, I wondered how I'd been discussed during morning rounds in my hospitalization on the Haven.

From the outset, the deference with which the recruited patients addressed me was unsettling. I fought the urge to clarify that I was actually their equal, not the authority they thought I was. All of this pretending quickly caught up with me, and in a matter of months, I was spending most nights rip-roaring drunk, alternating between arguing with Mark, my boyfriend at the time, crying, and staring numbly at the wall. I began to call in sick, back out of interviews with study participants, and drop the ball on transcriptions. Phillip was patient with me at first—after all, I wasn't getting paid—but eventually expressed his frustration. Ashamed, I stopped showing up altogether, stopped returning his calls.

• • •

I eventually managed to put my act back together enough to get a paying job as a research assistant for two professors in a graduate department at Harvard. As an employee of the university, I was allowed to take classes for free. Still loosely connected to that pipe dream future as a psychiatrist-anthropologist, I signed up for chemistry, but within minutes of the start of the first class, I felt my throat begin to close. Tunnel vision set in. I couldn't breathe. I rushed out of the room, not realizing until the next day, during therapy with Weinberg, that I'd had a panic attack. Devastated, I dropped out of the class and permanently abandoned the possibility of ever having a future in medicine. Within a year, I'd quit that second research assistant job, as well. As Weinberg would write of me in her summary notes about the chemistry class experience, "This was quite a disappointment and particularly alarming to be confronted by her inability to engage in the kind of academic work she could, at one time, have done with no difficulty and sessions addressed the grief associated with the loss of her sense of a competent self."

As I forced myself through the motions of living, Weinberg steadily increased my mood stabilizer, Lamictal, my antidepressant, Lexapro, and the benzodiazepine I used at night, Klonopin. I continued to drink frequently. Any sex I had with Mark was anesthetized; we mostly fought and made up and watched *The Sopranos*; he spent many evenings sitting alone on the fire escape, smoking joints and drawing ink sketches of solitary trees, while I lay in bed tranquilized by my prescribed Klonopin. We felt closest when we were driving around aimlessly listening to loud music—Cold War Kids, Neutral Milk Hotel, Animal Collective—all of it an effort to delude ourselves that we were enjoying our time together. On the rare occasion that I visited my family, I swept in like a tornado, devastating holiday dinners with my defensiveness and ire before sweeping out just as fast. There were some especially dark times in the apartment, like when I locked myself in the bathroom and sliced up my forearm with a serrated knife while Mark pounded on the door, or the time when, alone, I had to call Weinberg at two in the morning to keep from overdosing. I remember the distinct nerves in her voice, the growing steadiness as she told me firmly to take extra Seroquel and stay on the line with her until I fell asleep. She called me first thing the next morning. I was in her office a few hours later for an extra appointment and left with an upped antidepressant dose.

A year into my relationship with Mark, we decided the time had come to end things. Weinberg expressed approval of the decision, which steeled me against any regret I felt at leaving behind the comfortable discomfort of our dynamic. Mark moved to Kenya to teach art to young children. I stayed exactly where I was.

FIFTEEN

The Anatomy of
Treatment Resistance

By the summer of 2007, I'd been a compliant psychiatric patient for six years, spending countless hours in intensive psychotherapy, taking so many different meds in ever-increasing combinations and dosages: Depakote, Seroquel, Prozac, Effexor, Provigil, Ambien, Lamictal, Klonopin, and many more. I'd been inpatient and outpatient and in group after group after group. Where had all of it gotten me? I couldn't hold down a job. I was utterly unable to make it through a day without obliterating myself with alcohol. I was completely dependent on my family for financial support, adorning myself in the accoutrements of responsible, independent adult life while actually living none of it. I had no meaningful friendships, nor any idea what I cared about. I was physically, sexually, and creatively numb while simultaneously feeling like an emotional live wire, a rabid animal.

In therapy, Weinberg helped me understand why it had come to this: my mental illness had progressed. It wasn't just simple old bipolar disorder that I now had. It had morphed into the treatment-resistant variety.

The phrase *treatment resistance* came into pharmaceutically oriented use in the late 1950s, a few years after the first wave of psychiatric drugs—the central nervous system "disease-causing" major tranquilizers, in the words of French psychiatrist Pierre Deniker, that today are classed "antipsychotics"—had spread through hospitals across the country. Doctors had initially been excited by these promising new medical interventions but noticed before long that some patients didn't seem to respond in the way they wanted them to. The earliest reference to this phenomenon that I found in the medical literature came in a 1958 article in *The Journal of Nervous and Mental Disease* titled "The Treatment of Drug-Resistive Chronic Schizophrenics," which describes a subset of patients who appeared not just to have been nonresponsive to treatment but to have gotten worse while on it. "There is now no doubt that [these] new drugs . . . are very important in the treatment and management of schizophrenia," begin the authors of the piece. However, they continue, "it is becoming increasingly apparent that despite all efforts there remains in all studies a group of apathetic, chronic schizophrenics who simply fail to show any appreciable response to medications." They go on to say, "Although the group as a whole tended to be quiet, apathetic, and withdrawn, these particular patients were remarkably so and generally would have been described as not only chronic, but deteriorated."

Fast-forward forty years to a 2001 article in *The Journal of Clinical Psychiatry* titled "The Definition and Meaning of Treatment-Resistant Depression," written by Harold A. Sackeim, PhD, the ECT proponent whom Columbia University described as "one of the founders of the field of brain stimulation." "Treatment-resistant depression is a major public health problem," he begins, before going on to explain that up to 40 percent of depressed patients do not get better from taking antidepressants, with "getting better" defined as "at least a 50% reduction in symptom scores." (As of 2020, there were nearly 39 million American adults taking an antidepressant, according to a Medical

Expenditure Panel Survey conducted by the U.S. government.) Further, he says, around 50 percent of those who *do* improve still "have significant residual symptoms that continue to have an impact on function. Thus, broadly speaking," Sackeim summarizes, "only between 20% and 40% of patients receiving their first treatment for a major depressive episode are expected to achieve a relatively asymptomatic state." A vocal proponent of ECT, which is commonly used for treatment-resistant depression, Sackeim received over $5 million in funding from the NIMH (National Institute of Mental Health, which is part of the National Institutes of Health [NIH]) between 2000 and 2006 alone, much of it earmarked for researching ECT and depression. In 2017, in the conflicts of interest section of his *JAMA Psychiatry* editorial titled "Modern Electroconvulsive Therapy: Vastly Improved Yet Greatly Underused," Sackeim disclosed that he had consulted for nine psychiatric medical device companies and nine pharmaceutical companies.

In 2022, two decades after Sackeim's article came out, the European Group for the Study of Resistant Depression published the results of a study in the *Journal of Psychiatric Research* that attempted to address why so many people diagnosed with major depression fail to respond to treatment. It noted that over the past three decades, rates of major depression have doubled, with 322 million people globally living with the diagnosis as of 2015. "Even though a plethora of effective evidence-based antidepressant (AD) treatment options is available for MDD [major depressive disorder], the response and remission rates remain often unsatisfactory. . . . The most obvious approach to counteract outcome deficiencies might be a systematic and individualized exploitation of available treatment options." In other words, the authors propose, the reason why so many people have treatment-resistant depression is that they simply aren't getting enough treatment. The study, which was funded by pharmaceutical company

Lundbeck A/S (which markets, among its many psychiatric drugs, the antidepressants Trintellix, Celexa, and Lexapro, as well as Rexulti, an antipsychotic used as an adjunct antidepressant) and the majority of whose authors had extensive financial ties to pharmaceutical companies, observed 1,279 depressed individuals in ten different inpatient and outpatient settings across multiple countries, all of whom were on antidepressants and a third of whom were hospitalized. Would their outcomes improve once additional psychotherapies were added to their treatment? No, it turns out. In spite of ramped-up efforts at more treatment, fewer than 25 percent of the participants "responded," more than 34 percent were "non-responders," and more than 41 percent were classified as having "TRD," or treatment-resistant depression.

At the heart of this framing of a patient as "treatment resistant" are some powerful baseline assumptions. The first is that characterizing you, as a patient, by your relationship to treatment is a meaningfully informative way to understand you. The second is that psychiatric treatment is fundamentally safe, effective, and good, which in turn leaves you, as a patient, with one of two possible outcomes: If you feel better after taking a medication, it's because the drug worked. If you don't feel better—or, heaven forbid, you feel worse—it's because there is an obstacle blocking the medication from doing what it does, and that obstacle is, well, *you*. Your brain. Your fundamental biochemistry. The drug deserves the credit when one feels helped, but when the outcomes are unsatisfactory—whether in the case of those "failed," "chronic" so-called schizophrenics of the 1950s or me, in 2007, after Weinberg told me I had treatment-resistant bipolar disorder, or the "non-responders" and "TRDs" whom the European Group for the Study of Resistant Depression described in 2022—the onus is on the patient.

When I look through the conventional psychiatric literature on treatment resistance, I rarely see mention of other possible explanations for why people do not always benefit from taking antidepressants or other psychiatric drugs, of which there are many: Some people might be nutritionally depleted or have some kind of hormonal imbalance. Maybe some people are struggling with a physical ailment that's led to painful emotional by-products. Perhaps some people feel trapped in relationships that don't ignite them or in careers that they know, in their hearts, they never should have pursued. Maybe they're saddled with student debt, or they're raising kids on their own without support, or they've been through other stresses or traumas that they haven't had the time or resources to work through. Or maybe they are living in poverty and facing any of the multitude of other systemic socioeconomic obstacles to a thriving life that so many are faced with. Perhaps some people who don't feel benefit from psychiatric drugs simply don't want to be taking them in the first place, subduing the normally powerful placebo effect born from faith in their efficacy. Or maybe they're experiencing one or more of the many reported adverse effects of these drugs—effects such as emotional numbness, sedation, mental fogginess, anxiety, mania, and even suicidality, which mimic symptoms of psychiatric diagnoses themselves—and they simply don't realize it.

• ● •

I began dating a guy named Liam not too long after Mark. Our relationship wasn't pretty: yelling matches infused with venom and rancor; the sloppy, slurring desperation of wine bottles and cocaine lines; my threats to kill myself; a broken-down bathroom door; a visit from the police; my threats to leave him; his threats to leave me. I finally got myself a full-time job through his family connections in which I helped districts file school building permits. Within the first month, after calling in sick five times, I was put on probation.

By the summer of 2008, Weinberg had dramatically increased my medication doses, until I was on 400 mg of Lamictal, 30 mg of Lexapro, and 3 mg of Klonopin. I was blacking out several times a week by then—hefty doses of psychiatric drugs in combination with excessive amounts of alcohol on a nightly basis is a reliable way to disable one's hippocampus—but I didn't tell Weinberg or anyone else, for I found comfort in my growing absence of memory.

It was around this time that my arms and legs began to constantly vibrate, a sensation I can best describe as what it might feel like to be struck with a giant tuning fork. It grew so unbearable that I began to fantasize about ripping my skin off. I did not know at the time that I was experiencing akathisia, a known adverse effect of certain psychiatric drugs that causes an inner restlessness that can sometimes be so excruciating that people with no prior history of suicidal feelings impulsively kill themselves. I was desperate for Weinberg to fix this problem, so she again consulted Dr. Feingold, who, a year earlier, had directed her to increase my lamotrigine. He now told her to cut the dose in half, which she promptly did.

The visceral vibrations stopped soon after the dose cut, but in their place arrived a mental agitation that propelled me toward unusual activities: I began to chain-smoke cigarettes, which I'd quit five years earlier, at age twenty. I began staying up until the wee hours of the morning, peeling my body off the bed a few hours later, at seven, by promising myself a four-shot black Americano. I stopped eating all food except for jalapeño poppers, grew very thin, and suddenly felt compelled to expand my work wardrobe, accumulating shopping bags of business clothing and stiletto heels from Nordstrom Rack that sat untouched in my closet. I began to secretly hook up with a coworker who had a longtime girlfriend, became fixated on whether he actually cared about me, and talked endlessly about this with Weinberg.

After an especially sloppy, terrifying event at the apartment with Liam in which both of us were far from our best selves, I was inspired to leave him—at least for a few weeks. I moved in with my aunt Sara and uncle Bill in the Boston suburbs, lugging the shopping bags of unworn business clothes and high heels with me just in case. Liam wrote me desperate messages telling me not to leave him, the same kinds of messages I'd sent to him when he'd threatened the same. Though I hadn't agreed to get back together just yet, we began talking again. I knew in my heart I couldn't end things. It was far less scary to be lost together than alone.

The day before Thanksgiving, I drove in a near blackout to Maine, where fourteen family members awaited me for the holiday. I don't remember Thanksgiving Day. I drove back to Boston for work on Friday morning before returning to Maine the same evening, disheveled and spun out. On Saturday, my parents asked to speak with me privately.

"We can't watch you doing this to yourself anymore, Laura. We just can't," my mother said. I knew that she was referring to my relationship with Liam and to my rapid deterioration over the previous months. I stared out the window, feeling nothing.

"Laura, we know you're an adult," said my father, "but at this stage, we feel we have to step in. You just can't stay with Liam any longer. We can't sit back and let you fall apart like this." Tears were in his eyes. I said nothing.

As I looked out over the fields to the ocean, the thought casually crossed my mind that it was time to die. I felt instantly at peace with this, nodding slowly to myself. *My time here is done, I've given it a shot, just look what I've done to them, what I'm doing to them, think about all that I'll keep doing to them over the years to come.* I pretended to listen to my parents' heartache, to what they thought I should do, to their offers to help. "I'll come up and help move you out of that apartment first thing next week," my mother offered. I agreed, knowing I wouldn't be there to see it happen.

After they finished, we hugged. I went up to my room and closed the door. I dumped each of my prescription bottles—hundreds of pills, a month's supply of my three medications—into a mitten and poured some generic pain reliever tablets into the empty bottles in case anyone got suspicious. Packed my laptop in a backpack. Went downstairs, grabbed my coat, snuck into the kitchen to take a bottle of red wine and a corkscrew when no one was looking. I waited until everyone—my parents, sisters, grandmother, aunts, uncles, cousins— was close by enough that I could look at each of them one last time, and then I said in as cheerful a voice as I could summon, "I'm gonna go for a walk and do some writing. See you later."

SIXTEEN

My Suicide

As I walked to the sea, Maine's beauty ignited my senses, and I began to feel it, to really feel it: the insistence of life in the face of late fall's starkness, the colors and sounds and smells, all of it seeping through my chest, activating deep in my belly, moving up to the back of my neck, down my arms and legs, into my fingers and toes. I realized this must be what it was like to feel alive, and I pretended for a moment that I was, that I inhabited an actual human being's life. My throat clutched. Silent tears pushed themselves forth against my will. I took this visceral response as a blessing from this place. It was all going to be okay now.

I walked to the edge of the trees ahead, paused, turned back to look over the hardened fields, the woods, the bare bushes scattered like frozen tumbleweeds, the empty nests. There was the singular caw of a crow, the moan of wind through branches, the rumble of sea on rock. The house so far away now, holding my family in its cozy embrace.

A narrow path forged through dead brush stood between me and the sea. I thought of summer mornings in my youth when I'd follow my father through the fields here to watch him hack away at the overgrowth and spray poison ivy. The wine bottle clinked against my laptop in my backpack as I stepped through the brush. For reassurance,

I reached into my pocket to feel the scratchy wool of my mitten and the weight of all those pills tucked safely within it. I stepped onto the rocky ledge and suddenly, release. I felt instantly lighter, freer now that all I was left with was an endless expanse of sea and sky. It was as though the life back there were a distant dream, this blurry, dark amorphousness that had never really happened.

I stepped over four-hundred-million-year-old rocks, looking out over the glaring blue splendor of a world that would continue without me. I scanned the long stretch of shore for a good spot, choosing left, away from the path we usually took on family walks. I traversed ledges, skirted brackish tide pools with deliberate slowness, savoring each of these last steps, an unfamiliar solitude. Smiling, I wondered if this was peace of mind. The boulder up ahead was big enough to hide behind, a perfect place to stop breathing. With the sun more than halfway down, I knew I had the timing right, that the night would soon hide me.

I sat down, carefully placed my bag beside me, crossed my legs. The unforgiving rock pressed hard into my ankles, but I kept them there because it felt like something. I took a deep breath. Closed my eyes. Exhaled. For the briefest of moments, I was brought in close to myself, free from everything but right now, but it was short-lived. My history came hurtling back in as it always did: all that I had lost to treatment-resistant bipolar disorder, all that I could've been if I'd never gotten sick. Despite all the money and time and energy that my parents had spent on me, all the help I had sought from the best doctors and medications and treatment programs and hospitals over all these years, the only change my family and I had seen had been progressive deterioration. We knew that suicide was a possibility for me. We'd all been talking about it, fearing it, and it was here, finally. It was here, but in this moment, I was the only one in the entire world who knew I was about to die.

I took out the bottle of wine and placed it carefully next to me. I pulled the corkscrew from my pocket. I removed my laptop, turned it on, and set it on my lap. I pulled the wool mitten from my pocket and cupped its weight gently in my hand. I squeezed and released my fingers, watching them like they were someone else's.

I opened up a new document and began to type my goodbyes out on the screen. Tears made their way silently down my cheeks, falling into the corners of my mouth, insisting I taste them. My fingertips pushed goodbyes onto the keys, to my aunt, my cousins, my sisters. I stopped when it was time to write to my parents, and put my laptop down. I uncorked the bottle, closed my eyes, and took a few big gulps. Angling the mitten down, I watched a cascade of pills form a small hill in the palm of my hand—any larger and it would not fit down my throat. I couldn't help but consider the irony: the pills that I had once believed would save me would now end my life.

I closed my eyes, took a deep breath, and shoved them into my mouth. I washed their familiar bitter bite down with a long swallow. Another big handful poured, another deep breath, another shove, another swallow. Another big handful poured, another deep breath, another shove, another swallow. The mitten now empty. The pills settling in my stomach. After chugging the rest of the wine, I dropped the bottle, my belly cozy and warm.

I began my goodbyes to my parents but was feeling woozy. My head was heavy, my neck flimsy, collapsing to the side every few seconds under the weight of my skull before snapping back up. I moved in and out of consciousness, unsure of what was a dream and what wasn't. My line of sight narrowed; blackness crept in. I heard a ringing like a distant fire alarm, drowning out the ocean as it grew louder. My head cracked hard on rock—I knew because I heard the sound—but all I felt was warmth and freedom. With all the strength I had left, I pushed my hands against the rock and pulled myself up to a seated position. I didn't know sky from ground, or whether my eyes were closed or open, and it didn't matter, the pain was gone. I fell over again, peaceful, carefree, floating, so beautiful, more beautiful than anything I'd ever felt before, no way to get back, even if I wanted to, because my arms were gone, my body was gone, I was gone. I was gone, finally, at last, I was free. The last thing I remember is the ocean calling my name.

• ● •

Bright white light pushed through my closed eyelids. Buzzing reverberated through my head in waves. I was flat on my back, legs splayed, arms at sides, palms upturned. The light warm on my face, like summer; was I waking up from a beach nap? Something cold beneath me, a giant tray of ice. I didn't move—not sure I could have if I tried. New sounds around me now: Voices, growing sharper. Louder. The deep voices of men. "She's waking up," said one I didn't recognize.

"Laura, we're here. We're here. You're going to be okay." My father's voice quaked.

The coldness beneath my back was so demanding. *This just doesn't make sense, it can't be ice, it must be something else.* Hard, slick, metal: a table of some kind, I was lying on a table. I tried to open my eyes but couldn't, my lids too heavy.

Oh, no, no, no: I'm alive.

There was only one word to speak, but my parched throat scratched away so hard at "Why" that by the time it left my dried-out mouth it was a hoarse whisper. I sucked in air, licking my lips to get them damp enough to make it heard, pushing it out as a wheeze through the fire in my throat. "Why. Why. Why, why, why, whyyyyyyy?"

My father took in a loud breath and began to quietly weep. He knew what I was asking. "Oh, Laura, everything's going to be okay." His voice seized up as he spoke.

A wail now, surging forth from some animal part of me. I drew "No" out in a slow moan. Both of my parents, crying. Convulsions suddenly took over my limbs, shaking my arms violently, vibrating my torso. My legs clenched so tight I thought they might implode. Was this happening against my will or by it? All I felt was rage—so much rage at the breath in my lungs. There were the strange men's voices. A hustling of bodies. And then it all went black.

• ● •

I'll never have a comprehensive understanding of the events that unfolded between the time I slipped into peaceful unconsciousness on the Maine rocks and when I woke up in the intensive care unit at Massachusetts General Hospital in Boston. I've asked family members to share their recollections, but no matter how often I hear their stories, I never feel closer to grasping what really took place. My body was "there" through it all, but I was gone—and to where, I'll never know. Here's the little that I've been able to piece together about what happened.

When I went under, I recall that it was still light. When my father set out to look for me, apparently, it was nearly dark. He walked with a flashlight through the fields, past the stone walls and cranberry bog, toward the birch trees, and to the sea. Something in him said, *Go left*, and he listened. He found me not with his eyes but with his ears: the tide was low, the waves were quiet, and my rasping breath was loud enough that when he heard its unusual sound, he walked toward it, flashlight out. He found me lying on my side, cold to the touch, my breath shallow, slow, at the bottom of a five-foot ledge a little way down from the boulder I'd hidden myself behind hours earlier. I had a nasty black eye and bruising on my cheek from falling off that ledge. My father quickly took off his coat and covered me before turning to run back up the rocks, through the fields, to the house for help.

Once back at the house, he yelled that someone needed to call 911. He quickly gathered other family members, who climbed in my parents' SUV and drove back through the fields to the coast. Everyone picked me up and carried me over the rocks, in the dark, to the trunk of the car. My father drove back through the fields and to the house, where, by that time, an ambulance sat waiting. I was taken one town over to the nearest hospital, where doctors told my parents that my critical condition required me to be transported by medevac either north to Portland or south to Boston. My parents picked Boston because it was familiar, and my mother decided to travel with me in the helicopter as emergency technicians warmed my hypothermic body and tried to stabilize my dangerously erratic pulse. My father would drive the hour and twenty minutes south, leaving my sisters behind to come down the next day with Sara and Bill. A decision was made to tell Chase's school that she wouldn't be back for several days because her eldest sister had taken a bad spill on the rocks and was in the hospital. Nina told her employer back in Texas the same story: *Laura had a serious accident in Maine over Thanksgiving. She's in the ICU. Please keep her in your thoughts.* (This became my parents' and sisters' go-to story whenever they discussed me with someone outside the family, and would stay this way for several years.)

For a long time, I lived under the impression that it was my father who saved me, because he was the one to find my body; I eventually learned that my mother was the driving force behind my rescue. As the sun closed in on the horizon, an alarm bell went off in her: I'd been gone for a while. At first, my father tried to reassure her that I was fine, but she persisted. He eventually put on his coat, grabbed a flashlight, and headed out. What's always felt mystical to me is that my father knew where to go: of the many trajectories he could have taken that beamed out from that kitchen door—all the paths in the woods, the route toward the sandy beach to the south, right instead of left where the wooded path poured out to the sea—he was pulled to the very place where I lay dying in the dark.

After nurses transferred me from the ICU to the general medicine floor, I encountered, at my bedside, my sisters' tear-streaked, fatigued faces—faces I couldn't make out clearly for how blurry my vision was. This was a scene I had not prepared myself for, sure as I'd been that a month's supply of meds downed with a bottle of red wine was a foolproof plan for killing myself.

Nina, Chase, and I had waxed and waned in one another's lives over the years. There were times when we were close and times when we clashed with one another. On rare occasions, I'd been able to rise up as the helpful eldest sister they needed me to be—I was most reliable in the academic realm; if one of them called me up in a panic that a huge paper was due in two days, I could help her map it out— but for the most part, I'd long been settled into the role of person-constantly-in-crisis in our family. An excessive amount of my parents' energy had gone into managing and caring for me, which was understandably frustrating for Nina and Chase. I relegated my inability to be a reliable big sister to the long symptom list of bipolar disorder.

Yet they were there by my side in the hospital room as I came in and out of groggy sedation: Nina's muffled voice reading to me from a Harry Potter book, Chase squeezing my hand, saying, "Hey, Lo, we're right here," her voice shaking with shock, with terror.

There were wires connected to my chest and my head, IVs in my arms, a catheter inserted to capture urine. My throat ached from being intubated, and my arms and legs felt too heavy to move. Numbness had overtaken everything from my elbows to my fingertips, knees to toes. Air and time seemed blended in a thick, invisible sludge, and as my vision slowly grew clearer, I noticed the presence of an unfamiliar woman sitting in a chair by the door. She flipped through magazines, barely acknowledging my existence, from nine to five, when someone took over for the night shift. I'd learn she was my "one-to-one," another way to say "suicide prevention babysitter." In the bed on the other side of the curtain was a woman who had been diagnosed with an aggressive cancer. She was fighting for her life, I was told. I wondered if she knew that I was there because I'd tried to end my own.

When I came to enough to think of it, I asked to go to the bathroom to splash cold water on my face. It took a while to sit up, and I winced at the tug of the catheter as I slid my legs over the side of the bed. I clung to the IV pole for dear life to stand but had to quickly sit back down, too weak, too dizzy. A nurse gave me a walker, and I shuffled at turtle pace toward the bathroom as she pulled my IV pole and kept my bicep in a death grip. The rubber nubs on the bottoms of my hospital socks felt like all there was keeping me connected to the floor.

At the sink, I lifted my gaze slowly up the loose hospital gown, arms covered with scabs and IV inserts and tape and tube, the sticky residue of old adhesive gauze secured over elbow creases. The whirring air around me was punctuated by a most terrible ringing in my ears. My face in the mirror, its sallow skin, its gauntness, the giant black eye and bouquet of green, yellow, and purple across my cheek. I asked the nurse in a hoarse whisper what the wounds were from, wondering how it had come to this—how I'd failed not only at life but at death, as well.

Days after my admission to gen med, my insurance company informed MGH that it would no longer cover my stay there; in its estimation, such a high level of medical care was no longer necessary, and I was ready for a psychiatric hospital. I couldn't stand, let alone walk on my own. My echocardiograms showed ongoing heart abnormalities and my blood work indicated problems with my liver. My outraged mother threatened legal action should the hospital agree to the insurance company's demands. Through her efforts, negotiations took place, and I was able to recover several days longer on the medical unit.

When it came time to leave, I was transported to McLean Hospital, where, seven years since my first therapy appointment with Dr. Bachman, I would finally see the inside of a locked ward.

SEVENTEEN

A Fresh Hell

At McLean, I was wheeled on a stretcher past the security window and down the basement hallway to the elevator. When we arrived at the entrance of the short-term unit (STU), I tried and failed to stand. I was taken right to my room, where I lay down and weakly asked if they could turn the lights out, please, because keeping my eyes open didn't feel possible at the moment.

While I was in the ICU, doctors had abruptly stopped my Lamictal, Lexapro, and Klonopin in an effort to reverse the damage my overdose had caused my organs, especially my heart. During the rest of my time at MGH, IV sedation had insulated me from the effects of this. Now, at McLean, the physiological consequences of both the overdose and the abrupt cessation of my meds hit me with full force, though none of us—not the staff, nor I, nor my parents—had any awareness that the latter was a factor in my misery.

Every fiber of my being screamed out in agony. I couldn't eat, and taking tiny sips of water was my best attempt at self-nourishment. After the staff realized how medically unstable I was, they moved me to the room nearest the nurses' station, where I stayed quarantined. The remote-controlled hospital bed they brought in for me was a godsend, as vertigo made it impossible to sit myself up; it felt like I was getting tossed about on a boat during a hurricane. Gravity had become a disruptive force rather than a rooting one.

I was kept on low-level sedation with a new benzodiazepine and antipsychotic. On my second day, according to my medical records, I made a brief trip to the dining room with the aid of a wheelchair. Otherwise, I stayed bedridden with the door closed, lights off, shades drawn. "They had you strapped to that bed and didn't let you out of there," one fellow patient told me fourteen years later, as we caught up over a meal. He hadn't realized at the time that I was not there as an involuntary patient, for how isolated they had me from other patients at the start of my stay. "And man, you ate a lot of charcoal. You were puking that shit up. You looked green." I lay for endless hours in that hospital bed, curled in a fetal position with eyes pinched closed, wide awake into the night, shivering under drenched sheets because of my incessant cold sweats. It was reported in nursing notes that I "completed zero self-care activities." Mental health workers cycled through my room every fifteen minutes to check in on me, though I was unable to respond beyond weak nods and headshakes. In my notes, a nurse quoted me as saying, "I don't want to be alive but I have no intent to act." I knew that latter point was key to emphasize if I was to get out of there as fast as possible and off myself once and for all.

Unable to sleep, I was given more drugs. My psychiatrist wrote that a next step to consider would be Haldol—a first-generation antipsychotic drug with a particularly nasty adverse effect profile that includes heartbeat irregularities, the disabling of gross motor skills such that a person begins to shuffle instead of walk, muscle spasms, and, sometimes, a potentially deadly condition called neuroleptic malignant syndrome, which causes fever and the breakdown of one's autonomic nervous system.

My psychiatrist requested an urgent medical consultation for my dizziness and nausea and to find out when it would be safe to start me on lithium. I had elevated liver enzymes, elevated creatine phosphokinase (a sign of injury to muscle tissue, the heart, or the brain), and prolonged QTc (a heart condition that can cause rapid, chaotic heartbeats). The doctor told my psychiatrist not to start me on lithium, suggesting instead that I get a cardiology consult. A nurse wrote that I appeared to have symptoms of alcohol withdrawal. Nowhere in my notes was any mention made that I might have symptoms of psychiatric drug withdrawal.

Over the coming days, more urgent medical consults were requested for increased dizziness and weakness, an increased respiratory rate, an increased pulse. It's hard to make out much of what the consulting doctors wrote in my records, but I was able to decipher diagnoses of dehydration, persistent rhabdomyolysis (a condition resulting from muscle injury in which various elements of muscle cells are released into the bloodstream, potentially leading to serious conditions such as renal failure), and ICU neuropathy. It was suggested that my problems were caused by "intubation/ICU stays/immobility."

Those early days on the STU were a new fresh hell. I felt like a trapped, dying animal: my body seemed to be shutting down slowly while my primal instincts to survive were on overdrive. The racing thoughts I'd spent years talking about in therapy surged to warp speed, words pinging and skidding around my skull, pelting me with notions that were simultaneously violent, illogical, paranoid, rational, and baffling. I fixated on what Liam was doing, whether he was okay, what I'd do without him. (My parents, apparently, had broken up with him on my behalf while I was in the coma—they'd quit my school building permit job for me, as well.) I ruminated on all the disgust and loathing that I was sure the staff felt about me. I dwelled on all the mistakes I'd made in my life, all the letdowns, all the hurt I'd caused, all the failures.

• ● •

After I'd been on the STU for about a week, the unit psychiatrist took the following notes after speaking on the phone with Weinberg:

- *Clearly has BPAD [bipolar affective disorder]. Probably rapid cycling*
- *Past Sx- dprsn, eating DO, cutting, obsessional preoccupations*
- *H/o Provigil abuse to self-medicate mood disorder*
- *Suspects predominant, chronic hypomania*
- *Albert Feingold—saw her—wonders if current episode is manic*
- *Quite psychotic at times*
- *Wants pt to go on lithium*
- *Dr. Feingold—points to literature re: suicidality and mania; don't do anything else; just start with lithium*
- *Never euthymic in past 5 years*
- *Never been able to talk pt into detox or hospitalization*
- *Can't stand living with no ability to think, failed relationships*
- *Pt suggests "maybe I'm borderline." Dr. Weinberg—feels this is NOT accurate. Dr. Weinberg feels thinking, relationships will improve. Doesn't feel this is Axis II*
- *Wants "couple weeks" in hospital on lithium*
- *Feels pt. is very suicidal; has been able to call during crises; overdose not planning*
- *Fighting with parents; suddenly, everything cleared; in a fugue; thought—must kill self; organized, researched, planned attempt. "It just took over and it was done."*
- *Close relationship with pt; utterly shocked by this attempt*

- *Can be disorganized to point of psychosis when manic*
- *Hard to treat her alone; will she be able to live independently around Boston?*
- *Doesn't think pt will be able to live alone and do day program; "lots can happen in three weeks."*
- *"This has been a wild ride for a long time."*
- *Feels self + family have over-extended themselves.*
- *Plans to visit on Saturday AM*

There is such urgency to these handwritten notes: the underlined and capitalized words, the show of unquestioning obedience to Dr. Feingold's pharmacological commands, the dramatic quotes from Weinberg. Had I known then how much effort was being invested in strategizing about ways to manage me, I wonder what I would have felt. For so many years, I'd craved this level of attention—oh, how proud I would've been to have read these dramatic expressions of clinicalese—but by the time I arrived on the STU, I'd grown so tired of myself, so hopeless at the seeming inescapability of my mentally ill life, that I can't help but wonder if I wouldn't have cared at all. What strikes me even more was my suggestion that "maybe I'm borderline." I can't recall saying this, let alone thinking it. If Weinberg so adamantly disagreed with this idea, where had I picked it up?

My body made slow progress toward recovery. I was eventually able to keep down small bites of saltine crackers and sips of ginger ale. In spite of the constant migraine and light sensitivity, I began to open my eyes for up to ten seconds at a time and made more frequent trips out onto the ward in my wheelchair, pulling myself along the hallway, inch by inch, by gripping a side rail on the wall.

Desperate for relief one day, I headed to the nurses' station. I pulled myself up out of the wheelchair, winded from the exertion, and leaned on the counter.

A nurse came over. "Yes?"

"H-h-h-hi, p-p-p-please, c-c-c-c-can y-y-y-you help me." My jaw was clenched involuntarily. My arms and legs shivered in near convulsions, and my teeth chattered so hard I was worried I might bite my tongue. "M-m-m-y thoughts, c-c-c-can't s-stop them. Wha-wha-what's wrong with m-m-me?" I gripped the counter tightly in an effort to still my vibrating self.

"Aw, hun, I'm so sorry. Listen, this'll be sorted out soon. Your doctor's waiting until you're medically cleared to start meds. We'll get you right back on as soon as you are, m'kay? Right now your bipolar is untreated, so you might be feeling a little manic. But as soon as your labs are clear we'll get it under control. Hang in there, m'kay?"

When I grew strong enough to switch to a walker, I began going to the dining room for meals. Other patients asked me about my black eye and bruises, why I couldn't walk. I told them softly what had happened, empty of the pride I had once felt about how sick I was. All I could think about was how I'd failed at dying, how trapped I was, and how long it would take before I had the chance to once and for all kill myself.

One of the mental health workers, Harry, took an interest in me. He'd bring me to a meeting room with soft purple walls, where we'd sit in rocking chairs and talk about the meaning of life. He told me that I had a reason for being here, that I'd survived for a purpose I would soon discover. I tried to convince myself that maybe he was right but couldn't grasp how it was possible.

Because the numbness in my extremities wasn't getting any better, a team of Harvard Medical School neurology residents came in to evaluate me with one of their professors. I was escorted into a large room and asked to sit before a U-shaped table filled with young doctors around my age. The professor proceeded to demonstrate a neurological examination, poking and prodding various parts of me while discussing me in the third person. He asked his students for their educated opinions. I was thanked and informed that I could leave.

Nine days after my admission, I was medically cleared to start lithium. My concerns about the weight gain this drug was notorious for inducing were promptly dismissed as superficial; was I really worried right now about my appearance when my life was at stake? My hesitancy was met with the strong reminder that Dr. Feingold believed lithium was my best chance at survival. The unit psychiatrist reassured me that it was a tried-and-true medication not just for the treatment and prevention of mania but for preventing suicide, as well, and that it had been around for a long, long time. Yes, I'd have to get regular blood tests to ensure my levels were in the proper range, but I'd quickly adjust to them; all patients did.

EIGHTEEN

Lithium

Before I started lithium, which the unit psychiatrist told me was the "gold standard treatment" for bipolar disorder, he advised me of its biggest risks: possible thyroid problems and kidney damage, the latter of which he reassured me would likely not happen provided my blood levels were carefully monitored. "Make sure to stay hydrated," he said, "and take in consistent amounts of water and salt. Changing around how much you're ingesting can interfere with your levels." (Excessive thirst and urination are two of the most common adverse effects of lithium use; these are typically associated with the emergence of a condition called nephrogenic diabetes insipidus, in which the kidneys lose the ability to concentrate urine.)

No one informed me that lithium is also a neurotoxin—a substance that can damage nerve tissue—or that, historically, its purported psychiatric benefits have been linked to its toxicity. By impeding activity in the central nervous system, lithium can leave anyone who takes it—not just those who've been deemed manic—feeling slowed down, cognitively dulled; so, too, would regular consumption of other neurotoxins such as lead, mercury, or arsenic. Signs of low-level lithium toxicity include mild hand tremors and tiredness; at the other end of the spectrum, seizures, coma, irreversible brain damage, and death.

While lithium had been tested as a treatment for various physical conditions as far back as the midnineteenth century, it wasn't used as an antimanic agent until 1949, after an Australian psychiatrist named John Cade injected lab animals with high doses of lithium carbonate and noticed they became sedated. "Those who have experimented with guinea pigs know to what degree a ready startle reaction is part of their make-up," he explains. "It was thus even more startling to the experimenter [Cade himself] that after the injection of a solution of lithium carbonate they could be turned on their backs and that, instead of the usual frantic righting reflex behavior, they merely lay there and gazed placidly back at him." At the Bundoora Repatriation Mental Hospital, a two-hundred-bed facility in Victoria where he was director, Cade decided to test the drug on ten manic patients, following them over the course of weeks or months to see how they did. Within days, he describes, one patient was "distinctly quieter" and "appear[ing] practically normal." Another had "commenced work in the garden." One "mischievous and interfering" patient on the ward, who "had long been regarded as the most troublesome," became less so on lithium, a response that, to Cade, "was highly gratifying." He compiled evocative case summaries of each patient's progress—in spite of five experiencing symptoms of lithium poisoning along the way, nine out of ten were still on it and apparently no longer manic at the time of his writing. Cade published his results in a paper, concluding, "There is no doubt that in mania patients' [*sic*] improvement has closely paralleled [lithium] treatment and that this criterion has been fulfilled in the chronic and subacute cases just as closely as in the cases of more recent onset." But this declaration was just part of the whole story, and premature: after he submitted his paper, two of the ten patients would stop the drug because of extreme neurotoxic reactions, another simply wouldn't stay on it, and one who did stay on it—that "mischievous" patient, called "WB," whose response Cade had been most pleased with—would die of lithium toxicity eight months after the paper's publication.

Half a year before Cade was to publish his glowing report on lithium, coincidentally, the U.S. FDA banned its use. ("One can hardly imagine a less propitious year in which to attempt the pharmacological rehabilitation of lithium," Cade would later recount.) Lithium chloride, which doctors had been prescribing to heart patients in need of a table salt alternative for their low-sodium diets, had led to multiple deaths. "Stop using this dangerous poison at once," declared the FDA in *The New York Times* in early 1949.

In the years following the publication of Cade's paper, as more psychiatrists began to use the drug outside the United States, it was generally understood that psychiatric patients were essentially being treated with lithium poisoning. "The lithium level necessary to terminate mania is probably always reached only by near-toxic dosage," explained a team of Australian doctors, in 1951, who'd written up their results from treating over one hundred manic patients for anywhere from two weeks to more than a year. They described a long list of symptoms of lithium poisoning they observed in their patients, noting, "Most . . . resemble those of Addison's disease or sodium depletion. The suggestion that lithium owes its effect, at least in part, to a displacement of sodium from the body fluids and tissues appears to be mainly based on this similarity." (Addison's disease is a potentially life-threatening adrenal gland condition that causes deficits of hormones that help regulate basic functions like metabolism, electrolyte levels, blood pressure, blood sugar, and sleep, along with the body's stress response. Depleted sodium levels can cause headaches, fatigue, nausea, muscle weakness, seizures, coma, or death.)

According to psychiatrist and Brown University professor Walter A. Brown, when Cade was asked about the outcomes of his 1949 experiment years later, in the 1960s, he apparently omitted the inconvenient fact that the "mischievous" WB had died and described his lithium treatment as a success story—this in spite of the fact that Cade himself had lost faith in lithium due to its toxicity not long after publishing his paper. In 1952, when Cade took over as superintendent of the Royal Park Mental Hospital in Melbourne (where he would remain for the next quarter century), according to Brown, he prohibited any use of lithium at all. "We will never know if Cade's silence on this matter was a deliberate attempt to conceal a painful truth or in part or whole an unintentional lapse," says Brown. "Whatever the case, in omitting WB's fatal lithium toxicity from the retrospective versions of his lithium discovery, Cade painted a mistakenly rosy picture. . . . WB's happy outcome became an integral part of the lithium story."

One team of neurologists, addressing concerns of lithium and brain damage, suggested in a 1979 paper that "early detection of toxicity would be assisted by serial EEG monitoring of patients on lithium and perhaps by more frequent and more detailed clinical examination with urgent reassessment in the event of any abnormality being found." This proactive recommendation seems to have been a one-off; in subsequent decades, while researchers have continued to publish about lithium-induced brain injury, there seems to be little if any emphasis in clinical guidelines on what doctors can do to preclude it altogether. The International Society for Bipolar Disorders, for example, does not mention once in its "consensus guidelines for safety monitoring of bipolar disorder treatments" that lithium-induced brain injury is even a possibility. In the two years that I was to take lithium, I never once had an EEG to detect whether my brain activity had been dulled, nor did I hear this even mentioned as an option.

Because most American psychiatrists were well aware of lithium's toxic nature—and because there was no industry incentive to produce it, because it was unpatentable—the drug remained unpopular in the United States until 1970, when growing pressure from lobbyists like the lithium task force of the American Psychiatric Association pushed the FDA to finally approve it for the treatment of acute mania. Only a handful of controlled lithium studies had been conducted by that point, each with significant limitations and flaws. In one done at the Aarhus University Psychiatric Institute in Denmark, thirty-eight manic patients, who'd had their other medications abruptly stopped before the trial, were put either knowingly into an open lithium group or into a blind group in which they were switched back and forth at random between lithium and a placebo every couple of weeks. Ward staff tracked mania levels in daily records by noting a simple +, ++, or +++; how long these patients were followed was left unclear beyond "two weeks or more." Without distinguishing between patients who knew they were on lithium and those who didn't, researchers concluded that fourteen patients had a "positive" effect on lithium, eighteen a "possible" effect (meaning that there were other factors that made it hard to assume it was lithium that had helped), and six a "minus" effect. This study would play a key part in getting lithium its FDA approval.

A few years later, in the mid-1970s, the FDA expanded lithium's approved uses to include mania relapse prevention—again, based upon limited, flawed evidence. One study split fifty patients diagnosed with manic depression into two groups. All the patients had already been on lithium for between one and seven years. One group continued on lithium while the other group had its lithium stopped abruptly and was started on a placebo. Over the course of five months, it was reported that none of the patients in the lithium group relapsed, while twelve did in the group who'd had their lithium stopped cold turkey. No mention was made that perhaps people in the latter group weren't having relapses of manic depression as much as they were experiencing symptoms of acute lithium withdrawal—in fact, quite the opposite. Because relapses didn't happen simultaneously, the authors drew the conclusion that "there was no indication of rebound or abstinence effects."

More recently, researchers have acknowledged the fact that stopping lithium can cause debilitating withdrawal symptoms. One prominent bipolar researcher at the University of Oxford (who reported financial ties to more than fifteen pharmaceutical companies between the years of 2012 and 2015 alone, so is by no means what one might call antimedication) said of lithium in 1994, "Frank manic symptoms are the defining feature of significant withdrawal effects and appear to be of a comparable severity to those seen in manic illness generally, often requiring hospital admission." Yet even with an acknowledgment like this, mainstream psychiatric researchers rarely seem to conclude that perhaps a better long-term solution for those already on lithium is in fact a slow, careful taper of the drug, rather than continuing it indefinitely—and that in the case of someone who's been diagnosed manic for the first time, perhaps the best step is to try to avoid lithium altogether. That same Oxford bipolar researcher acknowledges that the scientific literature on lithium discontinuation makes clear that the rates of mania recurrence are "so high" in patients who've discontinued their lithium "that they appear likely to exceed appreciably those expected from the spontaneous recurrence rate in untreated bipolar illness." To put this more bluntly: patients who stop lithium are more likely to have a manic relapse almost immediately (within three months) than are patients who were never exposed to the drug in the first place. Despite this, as of 2024, the American Psychiatric Association's current Practice Guideline for the Treatment of Patients with Bipolar Disorder recommends lithium as a first-line treatment for various bipolar-related interventions, and the UK's National Institute for Health and Care Excellence (NICE) instructs doctors to "offer lithium as a first-line, long-term pharmacological treatment for bipolar disorder."

The sweeping assumption among psychiatrists that their patients' respective collapses into dysfunction upon stopping lithium is proof that they need the drug has also long been the assumption of many of those patients. "As long as I take those three pink lithium-carbonate capsules every day, I can function," explains Jaime Lowe in a 2015 *New York Times Magazine* piece titled "I Don't Believe in God, but I Believe in Lithium." (In the article, she maps out the geological, medical, technological, and cultural history of lithium, interweaves her own story of taking lithium for twenty years, and grapples with the fact that she's recently learned the drug has irreversibly damaged her kidneys.) "If I don't [take lithium]," she says, "I will be riding on top of subway cars measuring speed and looking for light in elevated realms." What strikes me most each time I read Lowe's heartfelt piece is the multitude of raw, lengthy-sentences-separated-by-semicolon-laden paragraphs in which she describes all the chaos that ensued after she decided to stop her lithium in 2000. (After seven years of doing well, she'd begun to wonder if, perhaps, she'd been "given the wrong diagnosis" as a teenager or "was past the point of having manic episodes.") Her life fell apart after she stopped taking lithium, she explains, which solidified her conviction that she needed it. "After that episode, I went back on lithium and stayed on it, despite the health risks. . . . I was scared by what happened when I went off it," she recounts. "I worry that without lithium I will lose my job, my partner, my home, my mind . . . because I've been through all this. I don't believe in God, but I believe in lithium."

"In my view," wrote critical psychiatrist and University College London professor Joanna Moncrieff in a 2015 response to Lowe's *New York Times Magazine* piece, "the evidence that lithium helps prevent episodes of manic depression is far too weak to outweigh the harms it can cause. . . . Long periods of remaining well are not necessarily evidence of a treatment's effectiveness. What we would need to demonstrate the efficacy and value of lithium is a prospective randomized trial in which people who had not previously been on long-term drug treatment were randomly allocated to start lithium or placebo. At present, my view is that the evidence that lithium *might* be effective is not strong enough to justify such a trial, given the health risks associated with it." In her article, Lowe doesn't mention that stopping lithium has been documented to cause serious withdrawal symptoms that can include mania, or that the drug was originally understood to work precisely through its toxicity. In fact, the one time the word *poison* is mentioned, it's in the context of her first experience on a psych ward, where she'd landed, as a teen, after she stopped sleeping and spun out into paranoia and racing thoughts, according to her medical records. "After I was admitted to the institute's adolescent ward," she explains, "I thought the nurses and doctors and therapists were trying to poison me."

When I read Lowe's story, I can't help but wonder if she's ever been asked the questions that no one ever asked me and so many of my fellow ex-bipolar friends back when we believed in our meds: *What if the mania that came on when you stopped the drug wasn't actually untreated bipolar disorder but a symptom of withdrawal? What if, after your insomnia set in all those years ago and you ended up on that psych ward, doctors had addressed your sleep issues instead of putting you on lithium—would you ever have gotten manic again?*

Around the time I was started on lithium while hospitalized on the STU, my psychiatrist requested further testing, writing:

25 yo SWF Harvard grad adm via ICU s/p [status post] very serious OD attempt with exposure to cold/elements in late

November. H/o BPAD I, presented in mixed episode at McLean.
O/p [outpatient] MD strongly questions possibility of fugue-like
state at time of OD. Questions for consult—diagnosis? Possi-
bility of dissociative element? Current suicidality?

A psychologist was brought onto the unit to conduct a battery of neuropsychological tests on me. Some were to assess my cognitive functioning, others, my personality, still others, whether I'd been properly diagnosed. He sat across from me in my room as I reclined on my hospital bed, and ran me through hours of questionnaires and interviews. I was even given the Rorschach "ink blot" test, which I didn't realize was still a thing. I described one red-and-black picture as a beheaded alligator on a surfboard dripping blood. In the report, he declared me psychotic.

Two weeks into my stay on the STU, according to my records, the nursing staff officially removed me from a stringent "self-harm protocol." (They'd noted on the date of my admission that I met the criteria of "harm to self," "self-concept disturbance," "impaired level of desired daily activity," "altered sleep," and "altered nutrition/ hygiene.") I'd been on lithium for a few days by then, and my mind felt somewhat quieted down, my body less tense; I couldn't have possibly detected the inklings of havoc the drug would soon be wreaking on my endocrine system. Whether lithium was actually helping me I couldn't say, but what I knew for certain was how soothing it felt to spend time with Harry, the mental health worker who made sure to check in with me each day, and that Pam, the head nurse, could get me smiling in spite of myself with her grandmotherly warmth and sarcastic humor. It had taken me fourteen days to trick them—and to begin to trick myself, as well—into believing I was grateful to still be breathing.

Condition on Discharge

CONDITION ON DISCHARGE: *The patient is a pleasant, well-dressed and groomed woman in no acute distress. She is alert and oriented x3. Her speech is clear and articulate with normal rate, rhythm, and volume. Her thought processes are organized and linear with no racing and no flightive ideas. There is [sic] no overt or reported hallucinatory experiences. There is no overt or reported delusional content. She describes her mood as "okay, better, just a bit anxious about discharge." Her affect is mildly anxious with full range and almost no tearfulness. She describes subjectively improving concentration and states that she has been able to read several books in the past week since starting on lithium. Memory, cognition, and fund of knowledge are intact. Insight is fair, and judgement [sic] is also fair. The patient adamantly denies any thoughts, impulses, or plans to harm or kill herself or anyone else.*

DISCHARGE DIAGNOSES:

Axis I: Bipolar affective disorder type 1, mixed, without psychotic features.

   Alcohol abuse.

Axis II: None.

Axis III: Rhabdomyolysis, resolved.

   Acute hepatitis, resolved.

   Nausea.

   Vomiting.

   Dizziness.

   Myalgias.

Axis IV: At time of discharge includes: Current unemployment.

Axis V: At time of discharge is approximately 55.

NINETEEN

Realistic Expectations

I was discharged from the STU after a few weeks—this was considered a long stay for the short-term unit—and moved into my parents' house to begin an intensive outpatient program at NewYork-Presbyterian, where I'd last been four years prior. In my estimation, my stay had been far too quick; most of the time, I felt out of body, like nothing was real. I was still debilitated by anxiety, physically weak, entirely numb in my extremities, and plagued with frequent headaches, profuse sweating, and cognitive fog, but because I was no longer actively suicidal, the unit staff had decided my stay had been a success. When not in treatment, I sat in the basement doing jigsaw puzzles, eating giant bowls of oatmeal covered in fat-free half-and-half and Splenda, and watching reruns of *Law & Order* while cuddling our family's two panting, bad-breathed terriers. Trapped in a kind of psychiatric limbo, I had zero confidence that treatment would ever begin to help me, but couldn't yet muster the will I knew it would take to kill myself.

I immediately returned to drinking alcohol at night, careful to hide it from my parents and treaters at the program. I did some SAT tutoring with the uninterested children of very wealthy parents. I reconnected with a handful of old friends from my youth who all had full-time jobs and their own places to live, some now married. As we drank wine and cooked elaborate dinners in their kitchens, I feigned normality. When I finally spilled about my psychiatric history, they simply couldn't fathom that I was fresh off the psych ward, my body still recovering from an overdose.

Less than two months after I'd started lithium, I saw my GP for a routine physical. She noted my concerns about how much weight I'd gained, along with the lengthy catalog of physical ailments I reported: excessive fatigue, shin splints, headaches, weak nails, and hair loss. She ran some blood tests and, on a Saturday morning, called me up: Was I okay? Could I stand? Was I able to get up a flight of stairs all right? Confused, I answered in the affirmative—I mean, sure, I was incredibly tired when I did all of these things, but that was nothing new to me.

"Why are you asking?"

"I got your blood work back. Your TSH is 118."

"Uh, what does that mean?"

"Thyroid-stimulating hormone. The amount of it in your blood indicates whether your thyroid is working properly. Normally, it's meant to be somewhere between 0.4 and 4.0. Yours is 118—at first I was sure it was a testing error, so I had them run it again. It actually is 118. I've never seen anything like this."

"So . . . what does the number actually mean?"

"The higher the level, the less active your thyroid function is, so you have severe hypothyroidism. Clearly, the lithium is impairing it. I'd like to run a complete panel to see if we can figure out what's going on here. In the meantime, you'll need to get right on Synthroid."

"Synthroid?"

"It's a drug that mimics the functions your thyroid is no longer able to do properly."

I didn't ask any further questions, as none occurred to me, and went right to the lab and had several vials of blood drawn. The additional tests revealed that in the seven or so weeks since I'd started lithium, I'd gotten a thyroid autoimmune condition called Hashimoto's disease, which meant my immune system had begun to produce antibodies that were now attacking cells in my thyroid. Symptoms included weight gain, weakness, fatigue, hair loss, and dry skin. I wasn't sure whether my hypothyroidism was the result of the autoimmune condition or vice versa or neither, and don't recall asking my doctor to clarify (Hashimoto's does, indeed, cause an underactive thyroid gland). I do recall that my doctor seemed clear, given the timing and rapidity of onset, that lithium had set off this condition, which I was told was considered incurable.

I was upset about the prospect of having to struggle with these new issues for the rest of my life, brought this news to the new psychiatrist I'd begun to see near my parents' house, and asked if I should stop lithium.

"No, no," she interjected. "This really isn't a problem. You're lucky: out of all the autoimmune conditions you could have, Hashimoto's is by far the most easily manageable. Synthroid's been around forever, and it's very well tolerated. We'll make sure your primary doc titrates you up to the proper dose. That should resolve any thyroid-related symptoms."

Influenced by a potent mix of self-loathing and the cognitive effects of polypharmacy, I felt confused and self-conscious about how strongly I'd reacted to this turn of events. I steeled myself for life with an additional incurable disease, nodded silently in agreement, and told myself that it was silly of me to have gotten so upset.

About six months after I tried to kill myself, I felt ready to move back to Boston. I reassured my parents—myself, as well—that I could find a tutoring job there easily. My father hesitantly consented to once again cover the cost of my rent until I was able to pay on my own, and when I called up my former landlord, I was happy to learn that another unit was available in my old building. I moved back in and got a job coaching a girls' squash team at a prep school in the suburbs. At night, I got drunk and often ordered a large cheese pizza and Cinna Stix from Domino's before eating myself into painfully distended–belly oblivion and passing out. I began to see a new shrink named Dr. Littwin, a tall, gentle, elderly man with a white beard and moth-eaten wool sweaters. Though he was a psychiatrist, he didn't prescribe medications; if I wanted those, he told me, I'd have to see a psychopharmacologist colleague of his down the road by the name of Dr. Feingold—the same Dr. Feingold who happened to be Weinberg's mentor and had been directing my treatment through her and the STU. During our fifteen-minute med appointments, Dr. Feingold ran through a quick checklist of symptoms. (He was always especially curious about how much sex I was having; years later, when looking through my records, I observed that two of his most used descriptors for me were *hypersexual* and *promiscuous*. He even threw *erotomania* in there on at least one occasion.) He had me on two mood stabilizers, an antipsychotic, and a benzodiazepine (lithium, Lamictal, Abilify, and Ativan, respectively). I saw him once every couple of months.

In therapy, Dr. Littwin attempted to explore the broader social forces that he felt had shaped my ongoing struggles with body, sexuality, womanhood, and self, and he seemed especially concerned about my knack for dating self-destructive men and drinking myself into blackouts. At the mention of any of this, I swiftly changed the subject, convinced as I was that the source of my troubles was faulty brain pathology. I never took him seriously and frequently skipped appointments. A few years later, in 2012, after I requested my medical records from him, Dr. Littwin would write of our treatment together:

I was struck by how much trouble and unhappiness you seemed to have had in your life, despite being a very bright, attractive, well educated, athletic young woman who came from a family of means. You described hating becoming a woman at menarche, having many problems regulating yourself—depression, drug and alcohol use, cutting, hyper-exercise, anorexia/bulemia [sic], perhaps hyper-sexuality— . . . *that the last time you remembered feeling happy was in the 7th grade and that in the 8th grade you were diagnosed as having bi-polar disease. I was unsure what to make of the latter, since many depressions are given a "medical" name by psychiatrists, ascribing the problem to "chemistry" and neglecting the context and specificity of why someone is having those particular life problems at that particular time.* . . . .

Over all, I think that although we connected in some ways, our attempt at treatment never really got off the ground. I don't think we could create the needed support structure with you living alone and being unable to manage and regulate yourself. Had anything like it been available, I would have preferred that you were in a therapy oriented open hospital or day hospital, until you felt solid enough to live and put together a meaningful life on your own with the help of the treatment. However, such places no longer exist in Boston and although we tried to create a sense of security, the aloneness and worthlessness were too much for us to deal with.

Of all my former psychiatrists, he was the only one who ever invited me to step back and rethink the diagnostic paradigm in which I so deeply believed. I just wasn't ready yet.

• ● •

In January 2010, I began to consider that my drinking was perhaps getting a bit out of control. There were the drunken, sloppy pickles I was getting myself into with driving, men, and food, the last of which concerned me the most: I couldn't stop binge eating and no longer fit in any of my clothes. I brought my drinking up with my father, who'd had the wherewithal to quit alcohol himself decades earlier, when he'd realized he'd become a little too preoccupied with whether he'd be able to make the one bar-car train out of Grand Central at the end of the workday. With the help of Aunt Sara, whom I was in regular contact with given our proximity to each other, we came up with a plan: I would try out *not* drinking alcohol for the entire month of February.

On February 9, I emailed them an update "which contains both good and bad news," I clarified at the start. I proceeded to give them a blow-by-blow description of the previous evening, when I'd spent an hour "pondering whether or not to get a glass of wine" and eventually "decided that I would." I rambled on about how committed I'd been to having only two drinks over the course of the evening and how, I was so excited to share, I'd succeeded! Afterward, I explained to them:

> i walked home, got right into my PJs, brushed my teeth and washed my face, got right into bed, took my meds, and told myself that i wasn't going to order any food. and i didn't! i hunkered down and watched one of my favorite shows on my laptop, and went to sleep at about 10:15. . . . so, yes, i did break this goal of going the month of february without drinking, but in many ways, i'm really proud of myself for last night. . . . i took care of myself, went to sleep early, slept really well, and got a

fresh start to the day. i just wanted to let you guys know. if you have time, i'd love any thoughts you may have.

lots of love,
laura

My father wrote back with a loving but skeptical reply, ending with:

I am so glad you shared this with Sara and me—that is a very good, healthy sign. But just remember not to let yourself slip back into old patterns. You must change them. Also, as I said before, always reach for a better thought when you don't feel so good. That will give you some relief, and relief, no matter how small, helps enormously and you can continue to keep reaching for more and better thoughts. It really can turn your mood around, I promise.

XO DAD

Over the years, I've met many parents in similar circumstances to mine with their psychiatrically diagnosed adult children. They are frustrated with the ongoing stall-outs, mishaps, and catastrophes of their struggling sons and daughters, sometimes even resentful of the ways they feel taken advantage of, but are also terrified about the possible consequences of challenging their kids or taking it a step further by cutting them off: Will their child collapse into breakdown? Get arrested? Become homeless? Kill themselves? Numerous psychiatrists had been reminding my parents for years, by then, that they needed to "set realistic expectations" for me (read: *likely can't hold down a job, live independently, or stay out of hospital for too long; might commit suicide*). When I asked my father a few years ago what he thought back then about my employability, he chuckled and said, "Not much!" It makes sense he was so terrified of disenabling me, convinced as he was that doing so might lead me to kill myself.

While my parents' generosity helped to insulate me from all those terrible things they worried could befall me due to my treatment-resistant illness, and kept me comfortably fed, clothed, and sheltered in a stable home, I was sheltered, as well, from reality. I knew nothing of the insecurities and fears that come from being a young adult setting out to build a life for herself. I was entirely unfamiliar with what it was like to find and hold down work in the face of personal struggle—let alone pay my own bills or manage money responsibly or even budget at all. Wholly unfamiliar with the satisfying sense of autonomy that comes from figuring out how to find one's way through the world, I got used to focusing my efforts on refining my skills as a patient. By the time I tried and failed at that sober February challenge, my father and I thought that success, for me, was managing the commute between therapy, my coaching job, and the grocery store in a car I owed no money on, before heading home to an apartment for which I wasn't able to pay rent on my own.

I think often about what would have happened had my parents cut me off financially after college. Maybe I would've killed myself on purpose or by accident or gotten myself in some other, lesser trouble. Or I might well have ended up hospitalized for a long stretch of time, thrown on new and more meds, then been instructed to get on disability and enroll as a "client" of whichever nearby community mental health center happened to have availability in one of its group homes, where my sparse monthly check would have been mailed to whichever staff person had been designated as my representative payee, and I'd likely have spent the following years becoming increasingly immobilized by and dependent upon institutional care. But perhaps facing the harsh starkness of young adulthood would have sparked something alive in me—in spite of the sedating layers of all my psychiatric treatment—that would have led me to the thrilling, terrifying, rewarding discovery of how the hell to take care of myself. I'll never know.

Just after midnight the following Sunday, which happened to be Valentine's Day, I stumbled through the emergency room doors of Greenwich Hospital, tears streaking my red face, hair drenched with rain, breath reeking of wine. When asked how I could be helped, I muttered something along the lines of "I have bipolar disorder and I think I'm gonna kill myself."

I came to, hours later, in a flimsy hospital gown in a small room enclosed by Plexiglas. A TV played the news up high on the wall of the common area. I was the only patient on this small observation unit, and a man sat in the walled-off nurses' station. The inside of my skull pounded. I had a terrible taste in my mouth, and the membranes of my nasal canals felt like they'd been burned. I needed water, I needed to brush my teeth, I needed a change of clothes. I needed to think through how the fuck I'd gotten here. I closed my eyes and rolled to my side, straining the mental mush for something graspable beyond the usual, murky residue of shame.

And then I remembered: Arriving, the night prior, at the house of a handsome squash player I'd met while watching a professional men's tournament a few days earlier. The lines of coke, the bottles of wine, the rug by the fire. His bed, and my spontaneous impulse to move my head down his body, ignoring my long-lived fear of oral sex (in high school, I'd half seriously diagnosed myself with a bad case of "peniphobia"). His reaction, *Oh, I can't, I'm so tired, I've already had so much sex today,* as he pushed me off. The jarring comprehension that whatever sex he was referencing had been with someone else, and then the speeding up of time, the fuzzy sound in my ears, the tunnel vision as I frantically put on my clothes and tripped down the stairs in my uncomfortable heeled boots and he stayed in bed. My guttural screams as I accelerated on winding back roads through the pouring rain and considered which tree to plow my car into—not that one, the next; no, the next; no, the one up there. *What a whore you are, you pathetic waste of oxygen, you're too fucking broken to get through a day without making a fool of yourself.* There was the hyperventilating as I sat in the driveway of my parents, who were away, and made a mental inventory of all the bathroom cabinets I'd have to go through to get enough over-the-counter drugs to successfully finish myself off. The baffling desire to not overdose that next occupied me, the desperate phone call to my father. His calm but urgent request that I turn the car back on and drive right to the hospital. The compelling urge, from a source that felt not of me, to listen to him. To save myself.

Now, in the observation room, I shuffled to the door in my socks to see if I was locked in. I couldn't decide whether to be happy or disappointed when I turned the handle and pushed it open.

I was transported back to the Haven at NewYork-Presbyterian that afternoon. Six years had passed since I was last there, in 2004, and what had really changed in my life? Yes, I'd managed to graduate from college, but beyond a diploma my mother had framed in gold leaf on my bedroom wall, the only real difference was that my bipolar disorder had progressed to treatment-resistant status. I wondered if they'd remember me on the ward, where I'd fit into their hierarchy of severity now that I had a serious overdose under my belt. I'd been a newbie inpatient last time; it was understandable that they hadn't grasped how sick I truly was.

TWENTY

Newly Sober

Relieved to once again be locked away from myself, I determined to get my act together during that third hospital stay. The unit had a stationary bike at the end of the hall: I would ride it every day! There was no way to order Domino's: I would no longer binge eat at night! The menu had so many healthy options to choose from: I would go on a fat-free diet!

This surge of motivation was short-lived.

The unit psychiatrist increased my lithium, assuming that I had been "medication noncompliant" because my levels were low. (Lithium levels are determined by the drug's "therapeutic index," which measures the ratio between what doctors consider a clinically beneficial dose and a physiologically unsafe one; lithium's therapeutic index is especially low, meaning that there is a tiny margin between a "therapeutic" dose and a toxic one.) I was started on two new drugs prescribed to keep people sober: Antabuse, which interferes with the metabolization of alcohol to make people violently ill if they drink, and naltrexone, an opioid receptor antagonist that is said to potentially lessen alcohol cravings. Just one dose of naltrexone had me totally knocked out, and when I brought this up in morning rounds, a nurse wrote, "She was encouraged to believe that this would lessen as she became more accustomed to it." Which it didn't. During my stay, I didn't shower or leave the unit once, nor did I ever end up getting on that recumbent bike. Instead of attending groups, I slept or watched cartoons in my room, too lethargic to perform the duties of a proactive patient.

My drinking was the predominant focus of mental health workers whenever they struck up conversations with me during the five days that I was there. At first, I avoided getting into it, as I didn't want to be forced to make promises I knew I'd break, but after feeling the relief of several days separated from a previous night's drunk, I opened back up to the idea of giving sobriety a shot, at least for a little while. I certainly wasn't going to call myself an alcoholic—*No way, not happening, I'm not one*—but I was willing to admit that in my desperate efforts to find relief from bipolar disorder, my drinking had gotten me into a whole mess of trouble. My treatment team reassured me that my mental illness might very well become more manageable if I stopped self-medicating with alcohol, and with the new hope this possibility brought, I agreed to focus on not drinking after I got out. When I left, I'd accumulated more consecutive time sober than I'd had since college (apart from the weeks I'd spent on the STU after my overdose).

In discharge planning, I'd been given the choice to move back in with my parents to attend a substance abuse program right there on NYP's campus or go back up to McLean to attend a substance abuse program there. I decided I'd return to Massachusetts, though I knew I couldn't live alone. Aunt Sara and Uncle Bill, who lived close to McLean, offered to let me stay with them for a few weeks while I got settled into the new program. The day before my discharge, a nurse wrote:

> *Patient is bright and in good spirits. States mood is good and*
> *relaxed. Feels motivated for treatment and is willing and able*

to focus on substance piece which she has not been able to or willing to do in the past. With some sedation and slurred speech for a few hours with naltrexone. Is willing to work through the discomfort and see if the effects resolve.

The next morning, as I was getting ready to leave, a mental health worker knocked on my half-open door with a thick, dark blue softcover book in his hand. He held it out, saying, "You know, this is there for you if you decide you want it." *Alcoholics Anonymous* was imprinted on the cover. I looked up at him, forced a smile, and took it.

"Just so you know, you don't have to think you're an alcoholic to try it out. They won't make you say you are. Once you're settled in Boston, you can look up meetings online and find one in your area. I bet there are tons of options."

"I'll definitely think about it. Thanks." I'd already agreed to admit myself into substance abuse treatment; wasn't that enough? I didn't want to kill myself anymore—at least, not for now—and if I was going to give life with bipolar disorder another try, getting rid of the excess turmoil that my drinking had been causing me seemed like my one last shot. Maybe *this* was why my meds had never helped me. Maybe *this* would be what freed me from the prison of treatment resistance.

In my admission notes to the substance abuse day program at McLean, my name is followed by a long list of diagnoses: alcohol dependence, cocaine abuse, bipolar I disorder (most recent episode mixed), eating disorder NOS, borderline personality disorder, and hypothyroidism. My medication intake form lists me on lithium XR, Lamictal, Lexapro, Abilify, Klonopin, and Antabuse (I'd stopped the naltrexone as soon as I got out).

In a lengthy admission form, I listed my bipolar disorder as "very serious."

In response to a question about the relationship between my substance use and life problems, I checked the answer "My problems are just as likely to have caused my substance use as to have resulted from it."

On my medical history form, I checked off my current problems as weight gain, sleep disturbance, low energy, poor concentration, diarrhea, constipation, bowel problems, menstrual problems, joint/back pain, muscle stiffness, headaches, memory problems.

For the question "Is spirituality an important part of your life?" I checked "Not at all."

For the question "Do you feel that issues of religion, spirituality, ethnic background, or culture may influence your use of substances or your recovery?" I checked "No."

When asked, "How do you feel about the spiritual nature of 12-step meetings?" I checked "I dislike it somewhat." I would've checked "I dislike it strongly" if I hadn't been worried that I might be judged as too closed-minded.

On my first morning, I lined up in a basement hallway to get Breathalyzed. The air was glumly lit, tinged with the depressing reek of stale cigarette smoke. We patients were tired and bedraggled, our hair unwashed, uniformed in hoodie sweatshirts. I glanced down and saw a lot of bitten nails and red cuticles, fidgety hands clinging to travel mugs and disposable Dunkin' Donuts cups. A staff person handed each of us a sterile mouthpiece as we entered the room one by one. When it was my turn, I popped the piece into a contraption held out by another staff person and blew. My result was recorded. I was told to take a seat.

For hours each day, sitting hunched in collective misery, we endured group after group led by overly exuberant counselors who popped in and out with loathsome buoyancy. Each of us had to fill out a worksheet in the morning that documented our sobriety efforts from the previous day: how many AA or NA meetings we'd been to, what kinds of coping strategies we'd utilized, how we were handling cravings. I wrote the same answer every time: 0, television, fine. When the day was over, we spilled like molasses across the parking lot, returning to our cars to face our respective miseries.

When I'd moved into Sara and Bill's house before the start of the program, I'd felt so much relief that I wondered if this was finally a turning point. My first week back at McLean shattered that optimism; day-to-day life without booze was far more jarring than I'd imagined. I had debilitating headaches. The sedation made it feel like I was moving underwater. It was as though a layer of protective insulation had been scraped off my eyes for how harsh and glaring life now was. Without any escape, I was forced up against the horrifying consequences of my bipolar disorder: the people I'd hurt, the humiliating things I'd done, the jobs I couldn't handle, the drain I'd been on my family, the self-destruction I'd pursued with such unrelenting commitment.

It wasn't really my diagnosis that I was afraid of. In a slumbering part of me lived the true source of my terror: change.

PART

IV

TWENTY-ONE

The Choice between Voluntary and Involuntary

Ruthless migraines and nausea kept me from two days of substance abuse treatment. I spent much of the first day curled on my side in a dark room before moving to the sofa in Sara and Bill's den to watch episodes of *Curb Your Enthusiasm* between disorienting, sweaty naps. When I returned to the program, I felt more lost and despairing than I could ever remember feeling. What was I doing with my life? Was this really all that was in store for me, the useless meds and treatment programs followed by mindless television watching, eating, sleeping, and waking up to do it all over again? This hell of unmanageable bipolar disorder?

Sara and Bill were going away that weekend to visit friends; I was simultaneously frightened by what self-destructive things I might do while alone in their house and excited by the possibilities.

I'd been assigned to work with a psychopharmacologist, Dr. Heathering, who was managing my medication while I was in the program. He was young—looked to be around forty—and had a receding hairline. His curly hair was so long, voluminous, and unkempt that it looked like he'd stuck his finger in a light socket. After I returned from my migraine hiatus, he asked if I'd been going to AA. I said no, he asked why, and I answered that it just wasn't for me.

I let him know how afraid I was of being by myself that weekend, and, knowing my history with suicide, Dr. Heathering asked if I was having any thoughts of harming myself.

I paused for a moment, not wanting to lie but not wanting to tell him the truth, that this treatment-resistant mentally ill life I felt so stuck in was, simply put, not one worth living. A part of me enjoyed the drama of the silence, which I knew he knew meant *yes*. Another part of me wanted to tell him that over the past few days, death had morphed from a soothing idea at the back of my mind to a presence of feeling that tingled in my hands and stomach, churning up a pleasurable swirl of thrill each time I picked up my Dopp kit of pills to feel its power.

Instead I told him, "I feel this way before I get suicidal. By next week it could be dangerous."

He sat up from his relaxed position. "Laura, given your history, this is really concerning for me. What do you think about heading over to the STU so you can get some extra support while your family's away?"

I pursed my lips and nodded in resigned agreement; at the end of the day, wasn't this simply my fate, to end up either dead or locked on a psych ward? I didn't really want to off myself, not yet. I wanted to be taken care of again by the kind staff on the STU—to see Harry, Pam, and the other familiar faces.

"Yeah, I guess that's a good idea. I'll go back to my aunt and uncle's house today to get some rest and pack up my things. I'm sure my aunt can give me a ride tomorrow so I can check in." Yes, the more I thought about it, the more I liked this plan. This was going to work out just fine. My fears quickly began to dissipate.

"Oh." He paused, looking at me like I'd said something to embarrass myself. "I'm sorry, that's not possible."

"What do you mean?"

"I can't let you go home."

"I don't understand."

"Well"—he paused—"you've shared that you're feeling how you feel when you're suicidal. Given that, I'm going to have to hospitalize you right now. It's protocol, I'm sorry."

"I didn't say I was suicidal right now!" I clarified. "And I just told you I was okay with going in, that I agreed with the plan. Why can't I go tomorrow? I want to be able to get all my things—I can't just go over there with nothing."

"I really am sorry."

I could feel my face flushing, and my heart was pounding so loud I was sure he could hear it. "This isn't fair. I'm not actually going to kill myself. You can't do this. I'm totally wanting to go, I'm not trying to be difficult." He said nothing, watching me with an apologetic look. I stood up and smacked my hand on my forehead in disbelief, overtaken by an emotion I hadn't felt toward a psychiatrist since meeting Anuja all those years ago: indignation. "Nope, I'm sorry, I'm not going to go right now." I shook my head, surprised by my defiance. What was coming over me?

Dr. Heathering stood up and set his shoulders back. "Laura, I am not going to allow you to leave." There was a forceful timbre to his voice. "It's as simple as that. It won't work out well for you if you try." He reached for the phone.

"What the fuck! What are you doing?"

"I'm calling security."

"This is absurd. You've gotta be kidding me!" I began to gather my belongings. I needed to get out of his office.

"I wouldn't do that if I were you." He turned away as someone answered at the other end of the line. "Yes, hello, this is Tim Heathering over in Oaks. I'm going to need some assistance up here escorting a patient over to AB1." He put down the receiver and turned to face me. "Security will be here shortly. Please stay where you are. You can call your family to let them know you're being admitted."

I'd always been diligent about doing what my doctors said, understanding in a detached, intellectual way that psychiatrists could commit people against their will who were perceived to be a danger to themselves or others. I just never imagined I might be one of them.

The elevator dinged a few minutes later. Shaky and bewildered, I followed Dr. Heathering into the hallway. My instincts told me I had to be deliberate in every action, that one wrong move could be dangerous. I remembered what had happened on the STU two years earlier to a petite MIT student whom I hadn't heard utter a single sound while she was there until the day she received a delivered bouquet of flowers, promptly hurled it across the hall, and began to scream at the top of her lungs, refusing to stop when nurses tried to calm her. She was eventually grabbed by two staff people who briskly dragged her, shrieking and kicking, around the corner to the isolation room, where she soon went silent. We didn't see her for many hours after that. I'd watched the scene unfold like it was happening to an entirely different breed of patient from me. *I'll never be like that*, I'd reassured myself. *I'd never do anything to upset them.*

Two bulky men in gray uniforms were now staring at me in the hallway, both with hands resting on their equipment-laden belts.

"Are you fucking committing me right now?"

"That's up to you," Dr. Heathering responded. "You can sign yourself in voluntarily, and if you do, that means I don't have to commit you. Otherwise, yes, I'll admit you involuntarily. It's your choice."

One of the guards put out his arm to guide me toward the elevator.

"Don't touch me."

"We won't have to if you don't make us."

• ● •

When Arnold met me and the guards at the STU's locked door, I was instantly flooded with warmth. A minute earlier, I'd been irate. Now I couldn't help but smile. He'd been one of my favorite mental health workers the last time I was there, and he looked exactly the same: a well-maintained, thin mustache tracing his upper lip, those soft brown eyes hidden behind wire-rimmed spectacles, the collared shirt tucked carefully into pleated, crisply ironed chinos that flapped loosely over his shiny loafers, the cell phone in a giant black case attached to his belt. "Lauraaaaaaa, hiiiiiii!" he said after he unlocked the door. I resisted the urge to hug him, remembering how strict he'd been about boundaries anytime one of us tried, always saying, "No, no, no, no hugging, no please."

This was exactly where I belonged. What was I thinking to have been so angry at Dr. Heathering for making me come straight here? Why had I made such a scene?

Sara arrived that night with my belongings and had even stopped at the market on the way to pick up some of my favorite snacks. She brought four books, carefully describing each one and why I might like it as she stacked it on my bedside table. She put her arm around me, rubbed my back, said, "You're going to be okay, m'dear." I nodded, unable to make eye contact. I couldn't deny how relieved I felt to be locked back away from myself. Now that I had some good trail mix, these books, and my sweat suit, what was there to be upset about? I was embarrassed for having been so unreasonable with Dr. Heathering.

After Sara left, I headed to the dining room for dinner, dropping a pile of flaccid carrots on my plate and ignoring the dried-out strips of meat drenched in thick, brown sauce. I thought about how lucky I'd been to have spent time on such a luxurious unit as the Haven, with its private chef, oblivious to the fact that McLean was still spa-like in comparison with the state hospitals I hadn't yet seen the insides of. A young woman was sitting alone at a nearby table, scrolling through an iPod with a furrowed brow. She had clunky headphones over her ears, gauze and tape wrapped around one of her forearms. Her dark brown hair was cut short and gelled in an up-flip, and every so often she pulled at the silver ring piercing one corner of her bottom lip with her teeth. She wore gray DHA sweatpants (dee-has, as we called them at Harvard, were the prized warm-up gear issued annually to varsity athletes; I had four sets myself). She noticed me looking at her and acknowledged me with a small nod, momentarily slipping her headphones off to tell me her name was Eve. I said, "Hey, I'm Laura," and got back to my reading.

The next day, as I walked the halls, I found Eve in a quiet corner drawing with pastels. The eyes of the figure on her page were jet-black; its mouth, agape with pain. The arms and legs were stretched so far it made me think of a body on a torture rack.

"Hey," I said quietly, not wanting to startle her. "Do you mind if I sit?"

She looked up unsurprised, like she'd been waiting for me. "Yeah, sure."

I glanced at the bandage on her wrist, which I sensed she wanted seen, and nodded at her DHA sweatpants. "What did you play?"

"Softball. But I left early. Haven't gone back."

"I was squash. Class of '05 but I finished in '06. Had to take a year off, got too messed up. No fucking idea how I made it through."

"I only made it partway through sophomore year. Shit got *really* bad."

"Can I steal a piece of paper and pen?"

"Sure."

I sat down, unlocking my wrist and letting my fingers take over to move ink into swirls and waves and outstretched hands, shapes they always seemed to gravitate toward on the rare occasions that I drew. We sat silently, the only sound the soft scratch of pastel and pen on paper. Nervousness leaked through Eve's tough veneer of gel-frozen hair and piercings: when a distant door slammed, she jumped; the specks of scabs on her forehead were clearly from picking; she constantly pulled at her lip ring; her hands shook incessantly, even as she drew, and she breathed loudly, like she never had enough air. She did nothing to hide the long, large zipper of keloid scar that moved up the underside of her upper arm before disappearing beneath the sleeve of her T-shirt. I was surprised by the overwhelming urge I felt to take care of Eve. I could tell, as we sat there together, that we were going to mean something to each other.

Eve and I talked for hours every day, pulled to each other by the irresistible force of shared experience. We'd both grown up in wealthy families, excelled academically, played numerous sports with facility. As we drew pictures and wrote poems together, we disguised our terror about the state of our lives with jokes: *Imagine if our fellow Harvard students could see us now—they'd be so jealous! Isn't it nice to not have to live in the real world?* We ordered takeout and tucked ourselves away at our own table in the corner of the dining room. We even showed up at the arts and crafts group in spite of its infantilizing offerings of nontoxic clay, nontoxic glue, children's rounded scissors, and little heart-shaped cardboard boxes to which we were encouraged to adhere colorful pieces of tissue paper.

When I eventually joined Eve on privilege level 3, which meant we could go out on the grounds together without a staff chaperone, we scoured the underground tunnels in unsuccessful pursuit of the hospital's old bowling alley. We got caffeinated coffee in the cafeteria and sat in the winter sun while Eve chain-smoked, observing all the professionals walking briskly to the closed-off spaces that only those with certain letters after their names had access to. I silently wondered whether in some alternate universe I might have been one of them, sensing Eve wondered the same thing too. In morning check-ins with unnecessarily merry staff people who were usually younger than us, we quietly rolled our eyes at each other, stifling laughter as we pulled the trigger of a finger gun at our temples when no one was looking. In our assessment, most of the other patients were ordinary people being overly dramatic about the challenges of ordinary living. We, on the other hand, *are very sick*, was what I thought, and what I assumed Eve thought too. Like me, Eve had been classified as treatment resistant, since none of the meds doctors tried on her ever seemed to improve her depression. Together, we wore this moniker as a badge of honor, stoic warriors with bodies bearing the scars of our internal battles. If we never again had the chance to be successful in society, at least we still had the chance to stand out in the realm of the mentally ill.

At dinner one evening, when I mentioned to Eve that I hadn't touched alcohol in about a month, her face lit up. "Hey, that's fuckin' awesome, dude," she said. "I've been sober almost two years myself, actually."

"Holy shit, two years, wow." This sounded like an eternity to me. "How have you done it? Do you still wanna drink?"

"Nope, haven't wanted to drink in a long time. I'm in AA. I'd definitely be drinking without it. Saved my life." The usual resistance pushed itself forth in me as I briefly entertained the thought of saying, *Hi, I'm Laura and I'm an alcoholic.*

No way, not happening.

"Have you been to a meeting before?"

I shook my head. "I don't know if I'm up for it, to be honest. I mean, I definitely have some problems with drinking, but I just don't think I can really accept the idea of being an alcoholic."

"I hear you. Totally get it." Her usually hard voice had softened. "Hey. Idea. How about I take you to a meeting once we're outta here so you can at least check it out. You don't even have to introduce yourself, and you definitely don't have to say you're an alcoholic. My home group is this awesome meeting in Lexington that meets every morning, back-to-back, at six and seven. I usually hit the later one and then head to treatment afterwards. Some of my favorite people go to that one. How about it?"

"What's a home group?"

"Oh, that's a group that you commit to going to regularly. You usually take some kind of service position in it, too. It's basically your home base in AA."

"I dunno, I'm really not sure right now. Can I think about it?"

"Of course. No pressure."

"I'm curious, though. How has it saved your life?"

Before Eve told me all the ways that finding AA had helped her, she told me the story of what her drinking had looked like. How after some difficult experiences in high school, she discovered that alcohol expanded her, helped her feel brave, powerful, free—temporarily, at least, until she woke up the next morning in more pain than the day before. How it always seemed to relieve her depression more than the meds did. How she eventually felt so reliant on it to get her through a day that she would deceive and manipulate to get the alcohol she needed. I couldn't avoid hearing myself in her words: different details, same pain, same compelling desire for relief. By the end of our conversation, the idea of checking out an AA meeting didn't feel so repulsive to me anymore.

• ● •

In my previous hospitalizations, the mere mention of discharge had reliably flooded me with panic. This time, when I was told I'd soon be let out, I felt exhilarated. I had my blossoming friendship with Eve. Sara and Bill had invited me to stay with them for as long as I needed. I'd attend a partial hospital program on McLean's campus for a couple of weeks, which I knew would provide structure to my days. There was only one part of the plan that I wasn't so sure about: I'd been informed that I had borderline personality disorder (BPD) and that after finishing the partial hospital program, I would start a long-term BPD program at the hospital's outpatient center.

Diagnostic and Statistical Manual of Mental Disorders,
Fourth Edition, Text Revision
Diagnostic criteria for
301.83 Borderline Personality Disorder
© 2000 American Psychiatric Association

A pervasive pattern of instability of interpersonal relationships, self-image, and affects, and marked impulsivity beginning by early adulthood and present in a variety of contexts, as indicated by five (or more) of the following:

(1) frantic efforts to avoid real or imagined abandonment. **Note:** Do not include suicidal or self-mutilating behavior covered in Criterion 5.

(2) a pattern of unstable and intense interpersonal relationships characterized by alternating between extremes of idealization and devaluation

(3) identity disturbance: markedly and persistently unstable self-image or sense of self

(4) impulsivity in at least two areas that are potentially self-damaging (e.g., spending, sex, substance abuse, reckless driving, binge eating). **Note:** Do not include suicidal or self-mutilating behavior covered in Criterion 5.

(5) recurrent suicidal behavior, gestures, or threats, or self-mutilating behavior

(6) affective instability due to a marked reactivity of mood (e.g., intense episodic dysphoria, irritability, or anxiety usually lasting a few hours and only rarely more than a few days)

(7) chronic feelings of emptiness

(8) inappropriate, intense anger or difficulty controlling anger (e.g., frequent displays of temper, constant anger, recurrent physical fights)

(9) transient, stress-related paranoid ideation or severe dissociative symptoms

TWENTY-TWO

The Father of BPD

A bipolar diagnosis made sense to me—the highs and lows and all the impulsive behaviors that came with them. Anxiety disorder, depression, binge eating disorder, even substance use disorder: all of these diagnoses resonated with me, as well. But not borderline personality disorder. Just mention of the term set off all kinds of bad associations in me: *Annoying, impossible, attention-seeking, manipulative, needy. Huge slut.*

These associations with the borderline label are not unreasonable; one need only do a quick internet search to find endless sources reinforcing these deep-seated judgments toward people so diagnosed. "Borderline personality disorder has long been one of the most vexing conditions encountered by mental health practitioners," one clinical professor of psychiatry declares. A psychologist describes how many colleagues of hers see borderline referrals as a "no-no, so much so," she says, "that it doesn't even have to be mentioned; it is a given." According to a professor of social work, "borderline has become the most pejorative of all personality labels, and it is now little more than shorthand for a difficult, angry female client certain to give the therapist countertransferential headaches."

A 2013 literature review of all studies done on the responses of mental health professionals to patients who've been diagnosed borderline concludes, "With few exceptions, most researchers have found that the majority of participants in various studies harbor negative feelings about and attitudes toward patients with BPD." The authors go on to list an impressive array of findings: professionals felt "uncomfortable, anxious, challenged, frustrated, manipulated, apathetic, and less caring." They saw borderline-labeled patients as "dangerous, powerful, unrelenting, more difficult to take care of, time-consuming, having poor coping skills, engaging in crisis behaviors, and demonstrating poor social interactions."

It stung to hear the diagnostic criteria. Fearing my humiliation might be used to reinforce how borderline I was, I resolved to keep my hurt to myself, instead focusing on the one undeniably good thing about enrolling in the hospital's Borderline Center: I'd get to be there every day with Eve, who'd been in it for a long time already.

My parents drove up for my intake with the head psychiatrist, Dr. Gunderson, after whom the center had been named. They arrived on the STU with a tray of coffee, which we savored in sticky chairs at the end of a hall. I worried what they thought of my greasy hair, pudgy face, hunching stocky shoulders, and overweight body hidden in food-stained sweats; wrapping my arms around my stomach, I avoided their eyes, picked mindlessly at a zit on my forehead. Dad reached out to gently swat my hand away. "Laura, don't." I came to and clasped my hands tightly in my lap, picking surreptitiously at my nail cuticles instead. I ripped one off and it started to bleed.

When it came time for the meeting, a staff person took us down to the basement and escorted us along the cement maze of poorly lit tunnels until we reached a curved set of well-worn mahogany banisters framing carpeted wooden steps at the end of a hall. Ascending the hospital's stark clinical underbelly, we emerged into an oak-paneled entryway with ornate trim, thick carpeting, old paintings and photographs. Outside Dr. Gunderson's office, I sandwiched myself between my parents on a sofa, bouncing my leg as my father checked the stock market on his phone and my mother leafed through an *Architectural Digest* magazine.

At five past the hour, the turn of the knob: there stood Dr. Gunderson. He was in his late sixties and had cinnamon hair and slightly tanned, leathery skin. He wore a blazer over a cashmere sweater, a bow tie peeking out over its top. His steel blue eyes were bright and penetrating.

The three of us rose in unison. "Mr. and Mrs. Delano, hello," Dr. Gunderson said, avoiding my gaze as he reached his hand first to my father and then my mother, who both told him their first names. Though he kept his eyes on them, I sensed he felt mine on his. He finally turned to acknowledge me. "And you must be Laura. Please come in."

• ● •

The first time I heard John Gunderson described as the father of borderline personality disorder, I assumed it was hyperbole. Many years after I left his program, I'd discover it wasn't: while the term *borderline* has been used in psychoanalysis since the 1930s, Gunderson and a colleague were the first to define the set of symptom criteria particular to the "borderline personality disorder" diagnosis, in 1975. Five years later, his diagnostic offspring would be incorporated into the third edition of the *Diagnostic and Statistical Manual of Mental Disorders*, where it's remained ever since, largely untouched. The Personality Disorders Work Group within the Task Force on *DSM-IV*, the edition in use when I was given the borderline label, was chaired by John Gunderson. Of the nine work group members, seven were men.

Feminist scholars have spent decades critiquing the psychiatric profession's predilection for pathologizing women's responses to oppressive social structures by diagnosing them as hysterical, crazy, or mentally ill. Psychologist Paula Caplan puts it succinctly: "After a woman has conscientiously learned the role her culture prescribes for her, the psychiatric establishment calls her mentally disordered." In ancient Egypt and Greece, the female reproductive system was considered, by men, to be the cause of much of what they deemed problematic about women. The term *hysteria*, which comes from the Greek *hystera*, meaning uterus, was first used in the fifth century BC by Hippocrates. Aretaeus of Cappadocia, in the second century AD, described the "wandering womb," proposing that "the womb is like an animal within an animal" and that, when on the loose in a woman's body (as men then believed that the uterus was free-floating), it could lead her toward all kinds of troubling behaviors. In the nineteenth century, hysteria was used to label women who didn't behave in the ways expected of them by their families. After having a breakdown following the birth of her child, American novelist Charlotte Perkins Gilman went to see physician Silas Weir Mitchell, who was famous for his "rest cure" for hysterical women; she wrote in 1887, at the end of her treatment, that Mitchell "sent me home with solemn advice to 'live as domestic a life as far as possible,' to 'have but two hours' intellectual life a day,' and 'never to touch pen, brush, or pencil again' as long as I lived."

By the time hysteria was removed from the *DSM*—it had been in the second edition as "hysterical neurosis" until *DSM-III*'s release in 1980—the term *personality disorder* had become the predominant way to box women's strong emotions and socially unaccepted behaviors into a medical category. After John Gunderson coined the borderline personality disorder diagnosis in the midseventies, it fast became the go-to label for frustrated parents, husbands, and psychiatrists eager to pathologize women who refused to cooperate. This is not something that the psychiatric profession has tried to hide; in fact, in one of the many medical journal articles that John Gunderson published on borderline personality disorder, "chronic anger/ frequent angry acts," "demandingness/entitlement, treatment regressions, and the ability to arouse inappropriately close and/or hostile responses in professional caretakers" were among the very criteria that he and his coauthors defined as borderline symptoms. Today, 75 percent of borderline diagnoses are given to women. It's been reported that up to 90 percent of people labeled borderline have experienced childhood trauma.

I knew none of this when I first met Dr. Gunderson, who had a large corner office looking out over McLean's courtyard that was replete with an old fireplace and walls lined with built-in bookshelves. In front of his colossal, leather blotter–topped desk were three stiff wooden chairs, in which my parents and I obediently took a seat.

"So, you're currently on the STU," he stated, eyes locked onto mine. I nodded, doing my best to keep my fidgeting hands out of sight. "And you'll be released to the partial hospital program in a few days." I nodded again. He looked down at an open file on his desk, atop which sat a stack of papers a few inches high, then back at me. "I've had a chance to take a look at your records. It seems to me that you'd fit quite well in our program." He paused. "Does that sound good to you?" He lifted his brow inquisitively. I nodded a third time, feeling a heightened self-consciousness, the cause of which I couldn't pinpoint.

Dr. Gunderson leaned forward and put his elbows on the desk. Interlocking his fingers, he settled his chin in the gap between his thumbs and pointer fingers, maintaining his gaze on me. "Would you like to hear about our program?" His tone was skeptical, as if I might not. I quickly nodded again. He went on to describe the comprehensive treatment team that he would assign to me, including a case manager, a specialized one-on-one dialectical behavior therapy (DBT) therapist who'd be on call twenty-four hours a day, a psychopharmacologist, a family therapist, and the outpatient group director. "We can also bring in any outside specialist you might need based on your current condition," he continued. "For example, from your notes, it appears that your eating disorder is causing you a great deal of distress. We often partner with an eating disorder specialist, who happens to be my niece. She'd be brought into the team and included in all meetings about your care. We'll have regular treatment reviews here in my office to track your progress."

"Okay, that all sounds good," I said.

"What I think would benefit you most, Laura, is to join our outpatient program here in the clinic—we can take you as soon as the partial program declares you fit to leave—and to move into our residence, which is located in Cambridge. This would allow you to get the most extensive support we have to offer, so that you get the benefits of the day program as well as the overnight resources of the residence—"

"I'm sorry, a residence? You mean, like a group home?" My voice interrupted him before I realized I had something to say.

"No, not a group home." He said "group home" like a rotting piece of garbage had been placed under his nose. "It's the Gunderson Residence. We've designed it for women who need access to intensive twenty-four-hour support."

"Nah, no, thank you, that's not something I'm interested in," I said quickly, shaking my head, surprised at how sure I felt of this, how easy it was to speak it.

"Can I ask why?" I couldn't tell how he felt about my response, which made me nervous.

"I dunno. I just don't like the idea of living in a house without any privacy. I, I'm not sure why, I just don't like it. I'd much prefer to just go back to my aunt and uncle's house. I feel at home there."

"Okay, then. You seem convinced of your choice. May I continue?" I was told that I'd be expected to attend a full schedule of groups each day for a minimum of five months. "Possibly longer," he continued, "depending on how we feel you're doing." Gunderson listed the names of each group I'd be in and, when he finished, looked again at me. I realized he was waiting for a response.

"Yeah, this all sounds fine."

"That's good to hear. I can imagine it would be quite difficult to be in a program like this."

"What do you mean?"

"Well, because you're a twenty-six-year-old woman and you're in a psychiatric hospital, and you'll be coming to one every day for quite a while. You don't want to be out there living life like other women your age? You did go to Harvard, is that correct? I have to imagine you didn't think this was where you'd be in your life by now."

I tried to respond but my mouth was frozen shut. My eyes went straight to the floor, and I had to exert every ounce of my willpower to hold back hot tears. I could feel my mother's outrage bubbling next to me and wondered if Dr. Gunderson could too.

As a young kid, I *had* believed I'd do something with my life, and by "do something" I certainly hadn't meant become a twenty-six-year-old chronic patient spending her days at a psychiatric institution on five medications. He was right, he knew it, and he knew I knew it, too.

Later that week, I was discharged to Sara and Bill's to begin the partial hospital program. Eve was discharged a day or two after me and, because she was already well established in it, returned straight to

the Borderline Center. We met up for lunch and made plans to head
to her home group.

The next morning, a little before seven, Eve directed me to a church
parking lot that was surprisingly full for such an early hour. "Nice,
it's packed today. Love it!" she declared. "I need a cig before we
go in."

"I'll stand with you." Though I'd chosen to come, the situation
suddenly felt out of my control. People were now streaming out of a
small building; most seemed to know one another, and Eve seemed
to know most everyone. Over and over, she high-fived, called out,
"Dude!" waited with arms outstretched to tuck the next person into
a hug while her cigarette hung loosely from her mouth with a precar-
iously long ash. She seemed like a different person here from the one
I knew on the ward, more confident, animated, even cheerful. She
flicked her cigarette, pushed out the last of the smoke in her lungs,
and wrapped her arms around me as she said, "C'mon! Let's go get
a seat."

A woman sitting at a table at the open end of a huge horseshoe of
chairs started the meeting by loudly announcing, "Hi, I'm Mary-
Beth, and I'm an alcoholic."

"Hi, Mary-Beth!" A collective of singsong voices filled the room.

"Alcoholics Anonymous is a fellowship of men and women who
share their experience, strength, and hope with one another that
they may solve their common problem and help others to recover
from alcoholism," Mary-Beth read from a piece of paper, rolling her
left foot on the ground as she spoke. I tried my best to shut out her
words, to protect myself from their meaning, but when she shared
her story over the thirty minutes that followed, I heard things that
made sense to me. She talked about feeling insecure as a teenager,
worrying what others thought about her. She talked about the fear
that she would never be good enough. She talked about the rush of

pleasure in that first sip of alcohol and how, over the years her drinking progressed, the liquid came to serve as her one reliable source of comfort. I couldn't deny, as she spoke, that alcohol had come to serve the same role for me as my life had unfolded with serious mental illness, and that, like Mary-Beth, eventually everything fell apart: the loss of our moral compass, hurting those we loved. She talked about her lowest lows without an ounce of shame or regret, her eyes emanating a peace that I couldn't help but trust. By the time she talked about getting sober, she had me hooked. She ended by telling the room that she was celebrating her twenty-fifth year of sobriety that weekend. We all roared in applause, me included.

After listening to Mary-Beth's story, I resolved to never touch a sip of alcohol again. I wasn't ready to call myself an alcoholic, but I was now convinced I'd figured it out: it wasn't mental illness that had caused my life to fall apart but the alcohol I'd been imbibing in an effort to deal with it. If I'd never started to drink so much after college, would I have been able to more effectively manage my bipolar disorder? Would my binge eating disorder have gotten so out of control? Would I have had so many inglorious encounters with men? Would my meds have actually worked? If I stuck with this thing, perhaps I'd one day be sitting in front of a crowd sharing my story, my alcohol-free bipolar brain finally well managed by pharmaceuticals, a glow of contentment in my cheeks, balance in my life, calm in my mind.

TWENTY-THREE

A Good Patient

Eve and I settled right into a daily routine: I'd pick her up at her group home at the crack of dawn to get our coffee before the morning meeting, we'd drive to the hospital for our respective programs, we'd meet up afterward to get another coffee and figure out which evening meeting we wanted to attend, I'd drive her home at the end of the night. I felt right at home in the dingy church basements, like this was where I had always belonged. Soon I was making plans for coffee with other twelve-steppers, going out to dinner with big groups after meetings, getting many dozens of phone numbers of so many kindhearted people who meant it when they said to call them anytime. Numerous women asked me if I needed a sponsor; finally I said yes to one of them.

Though I'd stopped drinking weeks earlier, it wasn't until I began to regularly attend meetings that my state of mind began to shift. To my surprise, I quickly clicked with the idea that I was an alcoholic— that I'd been one my whole life, in fact, well before I picked up my first drink at that slumber party in eighth grade—and before I knew it, "Hi, I'm Laura, and I'm an alcoholic" rolled easily off my tongue. Cleansing my bloodstream of booze had been one small part of the equation; I was still the same me, only more vulnerable without the trusty black cloak of nightly drunkenness. What I needed more than anything was to believe that I might be able to change. I needed hope, and now I had an unending source of it, offered freely to me each day in AA's halls through personal testimonies of transformation. No longer convicted by despair, I felt new space open up in me, and in it, the arrival of an unsettling question: *Who would I be off my meds?*

It cropped up in my quiet moments at first: in the shower, waiting for the next group to start while working on a crossword puzzle, in line at the store. The question had me entertaining what felt like wholly radical notions: *You've been medicated since you were a kid. You've never had the chance to really know yourself without pills. Your adult body has almost never existed free from psych meds. Maybe this is kind of a problem.* My bipolar disorder already felt more manageable; what would my life look like if it weren't just alcohol I no longer ingested but all my meds, as well? I still believed that my condition was incurable but wondered if I might one day be able to be like those people I sometimes heard stories about—people with the miraculous ability to manage serious mental illness without pharmaceuticals.

When it came time to begin at the Borderline Center, my new case manager wrote:

> *26 year old single Caucasian female with Bipolar Disorder, Eating Disorder, Polysubstance Dependence Early Remission since 2/14/10 and Borderline Personality Disorder. Laura is an intelligent and engaging woman with long standing [sic] dissatisfaction with self, body image, poor self-esteem, impulsivity, promiscuity, self-harm. Laura has had intermittent suicide ideation surrounding worsening depressive symptoms and relationship difficulties. She has had a near lethal suicide attempt whereby she overdosed and was in a coma for several days in November of 2008. She denies current suicide ideation*

and reports a miraculous and spiritual new lease on life since surviving and discovering the Alcoholics Anonymous community. However, due to her impulsive tendencies, long standing [sic] psychiatric symptomatology, alcohol and drug vulnerabilities, [and] near lethal suicide attempt in 2008 . . . ongoing monitoring and safety planning is necessary. Laura seems engaged and motivated for treatment and treatment planning.

I was diagnosed with five conditions in my official intake form: bipolar disorder, anxiety disorder NOS, eating disorder NOS, polysubstance dependence early remission, and borderline personality disorder. (My new psychopharmacologist, Benjamin, noted, "Overall, clearly has BPD [9 of 9 criteria].") I was admitted on lithium XR, Abilify, Lamictal, Klonopin, and Antabuse.

My first morning at the Borderline Center, Eve and I sat slumped in the waiting room as women wandered in and plopped down around us. Stealthily, I glanced up from my sudoku, intrigued by these strangers I'd be spending every day with for at least the next half year. At 9:00 a.m. on the button—I was taken aback by this, as I'd never met a therapist who actually started on time—Jerold, the outpatient program director, emerged from around the corner. The ends of his smile nearly touched his kind, wrinkly eyes. He had waves of thick, black hair and was tall and athletic, with ruddy skin suggestive of time outdoors. That day, he wore laced leather shoes, well-tailored paints, and a collared shirt tucked beneath a slim-fit sweater.

"Please come in," Jerold said warmly. We gathered our coats and bags and lined up in a row. I said hello as I walked past him. "Happy to have you here, Laura," he said with that same big smile. I could tell he meant what he said.

"How long have you been in Gunderson?" I asked Eve on a coffee break later that morning, the late winter air brisk on our faces as she smoked.

"Hmm, like, a year-ish in total? I've come and gone a couple of times. I'm the old-timer in the mix here, except for Edith." Edith was a gentle older woman who'd knitted continuously through the first group and spent her turn talking about her elderly cat's failing health. I'd noticed her fingernails were especially long and that her chestnut hair was about as greasy as mine. "She's apparently been coming to Jerold's groups for something like five years, ever since her daughter killed herself," Eve continued. "She doesn't do any other groups at the center, though. She's not even officially enrolled in it. I don't even think she's borderline. Not sure how that works."

I was intrigued by the backstories of the other women—in total across the program, there were around ten of us, though a few had graduated to part-time attendance—along with the singular young man, whose physician parents had apparently enrolled him after he'd gotten suicidal during his first year of college.

Eve broke down who was nice, who was obnoxious, who picked fights, who was the peacekeeper. "Things can get pretty wild in there—just wait for Interpersonal group. It's like a boxing ring. No, actually, more like a dogfight. They set it up that way on purpose, you know, to give us some practice at handling conflicts in real life. They just sit back and watch us while we go at it."

I shuddered at the thought.

A week later, Benjamin, my psychopharmacologist, upped the dose of my mood stabilizer, Lamictal. He also announced that he'd decided to bring me completely off Klonopin, the benzodiazepine I'd taken as prescribed for sleep. When I asked why, he explained that the drug was frequently abused by addicts, and given my early sobriety, it was too risky to continue me on it. I considered clarifying that I'd taken benzos nightly for upwards of seven years without ever once misusing them, but opted not to, as I didn't want to risk appearing hooked. It felt like the rug was being pulled out from under me: between Ambien and benzos, I'd taken some kind of prescribed sleep aid every single night for nearly a decade to address my incessant struggles with insomnia. How on earth would I ever sleep without a pill? I forced a nod in agreement. Benjamin cut my benzo dose in half immediately. I was completely unaware of how dangerous this decision was.

I stopped sleeping right away, by which I mean I was lucky if I got three straight hours in a night. Anxieties surged through the day in punishing waves—*It's too late for you to get your shit together. You'll never be in a healthy relationship. You'll never be able to get a good job. You're a human balloon—DISGUSTING! How are you ever going to function in the real world? You fucking WASTE of life!* Each evening, I'd tuck myself into the Laura-shaped divot on my aunt and uncle's sofa and systematically take down HBO shows: *Big Love, The Wire, Six Feet Under.* When bedtime came, I'd drag myself upstairs in dread of what lay ahead. The *South Park* episodes waiting on my laptop were all I had to save me.

During the day, I managed to convince myself that I was actually doing okay. In groups, I shared about my baby steps toward progress (more frequent showering, constructive calls with family, the occasional success of a night without binge eating), and at AA meetings, I could even smile, galvanized by my new friends and their hopeful stories. One night at the dinner table, I actually felt a swell of pride as Sara told me I was glowing after returning from a walk along the Charles River with my sponsor.

Nighttime convinced me that these positive shifts were pure delusion.

• ● •

I watched, aghast, as the BPD group spent precious time each morning in Self-Assessment providing moral support to one woman in the days leading up to her treatment review with Dr. Gunderson and the rest of her team. The scene looked more like preparation for a life-threatening military mission, not a therapy appointment. She was visibly shaking when she left group early to meet her parents on the morning of the review.

"They're brutal," Eve told me when I mentioned that my first review was coming up in a couple of weeks. "They take days to recover from."

I recounted my first meeting with Dr. Gunderson, when he remarked that I must not have imagined I'd be in a psychiatric hospital at this stage of my life. Eve nodded solemnly. "Exactly," she replied. "He tries to take you down. Like, he literally focuses on everything you're most insecure about and digs into it to deliberately humiliate you and bring out your borderline."

On the morning of my treatment review, I stared at the whirring noise machine on the floor outside Dr. Gunderson's office. It was the same model as Weinberg's: white, disc-shaped, slits around the circumference, like a miniature flying saucer. Aware that my entire treatment team was discussing me just a few feet away, I ignored the urge to flick it off so that I could hear what they were saying.

Eventually I was waved in. Dr. Gunderson, in bow tie and cashmere, was seated at his desk. He casually lifted up his hand, flipping it over to direct me to the seat in front of him. The team sat beyond him in a half circle. Jerold nodded gently, as if to say, *I see you, you can do this, I believe in you.*

Dr. Gunderson's blue eyes locked on mine. "Well. Why don't we get started." He looked down at the stack of my medical records in front of him.

"Okay." I made sure to give him and the rest of the team a smile. I was ready to have a productive treatment review; I wanted them to know this. I even had a pad and pen on hand to take notes.

"I've been getting updates from your team. It sounds like you're settling in quite well. Would you agree?"

I nodded. "Yeah, things have been going pretty well so far. Besides the insomnia, I think my eating issues feel the most problematic to me right now, I'd say."

"That's what Rachel's for," he said, referring to his niece. "I'm confident the two of you will make some good progress." I looked over at Rachel, who gave me a close-mouthed smile. In each of the sessions we'd had so far, I'd been distracted by her sharp cheekbones: Would she really be able to help me with my binge eating disorder?

Dr. Gunderson continued. "So, your parents aren't here today. How do you feel about that? About the fact they chose not to come?" The question took me off guard. I sensed a motive beneath his words that I couldn't quite nail down.

"Umm, I feel fine about it? It's really not that big of a deal. I know my dad couldn't get away from the office."

"It's not that big of a deal," he repeated.

"I'm sure they'll come to the next one . . ."

He stared at me for a few seconds before moving on. "So, you've been here for a few weeks now. Have you been developing relationships with the other patients?"

I was eager to answer this one. "Yes, I have, especially with Eve. We're going to AA meetings together every day, which has been pretty great."

Jerold chimed in. "Laura's been adding a lot to the groups. She listens carefully and contributes her opinions clearly and directly. It's really been a pleasure having her."

"Thanks, Jerold." I felt my cheeks flush.

The next morning, I relayed the good news to my fellow patients that my treatment review went just fine. A few provocative questions, but all in all, I handled myself okay, and the team and, most important, Dr. Gunderson, were happy with my progress. Everyone congratulated me for making it through.

I didn't know it then, but this would be the first and last treatment review in which I'd behave like a good patient.

TWENTY-FOUR

Iatrogenic Process

I traced my fingers over the smooth hardcovers on the "New Releases" display as I wandered the aisles of a Vermont bookstore, remembering how good it once felt to read, how I used to lose myself in pages, how the world opened up in the full bloom of possibility each time I occupied the life of a character. Though I still dragged my way through a book on occasion, I couldn't recall the last time I'd really gotten immersed in one. Years of cognitive impairment had made it nearly impossible for me to fully absorb words, to piece together meaning, often to remember what I'd read at all. I'd get through a paragraph, realize that I'd taken nothing in, and start over. And then I'd give up and turn on the TV instead. I blamed these issues on the progression of my bipolar disorder.

I was staying in a hotel with my parents, visiting my youngest sister, Chase, at college. My treatment team considered it a big deal that I'd come to Vermont, as they hadn't been confident in my ability to stay sober. Krystal, my therapist, had required me to write up a weekend schedule for her review that included which AA meeting I would attend each day and when I would check in with her by text. After lengthy discussion, she gave me permission to go.

As I browsed the store's shelves, I was struck by an ivory white face staring at me from a bright red book jacket. It was an illustration of a phrenology chart, one of those old, hand-drawn pictures of a hairless human head in which the skull area is broken up into different compartments. Each area of the skull, it was proposed by the nineteenth-century doctors who promoted this long-debunked scientific ideology, represented a different aspect of one's personality, but on this book cover, instead of personality traits like conscientiousness, destructiveness, or sociability, the compartments contained the names of various psychiatric drugs: lithium, Ritalin, Zyprexa, Klonopin, Tegretol, Wellbutrin, Lamictal, Prozac, Xanax, Risperdal. Nearly all of them, I quickly observed, were ones that I'd been on.

I picked up the book and traced my fingers over the title, *Anatomy of an Epidemic: Magic Bullets, Psychiatric Drugs, and the Astonishing Rise of Mental Illness in America.* The author was Robert Whitaker, a name I recognized from a psychology class I'd taken at Harvard. I didn't even read the book's description. I somehow knew, from the cover alone, that I needed to buy it.

When I got back to the hotel room, I lay down on my bed and began to read. I learned that the epidemic Whitaker referred to was the huge number of American adults and children receiving government disability payments due to diagnoses of mental illness. This number has skyrocketed over the past four decades: according to Whitaker, in 1955, 355,000 Americans were hospitalized for psychiatric reasons, which equates to 1 in every 468 adults; by 1987, there were 1.25 million American adults on disability specifically for psychiatric reasons, or 1 in every 184. The 2007 psychiatric disability rate, which Whitaker used in the book, had jumped to nearly 4 million people, or 1 in every 76. I considered that I very likely would have been included in this count had I not been born into a family with the economic means to insulate me from ever needing to go on disability.

When I first read these numbers, I considered possible explanations for their gargantuan rise: Perhaps clinicians had gotten better at diagnosing illnesses that were previously being missed, or maybe the stigma surrounding mental illness had been so successfully tackled that more people no longer felt afraid to get help. Or, on the flip side, perhaps the rise in psychiatric-related disability was because people weren't getting the treatment they needed.

In *Anatomy of an Epidemic*, Whitaker presents a very different argument. He sees these dramatically increasing numbers of disabling psychiatric conditions as a curious "medical puzzle" because they correspond directly to the dramatically increasing numbers of people on the very medications we've been told are effective ways of treating mental illness.

I quickly saw how relevant this puzzle was for me: If psychiatry had such effective treatments, wouldn't I have started to feel relief somewhere along the line? Despite spending so many years relying on pills and prescribers and therapists and programs and locked wards, I'd never actually felt lasting positive change of any kind. No lessening of my symptoms. No increase in my capacity to function. If anything, in fact, I'd gotten worse with each passing year I was on meds—so much so that twenty-seven-year-old me on a regimen of five prescriptions would have been entirely unrecognizable to eighteen-year-old unmedicated me, so desperate for help during the winter of those disorienting debutante balls.

Whitaker poses what he calls a heretical question: Is it possible that psychiatry's medication-based standard of care is actually causing people to become psychiatrically disabled? Is it possible, in other words, that the treatment is making people sick?

In his quest for an answer, Whitaker interviewed several individuals who'd struggled and eventually found themselves in front of a psychiatrist. Meds were promptly started, and what followed over the years to come was eerily similar to my own experience: the loss of the ability to attend school, to work; increasing mental and emotional turmoil; growing numbness; the destruction of physical health; the diminishment of career and life expectations; increased hospitalizations. The details and circumstances of our lives were all different, but the underlying trajectories were the same.

In one section, Whitaker recounted the story of a woman named Dorea, who'd been diagnosed with bipolar disorder and put on a treatment regimen that included Zyprexa, an antipsychotic I'd once been on. After starting medications, Dorea's life began to unravel: she slept during the day, gained thirty pounds, stopped laughing, decided to "scale back her career goals," and concluded "she probably wouldn't be able to handle the stress of postdoctoral research."

In 2003, according to Whitaker, Dorea happened upon research that got her questioning the safety and effectiveness of antipsychotic drugs. She decided to come off Zyprexa and eventually the other psychiatric drugs she was on, which she did over the course of three years, a process she described as "pure hell." About what it was like to be fully free from them, she says:

> It was fabulous. I was surprised to find out who I was after all these years. . . . When I was "bipolar," I had an excuse for any unpredictable or unstable behavior. I had permission to behave in that way, but now I am holding myself to the same behavioral standards as everyone else, and it turns out I can meet them.

Whitaker asks, "If you expand the boundaries of mental illness, which is clearly what has happened in this country during the past twenty-five years, and you treat the people so diagnosed with psychiatric medications, do you run the risk of turning an angst-ridden teenager into a lifelong mental patient? Dorea, who is an extremely smart and capable person, barely escaped going down that path. Hers is a story of a possible *iatrogenic* process at work, of an otherwise normal person being made chronically sick by diagnosis and subsequent treatment. And thus we have to wonder: Do we have a paradigm of care that can, at times, *create* mental illness?"

It was my first time hearing that adjective, *iatrogenic*. I looked it up and saw it meant "relating to an illness caused by medical examination or treatment." The room around me got instantly bright and clear and sharp, as though the word had swept away a distorting fog I hadn't before realized I'd been stuck inside. I looked over at my Dopp kit of medication bottles on the hotel's bedside table. I closed the book and stared at that drug-decorated head staring back at me. There was the sudden urge to hurl it across the room, to forget everything I'd just read in its pages.

I went into the bathroom to splash water on my cheeks. At the mirror, I tried to remember every single drug I'd taken since meeting Anuja all those years ago, as a fourteen-year-old. There were the antipsychotics: Seroquel, Geodon, Zyprexa, Risperdal, and Abilify. There were the mood stabilizers: Depakote, Topamax, Lamictal, and lithium. There were the antianxiety drugs: Klonopin and Ativan. The insomnia drug: Ambien. The narcolepsy drug: Provigil. The substance abuse drugs: Antabuse and naltrexone. And the antidepressants, all those antidepressants: Prozac, Effexor, Celexa, Cymbalta, Wellbutrin, Lexapro.

I thought about the list of psychiatric diagnoses I'd accumulated after accepting my first one, bipolar disorder, that freshman winter in college: major depression, social anxiety disorder, eating disorder NOS, binge eating disorder, substance use disorder, borderline personality disorder. Someone had even thrown obsessive-compulsive disorder in there along the way.

And of course, there were the physical issues I'd acquired since starting meds: Hashimoto's disease, the autoimmune thyroid condition I'd gotten soon after starting lithium. Irritable bowel syndrome.

Total loss of sexual function, such that I'd never had an orgasm in my life and felt numbness anytime I tried for intimacy, a numbness that drove me to booze and cocaine to feel something. The seventy-pound weight fluctuation. The chronic headaches and muscle pain. The clumps of hair in the shower. The flaking fingernails. The incessant sweating. The shocking decline in my cognitive capacities—my memory problems, my reading problems, my concentration problems, the problems I had articulating my thoughts.

I considered all that had happened during the decade after I embraced being mentally ill and the treatment that came along with it: the progressive loss of friendships and healthy relationships, the inability to handle being in college and the year off, the years spent bouncing around in short-lived jobs I could never handle. The financial dependency on my family. The many hospitalizations. The hundreds of hours of talk therapy. The constant thoughts of suicide. The overdose. The peace I had felt, that beautiful peace, as I lost consciousness on the rocks that November day two years earlier, so truly happy to die, happier than I could ever remember feeling.

Holy shit. It's the fucking meds.

I'd been confronted with something I'd never considered before: What if it wasn't treatment-resistant mental illness that had been sending me ever deeper into the depths of despair and dysfunction, but the treatment itself? What if, as a thirteen-year-old, instead of getting sent to a therapist, and eventually a psychiatrist who put me on Depakote and Prozac, I'd been able to connect with other young people who'd lost touch with themselves, who didn't know who they were, who were struggling to see how they fit into the picture of school, family, society, life? What if, at Harvard, instead of heading to a psychiatrist for help, I'd told my parents I needed some space and time away from school to sort out my struggles, earn some income for myself, and perhaps find an opportunity to be of service to others? If I'd had a chance to explore the deeper existential questions I was grappling with—ones about identity, performance, meaning, purpose, womanhood, body, and self—might I have returned a more centered, rooted person with a clearer sense of what my struggles meant, of who I was, of where I was going?

I collapsed onto the hotel bed and began to cry and then wail, a deep, long, low wail that undulated through me until my lungs exhausted themselves, at which point I rolled over and stared blankly at the ceiling. The significance of Whitaker's thesis hit me: if the treatment I'd been turning to for half my life had in fact been harming me, it meant that my life never had to unfold in the way that it did. Here I was, twenty-seven years old, all these years into a medicated existence. The damage had been done. There was no going back to do it differently.

I put the book down and didn't touch it for many weeks. I wasn't ready to read the chapters in which Whitaker unpacked the scientific reasons *why* all those years of psychiatric drugs had disabled me.

I'd assumed my future held one of two options: continuing with my tiresome efforts at unsuccessfully managing serious mental illness or killing myself. *Anatomy of an Epidemic* offered a third possibility.

TWENTY-FIVE

What the Hell Am I Doing Here?

A few weeks after my Vermont trip, Eve and I walked around Harvard Square one day after group, passing familiar shops and cafés. I'd long ago let go of the hope I'd had when I first arrived at Harvard—hope that I'd figure out my problems and forge ahead with working hard so that I could one day go somewhere, be somebody. Instead, I'd shrunk my life down to manageable proportions, accepting and embracing how sick I was. I'd given up on pursuing challenges in order to pursue the best treatment, and now, at twenty-seven, I was faced with the shocking prospect that I'd gotten it all wrong.

Motivated by a tiny spark of interest in expanding my daily purpose beyond psychiatric patienthood, I'd recently begun to volunteer as a squash coach and tutor for struggling kids in Boston. I'd even forced myself to lead a team in a tournament fundraiser for the urban squash program through which I was doing this work, putting together a roster of players who helped me raise money for the cause. I was going to at least one twelve-step meeting each day and continuing to make new friends in the halls. I met up with many newcomers before meetings to listen to what they were going through, invigorated by how good it felt to help someone else, to forget myself.

Before long, I decided the time had come for me to stop taking Antabuse, the drug I'd been put on to prevent me from drinking. I believed *I* was the one keeping me sober, not these pills, so this seemed the logical first prescription to go. For weeks, I practiced what I'd say to Benjamin at our next appointment, but at the end of May, as I waited outside his office, I suddenly panicked that I might upset him with my request. Disappointment from a doctor was not something I felt equipped to handle. I tried to look especially put together when he welcomed me in, to compensate for how much I was about to let him down.

"It's nice to see you, Laura. How have things been?"

"Good. You know, I think I'm really settling into the program. I'm enjoying groups, and I'm going to a lot of AA meetings with Eve, and I've found it all very helpful." I was sure to emphasize all that was going well for me: the friends, the volunteering, the successful squash fundraiser. Benjamin nodded his approvals, offering up "That's great to hear" and "Wonderful news" as he jotted down notes. "But I wanted to bring up something I've been meaning to share with you." I paused for a minute. "AA has been going so well, and I'm feeling good about my sobriety, and . . ." I trailed off before mustering the strength to continue. "And I think I'd really like to stop the Antabuse."

"I appreciate you letting me know." He considered the proposition. "How about this? I'm open to trying it out, provided that you agree to immediately reinstate if you have any cravings. Are you willing to do to that?"

Though I knew my answer was no, I told him yes.

At the end of our fifteen-minute appointment, I pushed myself to ask the bigger question. "I also wanted to ask, Benjamin, uh . . . I was thinking, y'know, things already feel more manageable since I haven't been drinking, and I just—I find myself wondering what things would feel like off my other meds. You know, to give myself a chance to see what my baseline really is? I can't help but wonder if I might be able to manage my symptoms better now that alcohol isn't in the mix."

"That's a very interesting idea." I could tell right away I wouldn't get the answer that I wanted. "We've already brought you off Klonopin, and now we're trying out cessation of the Antabuse. At this point, I don't think it's wise to discontinue Lamictal or lithium. Lamictal, especially, is very effective for borderline personality disorder. But I'm open to discontinuing the Abilify"—the antipsychotic I was on—"especially given that you're on a relatively low dose. As long as you continue taking your mood stabilizers."

I was ecstatic at the news. "Yeah, okay, that sounds like a good plan. So, can I just stop the Abilify?"

"Yes, but keep your bottle in case symptoms flare up and you need to reinstate. Let me know immediately if that happens."

I agreed. Removing Antabuse and Abilify was a start that I was happy with. I left his office carrying the same nagging question of who I might be off all my meds, but accepted that I hadn't yet gotten permission to find out.

One of my old boarding school friends was marrying a Frenchman at the beginning of July and had asked me, months earlier, to be part of a choreographed can-can dance that old friends of hers were performing at the rehearsal dinner. I had said yes, not wanting to disappoint her, but with the wedding fast approaching, I was regretting my response. What had I been I thinking, agreeing to launch my clammy, cumbersome body into synchronized high kicks in front of hundreds of people, including old friends who had no comprehension of the train wreck my life had become?

I focused my time in groups discussing my fears. How was I meant to connect with former classmates who'd spent the previous nine years getting graduate degrees and building successful careers and starting families? What would I say when they asked me what I was up to? *Oh, just hanging out at a mental institution!* How would I handle the inevitable stares when they saw a seventy-pounds-heavier me? My treatment team grew concerned that I would relapse. Krystal and Benjamin told me that, after discussing the issue, they'd decided I should reinstate Antabuse. I said I'd prefer not to, as I was doing just fine staying sober on my own. They disagreed. I refused to comply. Enraged by their lack of confidence in me, I fumed about them during groups. In clinical notes from this period, I'm called "reactive and willful." The way I saw it, I was actually beginning to see my psychiatric medications more clearly for what they were: instruments of behavior control wielded upon me by professionals who saw it as their right to decide what went in my body.

It was a right I'd once afforded them, but not anymore.

I managed to make it through the wedding weekend without drinking alcohol or sleeping much, coping with my jealousy toward anyone holding a wineglass by smoking nearly a pack of cigarettes instead, which almost made me puke. I hid my body in oversize shawls and shadows as my face feigned confidence with old classmates and an overwhelming number of mesmerizingly aristocratic and handsome French people. I returned to Sara and Bill's devastated by how pathetic I'd felt there, how debilitated the experience had left me. As with my previous experiences coming off psychiatric drugs too quickly, I had no idea about the biochemical chaos my doctors and I had gotten me into: after many years of chronic exposure to numerous psychiatric drugs, I was going through withdrawal from the benzodiazepine Benjamin had abruptly stopped over a few weeks in April and the Abilify I'd just stopped cold turkey.

The consistent tickle of angsty energy that had lived in me for years began to scratch viciously beneath the surface of my skin. Sometimes the energy twisted itself up in knots; other times, it flowed out in waves that pulsed through my limbs. As I had the last time I'd unknowingly experienced akathisia, I fantasized about slicing open my skin to let it out.

There were much worsened cycles of constipation and diarrhea. The sugar cravings and binge-eating episodes escalated. Even when I was able to successfully ingest a normal portion of food, my stomach now ballooned out to the point where I looked nine months pregnant; the pressure was so intense that I worried my stomach lining would split. This bloating was accompanied by shooting pain so excruciating that I'd have to lie on my side under layers of blankets and push gently on my belly. This happened several times a day. Sometimes I'd be at the mercy of my stomach for hours.

I had aches in my joints, near-daily headaches, back spasms, shoulders sore to the touch. My neck sometimes seized up uncontrollably, igniting a burning bomb at the base of my skull that jerked my face to the side before dissipating into a warm, dull ache that lasted an hour. My eyeballs occasionally spasmed, rolling up for a split second behind their lids and leaving me in the dark. Sometimes, while sitting in a chair, I'd notice that my entire body was involuntarily clenched: thighs locked, toes curled, shoulders activated, neck engaged, jaw flexed. When I lay on my back, my left foot wouldn't stop twitching.

At night, my mind forced me on its torturous theme-park horror ride, past all the memories and flashbacks of my failed life, through all the insults, criticisms, paranoias, and diatribes that ranted and raced their way through my head, looping on repeat, no off switch: *Look at you, you disgusting, defective, pathetic piece of shit. You're a greasy embarrassment. You made such a fool of yourself at the wedding—people were definitely laughing at you. You waste of oxygen. You're fucked. Why do you even try? It's too late.* I felt possessed by my own consciousness, saw no way out. The racing thoughts had me worried I was getting manic. My only nightly reprieve remained the distraction of TV shows on my computer, which I'd plug myself into at bedtime with the urgency of a scuba diver replacing a dislodged regulator.

I grew increasingly discouraged by what lay ahead for me. Was this simply what the first few months of sobriety from alcohol looked like—or was this actually my baseline state of bipolar disorder revealing more of itself now that I was off the benzodiazepine, Klonopin, and the antipsychotic Abilify? What did this mean for my chances of coming off the rest of my medications? Was I delusional in thinking that would ever be possible? I kept these concerns to myself; I couldn't risk reinforcing my doctors' convictions that it had been a mistake for me to go to the wedding without reinstating Antabuse, that I'd been too unstable, that I was exactly what they thought I was: dependent on them and their treatments, unable to strike out on my own in the world.

TWENTY-SIX

Wellness Check

After insisting I reinstate Antabuse for my friend's wedding, my treatment team had conveyed the message loud and clear that they saw me as an untrustworthy source of information about myself. I resolved to be more defiant, to speak up about what I felt. Before my next treatment review, Jerold described me as "rebellious." During my review, I told Dr. Gunderson and the rest of my team about my growing sense of confidence in my sobriety, how much more equipped I felt to navigate difficulties on my own, that I was finding groups not especially helpful, that I wanted to start challenging myself more.

Afterward, Dr. Gunderson wrote:

Is more emotional, but this is uncomfortable. Her suicidality is diminished but she remains concerned that she is a burden. She acknowledges that she intellectualizes, but says she is open about her conflicts/issues. She continues to rely on her parents but doesn't like to ask for help. She puts herself in risky situations (e.g. exposure to drinking) that test her abilities: "I should do it all by myself or I am a failure." Her stubbornness/willfulness is becoming more dystonic. She's deeply conflicted about living up to family standards. . . . She uses groups very well, but protests she would like to do fewer. She works part-time and is being encouraged to work more. She finds it very demanding, and wants to resume school/learning. She is very ashamed of her failure to live up to expectations. She is active in AA and remains sober, but she lacks a social life.

So much strikes me about this write-up: the rigid juxtaposing of opposing characterizations; the melodramatic descriptors leaving no space for nuance; the narrative through line of unflinching polarization. It's as though Gunderson's writing style itself were meant to reflect how he saw me: as a rigid, melodramatic, unflinchingly polarized woman, a textbook case of borderline personality disorder. Did he deliberately write me this way, knowing how much of my breadth and depth he was omitting in the pursuit of clear, clinical definition? Or did he honestly believe in the veracity of his analysis?

I can't help but wonder if he saw me pulling away from his program—no longer feeling dependent on my team, newly challenging their pharmaceutical recommendations, and questioning the proclamations they were making of me, my character, my person. Is it possible that in order to avoid facing my legitimate critiques of treatment, he decided to use my burgeoning noncompliance to reinforce just how borderline I was? (One study published in the *International Journal of Psychiatry Clinical Practice* states, "Borderline personality disorder (BPD) is a likely candidate for treatment noncompliance because this psychiatric dysfunction is characterized by inherent impulsivity as well as self-defeating behavior.")

For years, I'd been classified as treatment resistant, but a spark had ignited in me: it was time to resist treatment.

As I grappled with the collapse of everything I'd previously believed about myself, a new awareness emerged of the girl, the woman, the human, I might otherwise have been if I'd never sat myself down in front of a shrink as a freshman at Harvard. If I'd never taken medications, would I have stopped investing time and energy in maintaining the meaningful friendships I'd built at boarding school? Would I have had all that numbed-out, dissociated sex or so coldly cut off the young men who truly cared about me? Would I have done all that binge eating? All that cocaine? All that binge drinking? Would I have had to take the year off from school because of how suicidal I'd gotten? Would I have tried to kill myself? I tried to process the implications of what all those years of meds had potentially done to me.

I unwittingly journeyed ever further into intensifying benzodiazepine and antipsychotic withdrawal. The insomnia worsened. My mind felt like a toxic wasteland of paranoia, bitterness, and regret. I began to skip AA meetings, instead driving to Dunkin' Donuts after a long day at the hospital to sit in my car and gorge on a box of stale doughnuts. Jerold wrote of me in his notes, "continuing to beat up on self about body image," "filled with shame," "despairing."

In mid-August, during a psychopharmacology appointment with Benjamin, I brought him up to speed on my backslide, wondering if it was possible that I was still in the throes of early sobriety from alcohol. He wrote, "increased dysregulation, very focused on distorted body image thoughts, ruminating guilt, sleep has been disrupted." He offered me the antidepressant Wellbutrin, which I accepted out of sheer desperation in spite of all that I'd learned. I was still taking lithium and Lamictal.

According to Benjamin's notes, I reported feeling "more on track" a week later, and "more social." I got my six-month sobriety chip at a meeting and was able to savor the celebratory joy showered on me. But my sleeping problems remained, and not long after starting the Wellbutrin, I began to feel sedated during the day—the same kind of horse-tranquilizer sedation I'd experienced at Harvard. (Sedation is not a commonly reported adverse effect of Wellbutrin; my sense is that I might have been having some kind of paradoxical reaction to it, given how disrupted my central nervous system had been by all the recent drug changes.) I'd nod off on the drive to and from the hospital. My eyelids would droop when I sat down to lunch. I couldn't stay alert in groups, and, slumped in my chair, I frequently slipped into a strange half-awake state in which I appeared conscious to others but, by group's end, would have no idea what had happened during the previous hour.

And then, in late August, after I missed a session with my therapist, Krystal, she called the cops on me, and everything changed.

I'd seen Krystal twice a week for therapy throughout my time at the Borderline Center. She, like the other one-on-one therapists, was available twenty-four hours a day, the unspoken assumption being that we patients were so unstable and impulsive that we might go into crisis at any moment. Krystal had shiny, strawberry blond hair. She was fit and had a flower tattoo on the inside of her ankle that peeked out from beneath her tailored work pants. As she'd swivel in her chair, legs crossed gracefully, I'd look at the diplomas behind her and pine for the chance to go back and do my life all over again.

One afternoon, during the period of Wellbutrin-induced daytime sedation and on a particularly long break after morning groups, I'd gone back to Sara and Bill's house to take a nap. When my alarm went off to wake me up for therapy, I hit Snooze, and hit Snooze, and hit Snooze, unable to rouse myself.

About ten minutes after the hour, Krystal called. Too tranquilized to talk, I let it go to voicemail. She called again. And then again a few minutes later. She'd left two messages. I hit Play and the speaker button, wincing at the sound of her voice. In the first, she reminded me that we had an appointment, in case I'd forgotten. In the second, she let me know she was calling the police to do a wellness check on me.

Those words—*police, wellness check*—smacked me wide awake. I called her back immediately. "Hi, Krystal. Yeah, it's Laura. Don't call the police. I've been asleep. I am so tired. I couldn't wake myself up—"

She interrupted. "I've already placed a call. They're on their way."

"Call them back and cancel! Please!"

"Laura, I understand you're upset—"

"Yeah, I'm upset. I can't believe you would do this to me!"

"It's entirely within my right as your therapist to be concerned when you don't show up for an appointment. Wellness checks are the best way to ensure your safety. I felt it was important to make sure you were—"

"Please cancel it right now. Please!"

She finally agreed and we hung up. I spent the next hour sitting fuming on the sofa, fists clenched, completely done.

I informed Dr. Gunderson the next day that I wanted a new therapist. He informed me that he would not indulge my request, as each therapist is carefully matched with each patient, and it's part of the therapeutic process to work through conflict and unpleasant feelings together. I tightened my jaw to hold in my anger.

What a gift, that outrage. With each passing day it was moving me closer to a trustworthy source I'd long ago lost touch with: my instincts, my intuition, myself. First there was Dr. Heathering calling security on me, then the attempt by my treatment team to force me back on Antabuse, and finally Krystal's wellness check: these three encounters with psychiatric force had destroyed any last semblance of compliance I had left in me. I'd always assumed I needed permission from my psychiatrist to come off a medication, but it now seemed otherwise: It was my body. If I didn't want these pills coursing through my bloodstream anymore, I had the right to come off them. I immediately stopped the Wellbutrin, which I'd been on for about two weeks, and decided the time had come to drag myself to the gym. One night, as I was sucking wind on the elliptical machine, watching *Wheel of Fortune*, I looked around at all the joggers and bikers and weight lifters, these seemingly put-together people leading put-together lives. The usual thought occurred to me—*Imagine if you were actually going to a job tomorrow morning and not the psych hospital*—but this time, instead of the usual flood of shame, I closed my eyes and let my imagination invent a novel scene: me, living independently in a clean apartment, waking up alert and eager, fresh coffee brewing as I brushed my teeth and showered and combed my hair and put on clothes I felt good in, because I was in a body that felt like mine. I'd face myself confidently in the mirror, unafraid and unashamed of what I saw. There'd be the quiet minutes of solitude as I took sips from my mug and felt the morning sun beaming through my window, and then I'd head out the door to a challenging, purposeful job that allowed me to provide for myself. I'd work hard all day, go to the gym after work, followed by a twelve-step meeting, where I'd see my supportive friends and have the chance to help someone in the midst of struggle. I'd tuck myself into bed in the evening, pick up a good book, and look back on the day with gratitude.

I smiled and thought, *It's time to get out.*

There was no considering, no questioning, no doubt. I knew it clear as day the second it occurred to me: I was ready to stop being a psychiatric patient.

PART

V

TWENTY-SEVEN

A Rapid, Gradual Taper

In our next appointment, I told Benjamin that I'd stopped Wellbutrin and wanted to come off lithium next. "I've been educating myself about its long-term effects," I said, "and I'm concerned." I went on to describe my memory issues, the dulling of my cognition, and how I believed that the lithium might be part of the cause of these problems. "I'm also starting to wonder if I'm actually even bipolar. The longer I stay sober and the more involved I get in AA, the more I'm realizing that I think a lot of my issues were being caused by drinking, even by all the meds."

"Well, we've had questions about your diagnoses for a while," Benjamin replied after a pause. "Upon your admission, we were contemplating whether you'd been properly diagnosed bipolar, or whether you'd actually just been suffering from borderline personality disorder and alcoholism all along." This was news to me. Why hadn't this ever been mentioned? I wondered. He continued, "Let's entertain this hypothesis that you don't have bipolar. We can test out a very gradual taper off of lithium a few weeks from now and assess how it goes on a week-to-week basis."

"How gradual?"

"Around four weeks, most likely. Again, let's see how it goes."

Four weeks, to the uninformed me, sounded far too slow, but I agreed.

I began to build a semblance of a life beyond the confines of the hospital. I signed up with a trainer at the gym and asked him to teach me the basics of boxing so I could let my anger out. I enrolled in literature and writing classes at the local adult education center. I raised my hand in twelve-step meetings when the chairperson asked who'd be willing to serve as a temporary sponsor to newly sober women, and traveled with my home group to put on meetings in detox facilities and hospitals.

In groups at the Borderline Center, it was common for patients to vent about feeling pressured to find "get well" jobs, which was what our therapists called part-time work aimed at helping us lessen our reliance on the hospital while minimizing stress. The expectations were low. These jobs could be very part time. The income didn't matter (after all, most of us were already being taken care of financially by our families). In fact, no one seemed to care what the job even was, as long as you had one.

For a long time, I'd been one of those venters, convinced that taking on anything more than my volunteer coaching job would lead me to break down. Now I was motivated to earn income for myself, to take on more responsibility. It felt revolutionary to consider the prospect of being relied upon by someone who didn't know me as a psychiatric patient. I was determined to find a job that would challenge me and help me reconnect with the intellectual curiosity I hadn't felt in so long.

When I mentioned these ideas to my treatment team, they told me I shouldn't look too long or hard for employment. I disagreed. My resistance was interpreted by Dr. Gunderson as a sign of my stubbornness and pride, and I was told that I was being "too all-or-none" and setting myself up for failure—perhaps, even, that I was really just trying to avoid getting a job. I ignored these opinions, kept searching for interesting listings online, and eventually hit the jackpot: a research assistant position for an eighty-seven-year-old former Harvard professor and psychologist living just outside Harvard Square. I'd be working with him in his home office, helping to copyedit his forthcoming book and handle administrative responsibilities. I was interviewed and offered the job. We agreed I would work two half days and three full days a week, which would allow me to continue with a few of Jerold's groups at the Borderline Center—his were the only ones I felt open to continuing with. I was thrilled and scared and eager all at once; it occurred to me that perhaps the outside world saw me as less of a fuckup than I thought I was.

The more that life began to bud for me beyond the confines of the hospital, the less I wanted to put myself back inside its walls. Eve and I silently, slowly disentangled ourselves from each other. I started going to different meetings, making plans on my own. She could sense my momentum, I think, and what she felt about it I couldn't say. All I know is that we steadily drifted apart until we felt like strangers to each other.

In group one morning, a fellow patient described cheating on her girlfriend with a guy she'd just met. As she sat there bouncing her knee and talking lackadaisically about how she'd had no choice in the matter—"I mean, I'm borderline, right?" she said with a chuckle—I couldn't contain myself.

"I'm sorry, but I call bullshit," I interrupted. "What, you really think you had no choice? Don't blame it on being borderline. You had the power to say no. We all do."

The young woman stared at me, jaw agape. Benjamin, who was running groups that week while Jerold was on vacation, stepped in.

"Laura, I'm not sure what's happening for you right now, but I'd like to ask you to communicate more constructively in this group. It's important we maintain a safe and respectful space here."

I wasn't having it and kept talking, challenging the notion that we didn't have agency over ourselves. I shared my frustration with how we all seemed to just sit around and talk about how sick we were. "We're not actually *doing* anything with our lives," I said. "We're not *going* anywhere. It's like *this* is our job, to come here, sit all day, and talk about the same stuff over and over. All these silly little dramas in here between us are just a big distraction from the real world."

When I moved on to my concerns about the harmful effects of medications, Benjamin cut me off. I stood up and walked out early. In his notes from that day, he described me as "condescending" in my interactions with other patients and having "difficulty showing face in treatment."

He wasn't wrong: I was starting to find the Borderline Center and its culture appalling, but really it was myself I was truly appalled by, for having bought so deeply into it all.

In those final weeks at the Borderline Center, my symptoms, which I still didn't connect to medication withdrawal, continued to intensify. My metabolism seemed to stop working, and my weight increased to nearly two hundred pounds. On several occasions, I was seized by the urge to vomit and had to stop whatever I was doing to puke. Huge sweat stains the size of papayas lived under my armpits. My fingernails, which had long been flimsy and weak, began to flake off in layers, and my hair, which had thinned through my twenties, now fell out in clumps that I'd find bunched up in my clothes, on the seat of my car. I got instant, searing headaches and nausea from the tiniest hint of perfume, scented candles, and household cleaners. I was frequently itchy, but scratching never satisfied it, as the sensation seemed to skip around right beneath the surface of my skin.

When Benjamin began to reduce my lithium, a rancid, rotting stench started emanating from my sternum area. No matter how hard I scrubbed at my chest with soap or exfoliated it with a washcloth or coated it with astringent, the odor returned within minutes, leaving me nauseated by my own aroma. (Whether others could smell me I wasn't sure, as I didn't let anyone get close.) The lithium reduction also brought on tender, painful boils the size and firmness of peas that burst forth on my chest, neck, and cheeks. I'd spend an hour in front of the mirror, squeezing and pushing and inserting sewing needles into them to see if they'd empty out, which they never did.

The bright lights and clinking carts and trilling cell phones at the grocery store made it feel like I was on acid. My heart often seemed to skip beats. I was so overly sensitized to stimuli that the clicking sound of a closing door or blurry flash of a bird flying by was enough to make my chest pound violently, put the taste of metal on my tongue, and set off tunnel vision.

The best way to sum up this phase of psychiatric drug withdrawal is that the simple fact of life happening around me was enough to send my central nervous system into full-blown panic mode.

Sara and Bill's home was my haven. There was the smell of den fire wafting through the first floor on cold evenings. The clack of Sara's fingers on keys as she chatted with her daughters on Instant Messenger. The small vase of flowers she liked to set on the round breakfast table and the bottle of fresh-squeezed juice she always had on hand to make us "lemon seltzies," as she called them. When we'd go for walks at the reservoir and she'd listen to my ramblings, Sara would nod compassionately and run a hand down the side of my shoulder.

She'd say, "You're doing great. You really are," and while I could grasp, intellectually, that she was right in many ways—the pieces of my life were indeed starting to come back together—there was a civil war under way inside my body that made it nearly impossible to appreciate all that I was recovering beyond my terrain of flesh and blood.

TWENTY-EIGHT

Pharmaceutical Trauma

After realizing the harm that years of psychiatric medications had caused me, I'd concluded that I needed to get off them as quickly as possible. The logic seemed simple at the time: the faster I removed these meds from my body, the faster I'd recover.

I had no idea that I had it backward—that the fastest way to get off and stay off psychiatric drugs successfully for many people, much of the time, is to taper down slowly. And by "slowly" I don't mean over a few weeks or months. I mean potentially over years.*

---

* Much of the information that I share in this chapter about tapering off psychiatric drugs comes from the lay wisdom of countless thousands of ordinary people who were forced to figure out for themselves how to get off their meds successfully. Until recently, there was essentially no reliable information available from professional health bodies on how to safely taper off psychiatric drugs—and what was available was typically suggesting people taper far too quickly. Because of this, the only visible source to turn to for "evidence-based" taper protocols has historically been anecdotal in nature: the accumulated wisdom of personal accounts of tapering successfully and unsuccessfully that people have shared with one another online over decades. This is changing, as the expert knowledge base arising directly from personal experience is now being utilized in research and clinical settings, and a "deprescribing" industry of prescribers and mental health professionals is taking off, built largely on the methodologies developed by those of us with no letters after our names. (See Peter Simons, "Peer-Support Groups Were Right, Guidelines Were Wrong: Dr. Mark Horowitz on Tapering Off Antidepressants," Mad in America, March 20, 2019, https://www .madinamerica.com/2019/03/peer-support-groups-right-official-guidelines-wrong-dr -mark-horowitz-tapering-off-antidepressants/.) In 2023, the UK-based *Maudsley Prescribing Guidelines in Psychiatry*, considered by the NHS to be the "the essential evidence-based handbook on the safe and effective prescribing of psychotropic agents," published its first deprescribing handbook, much of it influenced by the knowledge base of laypeople. (See www.oxfordhealth.nhs.uk/library/cpd/maudsley-prescribing-guidelines-in-psychiatry

The basic organizing principle of the human body is homeostasis: We have evolved to maintain internal stability within all our bodily functions, whether they relate to temperature or blood sugar or oxygen levels or receptor function. When a natural physiological function is interrupted, damaged, or otherwise interfered with, the body alters itself to compensate for that change so that it can regain stability. Exposure to any psychoactive chemical—whether it's alcohol or caffeine or heroin or an antidepressant—disrupts neurotransmitter function. If that exposure is fleeting, the disruption may well be too. But things get more complicated when the exposure continues regularly for longer than a few weeks, sometimes even just a few days. What was initially a fleeting disruption may become a more substantive, lasting one, prompting the body, in its quest to maintain homeostasis, to change its structure and functioning in response. This now-artificial homeostasis is a sign of physical dependence: the body has changed itself so substantially that it now depends on that medication, in a purely physiological sense, to maintain this readjusted state of internal balance. In other words, whereas a medication is initially disruptive to a body that's never been exposed to it before, once that med has been taken regularly for long enough to cause physical dependence, it's the med's *removal* that becomes the disrupting force.

Had I known about physical dependence back in 2010 when I was a patient at the Borderline Center, there would have been two signals that could have helped me determine I was dependent on my meds. The first was that I'd developed drug tolerance, a condition in which the noticeable effects that initially emerge after a person starts a medication dissipate. This might seem like a good thing if it's an unhelpful "side" effect—what a drug company calls an effect that falls

---

-for-gps-and-practice-staff-in-oxfordshire/.) As of 2024, nothing of its kind has yet been published in the United States.

outside the scope of what its drug has been marketed to do, such as not being able to fall asleep after starting an antidepressant. Or it can feel like a problem if the dissipated effect is one the drug has been marketed for, like not being able to fall asleep after starting an antinarcoleptic drug. A good indicator of tolerance is the progressive increase of a medication dose over time; I think back to how my doctor started me on 0.5 mg of Klonopin per day, which initially helped me to relax at night, but subsequently upped that dose, as the years passed and my anxiety and sleep problems kept worsening, until I was on 3 mg per day.

The second sign that I was physically dependent was all those new or intensified mental, emotional, cognitive, and physical problems that emerged for me after I abruptly stopped my various medications, which I failed to recognize, at the time, were actually symptoms of withdrawal. Withdrawal symptoms occur because removing a substance the body has grown dependent on doesn't just snap its impacted systems back to their original structure and functioning. Instead, the removal can set off a state of biochemical disequilibrium that results in any of a wide array of issues that might be minor or major in nature, short- or long-lived. These issues can range from digestive and metabolic to hormonal, adrenal, sexual, and reproductive; cognitive and neurological to inflammatory and immunological; muscular to dermatologic to cardiological. Symptoms of withdrawal from prescribed psychiatric medications can include concentration issues, memory problems, and other cognitive difficulties; panic attacks and debilitating anxiety; paranoia or even mania and psychosis. Uncontrollable rage, homicidal thoughts. Suicidal despair. Withdrawal, for many people, looks like a more intense version of the very symptoms for which they were prescribed their psych meds in the first place. For others, it looks like the sudden onset of a terrifying, new mental or physical illness.

The range of withdrawal symptoms is vast because the numerous neurotransmitter systems altered by psychiatric medications—among them the cholinergic, histaminic, dopaminergic, norepinephrine, gamma aminobutyric acid (GABA), and serotonergic systems—are responsible for functions throughout the human body. For example, 90 to 95 percent of the body's serotonin is found in the gut, so when we're told that serotonin is the "feel-good hormone in the brain," this is a tiny snippet of the whole story. Serotonin also plays a crucial role in basic human functions such as appetite, digestion, bladder control, the vomiting reflex, temperature regulation, circadian rhythm, motor control, and respiration, not to mention memory, stress response, and perception. And when we're told that antidepressants—including selective serotonin reuptake inhibitors (SSRIs) like Prozac, serotonin and norepinephrine reuptake inhibitors (SNRIs) like Effexor, monoamine oxidase inhibitors (MAOIs) like Nardil, and tricyclics like amitriptyline—work in their respective ways by occupying serotonin and other neurotransmitter receptors (rather like how a key occupies a lock by fitting into it), which in turn creates a surplus of these neurotransmitters in the brain, this is an incomplete and crudely oversimplified version of what we know about how these drugs actually affect us (which is already very limited). When the human body detects the unnatural serotonin surplus created by an antidepressant, it responds by shutting down its own serotonin receptors in order to reduce that excess and return itself to a now-drug-altered homeostatic state. In other words, repeated use of an antidepressant can lead to the disabling of otherwise normal serotonergic function (and research suggests that, for some people, it can take years for these shut-down receptors to come back online once an antidepressant has been stopped). No wonder I was diagnosed with irritable bowel syndrome after a few years of taking antidepressants and that when I stopped them, I had among my many intense physical withdrawal symptoms spontaneous vomiting, excessive sweating, and well over a year of either total constipation or pure-liquid diarrhea. And again, serotonin is just one of numerous neurotransmitter systems that are disrupted by psychiatric drugs.

Understanding the profound alterations that had happened in my body as a result of developing physical dependence upon my medications would have helped to clarify what exactly was happening to me in the wake of trying to come off them. In spite of my fears at the time, none of the problems that emerged for me in the days, weeks, and months that followed were signs that I was relapsing or experiencing a new mental illness. They were not my baseline state off meds or proof that I needed them. They were not psychological reactions I was having because I wasn't ready to be med-free. My struggles were the physiological aftermath of iatrogenic harm. Of chronic pharmaceutical trauma.

It's hard to say what percentage of people on psychiatric drugs will have withdrawal symptoms upon stopping them. Recent studies looking at the frequency, intensity, and duration of withdrawal symptoms suggest the numbers are concerningly high. A 2022 survey of nearly six hundred people from twenty-nine countries who've taken antipsychotic drugs, for example, found that 72 percent reported withdrawal symptoms, and of those, 52 percent reported them as severe. And a 2019 systematic review that looked at twenty-four studies relevant to antidepressant withdrawal found that more than half of people, on average, experienced withdrawal symptoms, and of those, nearly half described their symptoms as severe. In their conclusion, the authors of the systematic review wrote:

> We recommend that U.K. and U.S.A. guidelines on antidepressant withdrawal be urgently updated as they are clearly at variance with the evidence on the incidence, severity and

duration of antidepressant withdrawal, and are probably leading to the widespread misdiagnosing of withdrawal, the consequent lengthening of antidepressant use, much unnecessary antidepressant prescribing and higher rates of antidepressant prescriptions overall. We also recommend that prescribers fully inform patients about the possibility of withdrawal effects.

So much of the withdrawal experience is unspeakable: there are simply no words in the English language that come close to capturing its otherworldly nature. The experience infused not just my every square inch but all that I could see, hear, taste, smell, touch; all that I believed and valued and thought about. Withdrawal hijacked my reality without my realizing it; it had to, after all, as these drugs altered not just the entire biochemical landscape of my brain and body but also my consciousness, my seat of self.

Some people assume that the hellish withdrawal symptoms experienced from stopping psychiatric drugs must last for a few weeks, and then the worst is over. But withdrawal from any kind of psychiatric drug—be it one classed as a stimulant, an antianxiety drug, a mood stabilizer, an antipsychotic, a sleep aid, or an antidepressant—can take much longer than a few weeks to recover from. A close friend of mine was taken off benzodiazepines and antidepressants (both of which she'd taken for a decade, as prescribed, for work-related anxiety) cold turkey by doctors at a detox facility she'd turned to for help. When my friend was sent home from that detox two weeks later, the vertigo, nerve pain, and depersonalization and derealization (the sense that you're outside your body and that the world around you isn't real) were so severe that she climbed into bed and basically didn't get out for years. (Many people have had similarly dangerous experiences in short- and long-term addiction facilities; one of the common pieces of wisdom shared among people who've come off their psych meds is to avoid these facilities at all costs.)

For years, that friend couldn't sit up for lengthy stretches of time because she had no equilibrium, and she was lucky if she made it to the end of the driveway and back because the panic attacks set off by the simple act of walking were so severe. Family members did her grocery shopping because she couldn't drive. This might sound like an exaggeration, and indeed, people going through prolonged symptoms of psychiatric drug withdrawal are frequently disbelieved because what they describe sounds simply too extreme. *It must be in their head,* friends and family think, especially when the person going through it "looks fine." I've heard countless anecdotes from former patients about their psychiatrists telling them that they couldn't possibly still be in withdrawal weeks or months, let alone years, after stopping their medication. "See what a hard time you're having off your meds?" their doctors tell them. "This is why you need to go back on them."

I often hear something similar from medicated people with whom I share that I no longer take psychiatric drugs. "Oh, I would never do that. My meds really help me," they say. But when I probe further to ask what "help" means to them, the response often goes something like "I feel so much worse when I don't take them" or "I already tried to taper off slowly and it really didn't go well." And when I ask what they mean by "taper off slowly," without fail I hear a few weeks or months or even sometimes a year or two—these rates, again, are far too fast for many people, who just don't realize it, as I once didn't.

The good news is that coming off psychiatric drugs does not, by default, have to be such a terribly disruptive and disabling experience. When people taper slowly enough to allow their bodies to gradually acclimate to the growing absence of their medication (for some, this might look like six months of tapering, and for others, five years or longer; unfortunately there's no way to know up front just how much time one's own body will need), the experience can often feel much more mild, manageable, and sustainable. Some people have come off slowly enough that they barely even noticed any symptoms of withdrawal at all—and on the flip side, perplexingly, a certain percentage of people who come off abruptly seem to have no or few difficulties. I know a handful of people who, after stopping their meds over a couple of weeks, say they had some headaches and diarrhea and were then basically fine; the problem is, one can never know in advance if it'll be this easy, and if a person ends up getting walloped by terrible withdrawal symptoms, there's no way for him to know in advance how long his body will need to restabilize.

Just how slow is "slow" when it comes to getting off a psychiatric drug? Thousands upon thousands of people's anecdotal taper experiences—which individuals have been sharing with one another on the internet for many years—have illuminated what you might call a basic principle of harm-reducing psychiatric drug tapering: making 5 to 10 percent reductions in one's daily dose per month, calculated on the previous month's dose, tends to result in a smoother, more sustainable withdrawal experience. For example, if I wanted to come off 100 mg of Drug X at a monthly taper rate of 10 percent, I would cut 10 mg in the first month (which equals 10 percent of 100), 9 mg in the second month (which equals 10 percent of 90), 8.1 mg in the third month (which equals 10 percent of 81), and so forth. This is called hyperbolic tapering, because a person makes progressively smaller reductions over time relative to her decreasing overall daily dose. If you imagine the gentle downward slope of a cereal bowl—as opposed to the linear hypotenuse of a right triangle—you have a rough visual of what these dose reductions would look like mapped out on an XY chart.

There is a logical biochemical explanation as to why this hyperbolic tapering technique can prove essential to ensuring central nervous system stability: because there is a hyperbolic relationship between the dose of a psychiatric drug and the effect it has on neurotransmitter receptors. To put this in more straightforward terms: the amount of drug that one takes does not correlate directly with the amount of neurotransmitter receptors that drug will interfere with; small doses can have very large effects on one's body, and vice versa. For example, the authors of a 2022 paper in *Molecular Psychiatry* show how the smallest available dose of the antidepressant Zoloft, 25 mg, already occupies 65 percent of the body's serotonin receptors, while upping to a large dose of 150 mg occupies only an additional 18 percent of serotonin receptors. (It should be noted that these are averaged percentages, as there can be variations in specific hyperbolic occupancy rates across individuals.) This means that the smaller one's daily dose gets during a taper, the more disruptive each additional reduction will be to the body's homeostasis, which is why making progressively smaller cuts over time is thought to help mitigate withdrawal symptoms. This also helps to explain why so many people have a hard time stopping what they've been told are "subtherapeutic" doses that are having a "negligible effect" on them. The truth is quite literally the opposite.

In March 2024, the UK's professional psychiatric guild organization, the Royal College of Psychiatrists, published a page on its website for patients looking for resources on stopping antidepressants that included detailed information about this hyperbolic tapering approach that had emerged in the lay withdrawal community. The American Psychiatric Association, as of 2024, provides no such information about this approach, either to its own clinicians or to the general public.

I knew none of this when I came off my meds in 2010, nor did I have any idea of the burgeoning online community of people from all over the world who were exchanging this information. (At the time, there were a small handful of forums; as of 2024, there are many dozens if not hundreds of Facebook groups for people looking to receive or offer support for coming off essentially any psychiatric drug, some of them with tens of thousands of members. Search phrases like "coming off mental health medication" on TikTok and you'll find an endless feed of personal video accounts documenting the trials and tribulations of psych drug withdrawal. On Reddit, posters are asking one another daily for information and advice. On r/AskReddit, over six hundred people responded to the question "How bad was your SSRI withdrawal?") I sometimes wonder whether I would have withdrawn more carefully back then had I found my way to those forums, or at least to a meaningfully informed understanding of psychiatric drug dependence and withdrawal. Would the outrage I felt at the harm those drugs had caused me have prevented me from properly grasping the speed paradox that so often defines the psychiatric drug tapering experience—that for many people, especially those of us who've taken these drugs for years, the "fastest" way to get off and stay off them is to go super slowly? And had I been able to grasp that speed paradox, would I have actually been capable of setting my anger aside to let those pills course through my bloodstream for many more months, if not years, in order to taper at a turtle's pace? It's easy to ponder these questions today, because my uninformed, brutal withdrawal experience turned out all right for me. I played Russian roulette, and I won—in large part because of all the material and emotional support I'd been given. Far too many of my friends and fellows haven't been so privileged or lucky.

Today, when I talk to people who are preparing to come off their meds, I share how important it is to pay attention to how they feel during their taper. If while reducing their dose they notice new or intensified problems—especially ones that feel unmanageable—I suggest that this may well be a physiological sign that they're going too fast. I explain that the standard guidance among laypeople is to pause one's taper (we call this "holding" in the psychiatric drug withdrawal community) to allow withdrawal symptoms to lessen to a manageable degree—or, if one prefers to be especially risk averse, to wait until they dissipate, possibly altogether—before proceeding with further reductions.

There is limited research into what factors determine whether someone will experience psychiatric drug withdrawal symptoms and, if so, how intense and long-lasting they'll be. After scanning the literature on antidepressant withdrawal, the authors of a 2023 review published in the peer-reviewed journal *CNS Drugs* suggest that factors like the length of time one has spent on a drug, which drug one is on, and the dosage one is taking may well play a role. Other factors might include one's genetics, metabolic function, and overall physical well-being; one's concomitant use of psychoactive drugs, supplements, or other pharmaceuticals; one's diet; one's personal beliefs; the nature of one's support system, stressors, and responsibilities; and, of course, the speed at which one tapers off one's medications.

A reliable understanding of slow tapering to minimize disruptive withdrawal symptoms, along with practical information about what that actually looks like and how to do it, is currently hard if not impossible to find in the medical or mental health system in the United States. I've heard from some people who say that after educating themselves about harm-reduction tapering methods and proposing responsible taper plans to their prescribers, they were told the slowness was unnecessary, even silly or ridiculous, and that they would "never get off meds at that rate." As a psychiatrist friend of mine once put it, "In medical school, we're taught how to put people on medications, not take them off." Which makes sense, given the essential role that psychopharmacology plays in so many psychiatrists' educations and practices. This same psychiatrist friend also says that were he not having a hell of a time getting off antidepressants and other psych meds he's been on for fifteen years, he *never* would have believed his patients when they told him about their brutalizing withdrawal symptoms, given how bizarre or extreme they sounded.

And when the FDA *does* require a pharmaceutical company to inform people about the risk of dependence and withdrawal for a particular drug in its official label—often this only happens after a class-action lawsuit—withdrawal is called "discontinuation syndrome," a clever euphemism invented by the industry, and a "gradual taper" is typically defined as lasting, at most, a few weeks.

Because we're still in the dark ages when it comes to public awareness about the reality of psychiatric drug withdrawal, many people end up learning about the importance of slow tapering the hard way: after they've already done it way too fast. They stop their meds over a matter of weeks, months, or even a year or two and, after getting walloped by hellish symptoms, turn to the internet to make sense of what's happening to them. There they find the vast numbers of online psychiatric drug withdrawal support groups and communities that house over a hundred thousand people, but by then, it's often too late. They are stuck on the nightmarish roller coaster of too-fast psych med withdrawal for a length of time impossible to know. Maybe a few weeks. Maybe several months. Maybe many years.

As I readied myself to leave the Borderline Center, I still hadn't realized that I was one of them.

TWENTY-NINE

Dear Mr. Whitaker

I told my treatment team that I felt ready to leave the Borderline Center. They told me, in turn, that I first needed a therapist in place to whom they could discharge me. After concluding this wasn't a battle worth fighting, I opted to return to Weinberg; this felt like the quickest, easiest choice, especially because it turned out she lived just a few minutes away from my new research assistant job.

I didn't know exactly what I wanted out of working again with Weinberg. In the past, I had craved therapy, eager as I'd been to pour my pain onto someone trained to receive and validate it, to tell me what to do next, to help me hang in there a bit longer. Now this felt unnecessary. Since I wouldn't need Weinberg's prescribing services once I was finished coming off my meds, what kind of help could she offer me that I couldn't find from a friend in AA? Weinberg had always treated me with compassion and care, but I couldn't deny that through the many years I'd seen her, my life had gotten progressively more dysfunctional. Had she really, truly helped me beyond being a smart, caring, interesting woman to talk to? I wasn't so sure. Whether she could help me now, when likely all she had to offer was more of the same, was a question to which my instincts told me I already knew the answer.

I left Weinberg a voicemail letting her know that I was coming off my meds and didn't want to go back on them, that I was looking for a therapist, and would she be willing to start seeing me again? She called back and said yes, she respected my decision to not take medications and would still work with me. For all my ambivalence about reigniting our relationship, I felt giddy at the sound of her voice.

I had a job, I had a therapist, I was an active member of AA. I was nearly finished with the lithium taper, and though I still had the Lamictal to go, I knew that once I was out of Benjamin's watch, I'd be free to stop (I was still oblivious to the dangers of quitting a drug so abruptly). My next task? To begin to make sense of the past fourteen years of my life.

• ● •

"Dear Mr. Whitaker," I began my first email to Robert Whitaker around the time I left the Borderline Center, "having just finished your most recent book, I feel compelled to write to you." I went on to describe the pressures and expectations of my privileged upbringing, my descent into the depths of psychiatric patienthood, and how I was now working to find my way out of the mental health system. I asked if there were any opportunities for me to write about my experiences at his website, Mad in America, which he'd named after one of his books. He replied that he'd be delighted to explore the idea, and we made plans to meet at a coffee shop in a few weeks' time.

Sara gave me a pep talk before I left to meet him. "Just be yourself," she reassured me. "Just tell him your story."

Just be myself. Just tell him my story. How would I know what that even was, when all the years of meds had led to a forgetting of myself, which was the very reason I was reaching out to this man in the first place?

He was seated at a small, lamplit table along the back wall of the coffee shop when I arrived. I waved as I approached, recognizing him from his author photo; he smiled and stood to shake my hand. He wore a black polo shirt tucked into charcoal gray jeans, his cheeks rosy beneath salt-and-pepper scruff. "Hi, Laura. I'm Bob. It's very nice to meet you."

He asked me about my history with diagnoses and medications. I spent the next two hours describing all that had unfolded following my first visit to a therapist at the age of thirteen, crying on and off, not sure if I was making sense, and wondering, at various points, if I was actually trapped in a strange dream for how surreal it felt to be putting words to all that had happened. Bob sat across from me patiently, asking questions with gentle curiosity and giving me the space I needed to release everything I'd been holding in. He shared that what had happened to me and to my body was unspeakably big, that it was a miracle I was still here.

It was Bob who first helped me see that what I'd been through *meant* something—that it wasn't simply wasted years of fucked-up-ness, of numbed-out disconnect and purposeless suffering. "You've got an important story to tell, Laura," he said. "Let's talk about how to help you get it out there."

Stuffy-nosed and red-eyed from crying, I looked at him and nodded.

"But first, how about another coffee? It's on me."

At the end of our meeting, Bob walked me through some tips for how to go about writing my story for his website. Each blog post would be a new "chapter," and we agreed I'd submit my first in a week's time. I told him I wanted to call the blog *Journeying Back to Self*.

By the time I got back to Sara and Bill's house, I was already panicking about how my family would react to my publicizing on the internet the fact that I'd been a psychiatric patient. Though I planned to share only about my own experiences, I feared they would nonetheless feel as though their privacy were being violated, or even that they'd be humiliated. And what about my current state? What if writing about my past threw me back into some kind of self-destructive spiral that would lead me back into the hospital? What if, after putting myself out there as this person soon to be freed from psychiatric drugs, I ended up having to go back on them?

The next morning, I sat down at the dining room table, opened my laptop, and looked blankly at my shadowy reflection in the screen. My head was instantly full of things to do: Brush the snarls out of my hair. Peruse the pantry for a snack. Scoop some grime out from under my fingernails. Scratch the dog's belly. I stood up and walked to the mirror, picked at a boil on my neck, walked over to the fridge. And then I was overtaken by the urge to stop. To just stop. *Stop running, Laura.* I'd promised Bob I'd send him something, and he was relying on me. I didn't want to let him down and now wondered if I actually had the power not to.

I sat back down, closed my eyes, and listened—not to the verbal rush hour in my head but for something deeper, for a quiet stillness sitting beneath the chaotic thoughts. It was there, I sensed, that the words awaited me.

After finishing my first post for Bob's website, I sent it to my father and Aunt Sara for their feedback. (My years as a psychiatric patient hadn't been easy for my mother—how could they be for any parent overwhelmed by concern and fear?—and so I had decided to keep from her, for the time being, what I knew would be a very raw, public process of personal reckoning, I think as a form of protection both for her and for me.)

"Just read the first part," my father wrote back. "My only concern is that mentioning you—Laura Delano—have spent time in mental hospitals, etc., could come back to haunt you in your professional career. I don't think it is a good idea for everyone to know this is you. Won't it be just as effective if you use Laura or some other handle?"

We went back and forth about his concerns. Sara, too, encouraged me to use a pseudonym.

I reached out to Bob for guidance. He said that he understood my family members' worries but reassured me I didn't have anything to be ashamed of. "It's simply telling a story of a process (diagnosis and medication) that is swallowing up millions of American children," he wrote. "You are bearing witness to that process, and that is the value of your blog. This is an important story (the medicating of children), and yours can become a voice in that story."

His words were all I needed to shift my focus off my family's opinions and forge ahead. By the time I'd written my next post and shared it with my father for feedback, he had already set aside his concerns about my outing myself to the world as a psychiatric patient.

• ● •

During my final treatment review with my team in Dr. Gunderson's office, I spoke about how well I was doing, how eager I was to leave McLean.

"To what do you attribute all this progress you feel you're making?" Dr. Gunderson asked.

I described how AA had been a lifeline for me. "Don't get me wrong," I said. "Things are still tough, especially with my eating issues, but I've really found a lot of hope from listening to people's stories in meetings."

Dr. Gunderson looked at me silently before jotting down some notes. "So, you think it's AA that's been most helpful?"

"Yeah, I do."

"I see," he said. "Benjamin"—he turned to face my psychopharmacologist—"how have things been going with Laura's medications?"

"Well, we've been successful with the lithium taper, wouldn't you say, Laura?" I nodded. He went on, "And Laura will continue with the Lamictal once she leaves us. She and I have discussed its importance in the treatment of borderline personality disorder."

I jumped in. "Well, yeah, I know we've discussed it, but I'm not certain I want to stay on it. I just don't see the point, to be honest. With the research I've been doing on these drugs, I'm feeling more and more like they're not helpful to me. Even that they've been causing me a lot of problems."

Dr. Gunderson stared straight at me as I spoke. For the first and last time, I stared back at him, long enough that he turned away.

As I left the hospital, I churned with terror and excitement at the prospect of no longer being a patient.

After I departed his program, Dr. Gunderson wrote:

> *She got a job as a research assistant and prioritizes it over her treatment. She attributes her success to sobriety. She says she's had no suicidal ideation and that her eating disorder is still active. She stopped seeing Rachel, but has valued seeing a trainer. She says she will not be suicidal again unless she loses her sobriety. She keeps appointments with Krystal, but resents "having to do it." She denies resentment, but prefers seeing Dr. Weinberg who "pathologizes" her less. She denies having BPD (or bipolar disorder) and wants to discontinue the BC. She has felt humiliated by being a patient. She knows how she wants to be seen. She takes Lamictal (and Synthroid) but wants to dis-*

continue that too. . . . She remains rigid, dichotomous (black-and-white) thinking, and denies her need for anyone.

• ● •

It happened for the first time not long after I left the Borderline Center. I was needlepointing in an AA meeting, when bam: a deep surge of sensation shot up from my groin, filling my belly with slow, warm twists of pleasure. It took me completely off guard and lasted for a minute. The sensation was intense enough to make me squirm in my seat, and then it was gone.

Over the coming weeks, the sensation surged forth at random points throughout the day. There never seemed to be anything in particular that set it off, but the pleasure was so intense that I felt self-conscious anytime it arrived. And then it linked itself to Bradley, who had gotten sober a month before me. He had sandy hair, vivid blue eyes, and strong dimples, and worked as a bridge painter. In meetings, I began to feel those pleasure twists spin up when I'd catch him looking at me. I'd blush, hoping I was successfully hiding the intense pulses activated beneath my skin. I knew, by that point, that I had no business being in a relationship with anyone—"Except yourself!" as my sponsor liked to say affectionately—but this didn't stop me from considering a less formal arrangement. The sensation, simply put, felt impossible to ignore.

One night after a meeting, Bradley invited me over for a movie. We cooked dinner together and, afterward, made out on his sofa while his pug snorted at us from the corner. As I sat there facing him, I felt every square inch of me ignite: my cells dancing, singing, celebrating, my forearm beneath his grip, my hair between his fingers. I was actually *connected* to this man. That I had no plans to pursue a relationship with him seemed beside the point.

A few weeks later, in Bradley's bedroom, I had the first orgasm of my life. I was twenty-seven. Afterward, as I looked up into the darkness, heart pounding hard, my skin's sweat cool against the air, I took in a slow breath, bringing the air deep into my lungs, and paused, feeling the thrum of animated neurons inside me. And then a surge of emotion brought the urge to cry with such force to my eyes that I had to hold my breath. And then I couldn't any longer, overtaken by a sudden, new grief—grief for all the sensation and connection and intimacy and pleasure I'd never had, years that were meant to be the most formative of my personhood, shaping my capacity for love, my relationship to my body, my sexuality, my connection to womanhood, grief for my long legacy of physical vacancy. Grief that I was sometimes so out of body during sex that I wondered if I was being raped.

I'd always assumed these were symptoms of how mentally ill I was. Only now, a few months off my meds, did I truly understand the depths of what those pills had taken from me.

• ● •

In early December, I announced to Sara and Bill what felt like huge news: I was ready to set Christmas as my deadline for moving out. The prospect of being alone at night was still alarming, but I knew that the longer I avoided figuring out how to be on my own, the harder it would get to actually do it. Sara reassured me that I was welcome back anytime, that their extra bedroom had my name on it.

A few weeks later, before I left, I poked my head through the kitchen door to look one last time into the dining room, where winter sun lit up the table at which I'd written the first few chapters of my blog for Bob's website over the previous months. I knew the gift my aunt and uncle had given me was far bigger than a spare bedroom.

They'd given me their presence. They'd cared for me free of judgment. They'd let me be exactly as I was, for as long as I needed to be there, and offered me the space that this required. They'd given me the time I needed to figure out that there was, in fact, a pathway through the dark, and that I was on it.

THIRTY

My Healing

One chilly evening after an AA meeting in early 2011, I strolled down Commonwealth Avenue with Sam, my sponsor. Sam carried herself with a grace that befuddled me; she "had what I wanted," as they said in the halls, and this was why I'd asked her to sponsor me. Now here we were, talking about God as we walked beneath rows of lit-up, leafless trees. I shared my resistance to the idea of turning it over to a higher power. I struggled to articulate the sensation of feeling trapped in my skin. I talked about how hard it was to not follow the compelling impulse to check out from the present with food. I talked about how unsure of myself I felt in conversation with others—how unfamiliar this strange voice coming from my throat sounded to me. Several months off all my meds, I was trying to figure out my baseline state of being.

Silence overtook us as we walked side by side, and it occurred to me that here, with this woman, on this brisk night, I was my full self: nothing hidden or compartmentalized, none of me trapped in performance. I was pouring out my most vulnerable thoughts without self-censorship, and, far from shriveling up in shame, I felt expansive. By the time we got to Fairfield Street, my senses had crescendoed: the holiday lights twinkling in the trees, the streetlights, the headlights, the lamplit apartment windows, all of them winking at me as if to say, *Yes, we've been here all along, waiting for you.* I turned my gloveless hands over, pressed my fingertips together, the touch of skin on skin: *Holy shit, these are my fingers.* The blood in my veins, the frozen earth beneath my soles, the heat off my skin, the icy air. There was so much beauty here, all of a sudden—such magnificent, mystical beauty— that it brought me to tears. *Life, this life, so much life ahead of me.*

And then a strike of fear: *I'm getting hypomanic.* The euphoria, the grandiosity, the heightened senses—these were telltale signs of an impending episode. I instantly regretted my decision to come off meds and leave the Borderline Center and be so arrogant as to think I didn't need them. My treatment team was right! Look what was happening to me; I was losing my mind! This was my true baseline, this madness—*this* was all there was in store for me.

And then an unknown force within me shifted my attention down and in, to the breath in my lungs, in and out, like ocean waves. The thoughts fell away, and in that stillness, clarity: I wasn't mentally ill. It wasn't a mistake to have gone off my meds. This tingling, joy, expansiveness, vibrancy, however scary it all felt—all of it was a sign of coming-aliveness, a sign that I was healing.

Healing: it's such a nebulous word. I use it all the time to describe the years that followed my withdrawal from psychiatric drugs but always find it unsatisfactory. Platitudinous, even, for the term has grown so pervasive in the American wellness industry that it's often now assumed to mean a kind of health perfection, an absence of pain, a completed renovation of one's faulty parts. Yes, a biochemical restoration process certainly unfolds after removing a psychoactive drug from a body grown dependent on it, but that's not what I mean when I say the word. Healing, for me, has happened in the realm of the metaphysical: in the shifts of consciousness, in my awakening vitality— that fingertip-touching, *I am actually, really here* kind of vitality that

can't be measured in a lab or blood test or X-ray or through a subjective, number-scaled, clinician-led questionnaire about so-called
mental health. In my experience, it's had nothing to do with the disappearance of discomfort and everything to do with its embrace. It's
been about extricating myself from any industry or institution—be it
psychiatric, mental health, holistic health, alternative health, wellness, or otherwise—that tells me I have a problem it has the solution
for. As a teenager on a bewildering quest for purpose and belonging,
I became an unwitting sleepwalker in a hazy daze of pharmaceutical enchantment. Healing, for me, has been waking myself up from
the spell.

• ● •

I intended to publish new blog chapters regularly, but many weeks
often passed between posts. I hadn't anticipated just how hard it
would be to make sense of my past free from the clinical language of
the *DSM*. Describing a memory without resorting to words like *gran-
diose, racing thoughts, emotional lability, hypomanic, rapid cycling,
depressive symptoms,* and *suicidal ideation* was like pulling teeth; I
sometimes sat frozen at my computer for an hour straight, stunned
by my lack of creativity, and when I managed to force nonclinical
words onto the page, it felt like I was writing fiction. How on earth
had I reduced my life to such cold, sterile psychobabble that I'd essentially stopped thinking of myself as being human?

The growing stream of meaningful reader emails from around the
world kept me going. I heard from older women who felt stuck on antidepressants and alone. A therapist who had been chastised by her colleagues for bringing up the idea of medication withdrawal with clients.
An emergency room doctor alarmed by the high percentage of patients
coming through his doors on psych meds. One young man who'd

been diagnosed bipolar years earlier and now didn't want to leave his house because his antipsychotic had caused him to grow large breasts. (Years later, in 2018, a judge would rule in favor of another man who'd had a similar experience while taking Risperdal and subsequently sued its manufacturer, Johnson & Johnson; the young man was eventually awarded $6.8 million in punitive damages. By 2021, J&J had settled nearly nine thousand lawsuits regarding Risperdal.)

One mother shared the story of her daughter, who, like me, had fallen apart when she entered adolescence. "We were completely astonished that this well loved and treasured child who came from a stable home could struggle so emotionally," she wrote. "We had no idea how to handle it and, of course, initially accessed the traditional mental health field." She listed the array of diagnoses, medications, treatment programs, and other interventions her daughter ended up interfacing with in the quest for relief, and the ways she continued to get worse. Eventually, they realized that none of it was working; instead of seeking more treatment, they decided to see what would happen if they stopped it altogether. "Is everything perfect?" she concluded. "Not by a long shot. But I try to focus on what she has accomplished. Your story gives me hope."

She asked if I was familiar with Viktor Frankl's book *Man's Search for Meaning*. "I might imagine you are," she said. "Seems to me you've found your meaning, your purpose."

I wasn't actually familiar with Frankl or his 1946 book, so I picked up a copy. He'd been a psychiatrist in Vienna prior to the rise of the Nazis, when he and his family were imprisoned in concentration camps; only Frankl and his sister survived. In the book, he outlined a philosophy of being he'd developed called logotherapy, which he believed had helped him and others endure the terrors of the experience. It was based on the simple notion that the objective of living is not to be happy but to find meaning. "If there is a meaning in life at all," he said, "then there must be a meaning in suffering. Suffering is an ineradicable part of life, even as fate and death. . . . The way in which a man accepts his fate and all the suffering it entails, the way in which he takes up his cross, gives him ample opportunity—even under the most difficult circumstances—to add a deeper meaning to his life."

This message resonated deeply. As a psychiatric patient, I'd come to see my suffering as the unfortunate by-product of faulty brain chemistry—as meaningless symptoms in need of pharmaceutical eradication. Frankl's message inverted everything I'd been taught by the psychiatric paradigm: far from being a sign of a broken brain, my struggle had *meaning*. It was happening for a reason. I needed to learn how to be with my painful emotions and make sense of what they were telling me about my life, instead of seeking to eliminate them.

"The true meaning of life is to be discovered in the world rather than within man or his own psyche, as though it were a closed system," said Frankl, which left me rethinking the utility of those countless hours I'd spent sitting before countless therapists, thinking about myself, talking about myself, and focusing on unpacking and analyzing my thoughts and feelings as if there were no more important task in the world. Helping people in AA and corresponding with people who'd reached out through my blog had given me endless opportunities to get out of my own head and be there for someone else. What a radical concept to consider, that a meaningful sense of purpose came not from trying to figure myself out but instead from shifting the focus off myself altogether.

After finishing Frankl's book, I went out for a brisk walk in the cold. For so long, I'd extolled the therapeutic encounter as my most valuable source of human connection; now, receiving help in the form of a paid, professional service seemed obsolete to me, and I to it. I made the decision then and there: my upcoming session with Weinberg would also be my final one.

THIRTY-ONE

Peer Support

I heard of peer support for the first time about a year after I began to taper off psychiatric drugs. The model emerged within the psychiatric context in the 1970s as a political response to the human and civil rights injustices people had experienced as patients in the mental health system—a system that "puts wealth, property, and power above the basic needs of human beings," as prominent ex–psychiatric patient activist Judi Chamberlin put it in 1978. When it came into being, peer support was envisioned as a mutually beneficial, nonhierarchical relationship between people who'd been through similar struggles; it was intended to happen in one's own natural community—in the coffee shop, over the dinner table, at a local meeting space—and outside a clinical setting, without institutional association. "When the emphasis is on people helping one another," Chamberlin explained, "the gulf between 'patient' and 'staff' disappears. Someone can seek help from others without being thought of as sick or helpless. The same person who seeks help can also offer it." In time, though, funding opportunities emerged, profit motives were catalyzed, and debates ensued among current and former psychiatric patients about whether it was a good idea to bring the peer support model into the mental health system. In the 1980s, proponents of institutionalizing peer support won out, and it began to be offered in clinical and eventually hospital settings. Systematized trainings and certification requirements were subsequently implemented to streamline a model, centralize control over it, and spread it far and wide, thus morphing it from an authentic human relationship into a paid, one-sided service. (In the 2000s, peer support was even made billable to insurance companies, though I never once encountered it during my time as a patient.)

In the fall of 2011, I was hired as a "peer specialist" at a state-funded Boston-area community mental health organization. (I was told I'd need to complete a lengthy, intensive "certified peer specialist" training and pass its comprehensive final exam within a few months after starting the position but managed to avoid ever doing this.) The simple fact that my long career as a psychiatric patient was the main qualification for a full-time job with health benefits, generous paid time off, and a high enough salary to afford me financial independence was all that mattered to me.

On my first day, I was given a photo ID badge that I was told to wear visibly while on the clock. Much of my time was spent in emergency rooms, where people in crisis awaited the arrival of me and whichever clinician I'd been partnered with for the day. My job was to connect with the person in crisis through my own experiences, listen to what she was struggling with, and help to advocate for her desires; my clinician coworker was tasked with conducting a psychiatric evaluation to diagnose the person and determine her next step, which was usually inpatient or outpatient hospitalization for the more serious cases or referral to a psychiatrist for a med consult for the ones deemed more stable. Many of the people we saw had voluntarily called a crisis line or taken themselves to the hospital, desperate for help; they were typically uninterested in hearing about my own experience leaving psychiatric interventions behind.

Others, however, had been brought to the emergency room against their will, whether by ambulance or in the back of a police car. Often it was because a concerned family member or friend had gotten the impression—rightly or wrongly—that the person wanted to harm herself. Or it was because the person was saying strange or scary things or yelling in a public setting. In almost every situation I saw involving psychiatric force, the person had yet to actually do anything harmful, wrong, or illegal—and on the extremely rare occasion when some act of violence *had* occurred, I now wondered, why on earth was this being seen as something medical in nature to be addressed by a diagnosing clinician?

When patients heard that I was there to help them voice their wishes, most of the people who'd been involuntarily brought to the ER begged me to get them out; I quickly discovered, to my dismay, that my peer support role afforded me zero authority. I was essentially a token, there to falsely signal to patients that the psychiatric evaluation process was a respectful one because someone who had once been a patient herself was now a visible part of it.

In a quest to better understand the human rights implications of forced psychiatric interventions, I tracked down the writings of an ex-patient activist named Leonard Roy Frank, who, as a young man in the 1960s, had stumbled upon the autobiography of Mahatma Gandhi, realized his graduate business degree and real estate job weren't leading him to a life of meaningful purpose, quit said job, grew a long beard, became a vegan, and consequently caused such concern in his conventionally minded parents that they involuntarily institutionalized him in a psychiatric ward, where he was electro-shocked thirty-five times and put into fifty insulin comas against his will. "When you lock someone up on the basis of what he or she thinks, you're really instituting a kind of preventive detention," said Frank in a 2003 interview. "You're saying the person may be danger-ous; but a person shouldn't be denied their freedom on suspicion of being dangerous. They should only be denied their freedom when they are found guilty of breaking the law and actually hurting other people."

Around 1.2 million Americans are forcibly detained in hospital settings for noncriminal, psychiatric reasons each year. In a 2020 report presented to the United Nations Human Rights Council, the UN Special Rapporteur on Torture stated, "It must be stressed that purportedly benevolent purposes cannot, *per se*, vindicate coercive or discriminatory measures. For example, practices such as involuntary . . . psychiatric intervention based on 'medical necessity' of the 'best interests' of the patient . . . generally involve highly discriminatory and coercive attempts at controlling or 'correcting' the victim's personality, behaviour or choices and almost always inflict severe pain or suffering. In the view of the Special Rapporteur, therefore, if all other defining elements are given, such practices may well amount to torture."

• ● •

When I wasn't in emergency rooms, I spent my time in three of my employer's group homes, which I quickly concluded would have been more accurately called small, unlocked psychiatric institutions beneath pleasantly painted siding. The more I got to know the residents, most of whom were considered chronic patients with severe diagnoses like schizophrenia, schizoaffective disorder, or bipolar disorder, the more I noticed a consistent theme: every single one of these men and women had experienced some kind of serious trauma, challenge, loss, or crisis prior to meeting the mental health system but had never been afforded the time, space, or support required to successfully find resolution.

There was Bill, who had long, stringy gray hair and frequently muttered to himself while cringing at seemingly nothing. He was in his fifties and had been on medications for more than thirty years; he was missing most of his teeth (and sometimes forgot to put in his dentures) and had diabetes and early-onset dementia. He'd first been institutionalized at sixteen after smoking some "bad grass," as he put it, and seeing bugs crawl out of the family television. In a panic, he'd told his parents, who proceeded to drop him off at a nearby state hospital, where he was promptly admitted to an adult ward, diagnosed schizophrenic, and started on potent neuroleptics. He stayed there for the next two years, at which point he was discharged to the first of numerous group homes he'd lived in for the three decades to follow. He'd been medicated ever since, as well, the number of his prescriptions growing through the years as his physical health and cognitive abilities simultaneously declined.

Or Maggie, a woman around my age who spent much of her time institutionalized in nearby hospitals because group home staff had only so much patience for her sporadic bloodcurdling screams. These screams, she'd once told me, were the only reliable method she had to release the pain of all the souls that were trapped in limbo inside her. Maggie called herself a shaman; everyone else called her schizophrenic. She had been an exceptional artist in high school. Her first encounter with psychiatry happened during freshman year of college, when she found that she couldn't focus, went to a psychiatrist, and was swiftly diagnosed with ADD and started on a stimulant. Within a few weeks, she'd stopped sleeping and started acting wacky. By the time I met her, she was heavily medicated, had been forcibly electroshocked on at least one occasion, and had been living in group homes and psychiatric hospitals for nearly a decade. She complained that the drugs she was forced to take made her gain weight and dulled her brain (when she was medicated and I'd ask how things were going, she'd take up to fifteen seconds before slurrily responding, a strand of drool often dribbling down from the side of her mouth). You could tell anytime she'd secretly stopped her meds cold turkey—she was expert at tonguing them—because she quickly lost all the weight and got her mind's sharpness back. The problem was, she also quickly stopped sleeping, which would reinvigorate her shamanic convictions. The screaming soon followed, along with annoyed staff who were convinced she was having a relapse. No one seemed interested in resolving her insomnia—let alone discussing whether she might benefit from tapering slowly off her meds the next time, instead of secretly quitting. Reliably, she'd be taken in an ambulance to the psych ward, where she'd be committed involuntarily and loaded up with a slew of new drugs, and the same cycle would start itself all over again.

After months of writing my blog, corresponding with readers, and working in the public mental health system, I had noticed a trend among the many people I'd connected with who had a history of what the *DSM* would call intense mania or psychosis: these states, nearly every single time, had been preceded by sleep deprivation, which emerged soon after skipping or outright stopping their meds too quickly or using other psychoactive drugs, or after experiencing overwhelming stress or trauma. This trend was so ubiquitous that when asked my opinion on the question of what to do to help someone who was spinning out into a seemingly unmanageable altered state, I now always began with a response along the lines of "Start by helping them get some sleep, and if you exhaust every strategy you can think of to do that, ask if they'd be open to trying a short-term tranquilizing agent like an antihistamine, a neuroleptic, or a benzodiazepine."

I now saw clear as day that the people I was spending time with at work all had meaningful reasons *why* they'd initially broken down, gone crazy, or otherwise lost their minds. When I sought out their stories, though, most of them seemed perplexed, sometimes struggling to answer. "What was happening in your life around the time you first got diagnosed and medicated?" I'd inquire. "No one's ever asked me that before," most replied. Not once had someone offered them what they needed to reckon with their issues without medicalizing them, or to sort out ways of navigating their pain à la Frankl's logotherapy. Instead, they'd been instantly reduced to a list of symptoms stripped from the context of their lives and declared in need of medical intervention.

What would have happened to that teenage Bill if he'd been given some time to come down from that bad batch of pot? To Maggie if she hadn't been put on powerful stimulants that have among their many well-documented adverse effects the risk of insomnia and psychosis—or, perhaps, if she'd attended a different kind of college in the first place, one better suited to someone with her artistic talent? Could their so-called chronic conditions have, perhaps, instead been rough patches in the road, difficult life chapters, short-lived episodes, if they'd never ended up in front of a diagnosing, prescribing clinician?

THIRTY-TWO

Connection

I diligently kept my father up to speed on all the connections I was making through my blog. "You have made awesome progress over the past year," he wrote after one update, "and I am so proud of you." Before long, he was mailing me clipped *Wall Street Journal* articles about the rising numbers of Americans on psychiatric drugs or the latest billion-dollar criminal fine levied against a pharmaceutical company. (He'd highlight the headline to make sure I saw it, before carefully folding the article up and leaving a sticky note on top that read "Thought this would interest you, XO DAD" or "Reaffirms everything you've been saying, XO DAD.") Whenever I panicked that I'd made a catastrophic mistake in putting myself out there so publicly through the blog, I thought of his pride. After so many years of endless crises and collapses, I finally had something other than a problem to connect with my father about.

It wasn't long before childhood and family friends found my blog and began reaching out to me and my sisters to share their own stories of encounters with the mental health system. I think this, perhaps more than anything, was the turning point for my family, whose long-held assumption that we were probably the only ones in our vast New England network of friends and contacts who'd been through what we'd gone through was now disintegrating. My father and I decided it was time to tell my mother about the blog, and that he should be the one to do it. I was worried about how she'd respond, but I also knew I had to walk through my fear and invite her into this new life I was building. Soon after, she reached out to catch up on how things were going and didn't mention my writing. We continued like nothing had changed.

At the end of the year, I emailed Dad and Sara to let them know I was at work on the suicide chapter of my blog. "i know this is a big deal—to out myself and the family in such a vulnerable way—," I explained, "but i firmly believe that i can help people in the midst of suffering if i really share how rough things got."

My father and Sara both expressed their concerns about protecting the family, especially my mother and sisters. "I do think you should share the next post with your family before you publish it," Sara said.

I shared a draft of the chapter with my parents and Sara, prefacing it with a request: "please keep an open mind and an open heart and remember how important it is to show readers out there how it is possible to be at the very bottom of life and come back to find meaning, purpose. . . . i'll await your response before i do anything else. love you guys so much, and i am just so unbelievably grateful to have you all in my life. boy am i feeling waves of gratitude right now!"

I received an email from my father first, who let me know my mother had read the post and was struggling with the idea of my overdose being detailed all over the internet. "I think it very important that you not publish this blog until we have thought about it and discussed it more," he implored, reminding me that my mother was "a very private person so this is very difficult for her to cope with in a way that you or I may not understand." He ended, "Please do not in any way get mad or annoyed with Mom. She is really hurting. XO, Dad."

I understood my mother's concerns, along with my father's

concerns about her, but I knew I needed to publish the blog post regardless of what they felt. I saw my overdose as the linchpin in my story of iatrogenic harm, and felt strongly that I could not just skip over it. I went ahead and posted the chapter. My mother cut off contact with me, and my sisters followed suit, wishing I'd put my family's needs at the forefront. While I respected their choice, I remained certain that I'd made the right decision. I knew I needed to speak out resolutely about all the things I'd felt and said and done that had, for so long, debilitated me with self-doubt and shame.

The connection I felt to the world around me intensified rapidly in the months after I published the chapter about my overdose. "Do you know the feeling of loving someone so much that you seem to feel their pain even more acutely than you feel your own?" one father wrote, before going on to outline the struggles his young adult son was in the midst of and how desperate the situation felt, since he and his wife had different perspectives on the utility of sending their child to a psychiatrist.

I heard from a mother whose twentysomething son had recently killed himself after living under the weight of a schizophrenia diagnosis and its long list of required drugs for many years. "Oh, Laura!" she wrote. "I see so many sad similarities between you and Tom." We struck up a regular correspondence in which I shared what I was up to and she shared memories of him. At one point, she sent me a hand-knit scarf, which I hung over my desk as a daily reminder of how lucky I was to still have a voice after "failing" to kill myself, and that I had a responsibility to keep using it.

I was blown away by the words of a woman I'd never met before who cc'd me on an email she'd written to close friends of hers after finding my writing:

[Laura's] blog details the history of her struggle, descending to the point where she makes a serious suicide attempt and is admitted to McLean. I'm hit by her keen descriptions of how her identity is stripped away during her teen years and college as she becomes a "mental patient" hiding behind a mask of perfectionism and helpless attempts at control. It is my story, and it isn't. Not my story because I lost hope in different ways, on a different schedule. Is my story because I also tried to overcome my self-loathing by Just Trying Harder. Indeed, my own adult history of Mental Patienthood is a drama in two major acts (and many minor ones), separated by a few years of "recovery" when I thought I had Finally Tried Hard Enough And Gotten Cured. Only to have all my fears and self-loathing double back later and strip everything away. Where the hell am I going with this? I don't think I mind the fact that everything got stripped away. Where the hell am I going with this? I can be human now that everything got stripped away.

I heard from a younger Deerfield graduate whom I hadn't known personally while there; he sent a lengthy message explaining all the ways he related to my story. I wrote back to let him know how appreciative I was that he'd entrusted me with such vulnerable memories, then shared about the hard time my family was having accepting how much I'd chosen to disclose in my blog. "I'm sorry to hear about your family's resistance," he replied. "I think telling your story is helping you confront your past, accept who you are now, and step forward into the person you will become. I see their side of the story too, but ultimately it's your life, your health, and your livelihood. . . . Although it may be a struggle for them, if you keep loving them I think it should work out in the end.

"You already know this," he said, "but you're not the only one who has felt like a commitment to living doesn't make sense. I have lived many happy days, so many it seems sometimes that I've lived all the life there is to live. And I have had bad days too. Vacuous, brittle, and unfounded days of profound indifference and apathy. But I've chosen to live them, nonetheless, and it touches me in the deepest way possible you've decided to live too."

It's hard to put into words the impact that talking openly about my psychiatrization and suicide had on helping me remember how to be alive here. (I'm easily brought to tears, to this day, just thinking about it.) After all those years of compartmentalizing, and hiding, and suppressing, of so much humiliation and shame, of feeling convinced that I was alone and didn't belong here, it took one terrifying choice to do something I'd never done before—to just fully be, as I truly was—to instantly burn away the smothering muck of a lifetime spent pretending. It wasn't until I began to give an honest answer to How are you? that I realized how revolutionary it is, today, to wear emotional pain on your sleeve without medicalizing it. I learned to bear struggle by sharing it with others, who then shared theirs with me in return. That connection offered what no doctor, pill, or psych ward could ever give me—the same realization I'd had that night in the bathroom mirror all those years ago but couldn't then recognize as wisdom: the "self" as this solitary thing held captive inside my body is, in fact, an illusion. I remember learning about the underground network of fungi that allows trees to communicate silently, to exchange water and nutrients with one another, to sense when a weakened or sick fellow needs assistance; what look like discrete trees to those of us standing on the soil above is actually one interconnected entity. Are we humans really any different? Do our emotions truly live within each of us, encased in these crenulated blobs of brain like we've been told? Or do they pulse and flow and surge between us, in this tumultuous, sensate ocean in which we all swim? I was right all along: I have no individual self. And what wonderful news that is. We're born sensitive and vulnerable; this is for a reason. We are designed to tell stories and bear witness and see ourselves in others. To absorb, and reflect, and mimic; to give, and receive, and commune. We need one another to be alive. We're built for tribes and villages and neighborhoods and potluck dinners. We're meant to feel it all, and bear it all, together.

THIRTY-THREE

Spiritual Disease

Two years into my sobriety, my sponsor let me know I'd done enough AA step work that she felt I was ready to start taking women through the steps as a sponsor. (It was standard practice in AA to defer to your sponsor's judgment regarding decisions like this.) I was still attending at least one daily meeting, frequently raising my hand to speak about whatever struggle I was actively grappling with and how the practice of "turning it over" to a power greater than myself was helping me find the strength to get through. (For a while, I'd struggled with the higher power idea, but after hearing that I could pick anything I wanted as my "HP" as long as it wasn't me, I settled on the ocean and was good to go.) People began to ask me to travel to meetings up to an hour away to speak from the podium about my experiences getting sober, to which I always said yes, excited to be of service. But by the time I got my three-year medallion, in February 2013, I was quietly readying myself to depart AA.

Alcoholics Anonymous had played a crucial role for me as I navigated life in the wake of psychiatric drugs, providing me with a free space for support each day—even twice a day when I needed it. In its halls, I found a family of kind, compassionate, and accepting people—people who had come from all backgrounds and walks of life and had all different kinds of belief systems but had been in the very same pain in which I'd been. The thousands of stories I heard in those halls showed me what it looks like to own the darkest facets of one's past free from humiliation—and that the more vulnerable a person can make herself when sharing about her struggles and her hope, the more opportunities there will be for others to see themselves in her words. Those stories helped me trust that the conflict I'd been in with my mother and sisters would one day resolve if I stayed focused on building a life for myself and "cleaning up my side of the street," as they liked to say in AA—and resolve, the conflicts did. (By Christmas 2012, we'd gotten back in touch. I look back on that year of separation as a gift, for it forced me to figure out how to make decisions independent of what anyone else thought of me; I think, as well, that we each got better at letting go of needing one another to be something other than we each were.) After shedding the *DSM*'s fatalistic psychiatric paradigm, I'd found a more hopeful one in the twelve steps, which helped me better understand the many deep-seated fears that had influenced all the destructive decisions I'd made in my life and start to hold myself accountable for the harm those decisions had caused others. The transformative nature of this framework felt radical: after so many years spent resigned to a helpless life of passively receiving unhelpful mental health treatment and taking no personal responsibility, I was now taking action through doing step work and helping others, which in turn had opened up for me the beautiful promises of peace, joy, and freedom outlined in AA's Big Book. AA helped me find the resolve to stop making excuses for my destructive behaviors by calling them symptoms of mental illness, to take responsibility for my words and actions, and to own up, to the best of my ability, when I took a misstep along the way.

But Alcoholics Anonymous had its limitations, and as my thinking grew clearer the more my brain recovered from psychopharmaceuticals, the more obvious these limitations seemed to me. At first it was the twinge of pain that I'd begun to feel each time I said "Hi, I'm Laura, and I'm an alcoholic." On the one hand, here I was, passionately writing and speaking out about the problems that come from reducing the dark complexity of what it means to be human to the simple label of "mental illness," and on the other, I was sitting in meetings each day, translating my own dark complexities into symptoms of a different incurable condition. For the first few years, I'd tried to justify this inconsistency by telling myself, *Well, AA calls alcoholism a "spiritual disease," not a medical one, so it's actually very different.* But was it really? Each time I inventoried my fears—fears that had long plagued me, I'd come to believe, because I'd always been an alcoholic, long before I ever had my first drink—and asked my higher power to relieve me of them, wasn't I still seeing myself as fundamentally different from "normal" people, as eternally defective, as needing an outside source to fix me? Eventually I couldn't deny it any longer: I'd left one institution—an institution that reduced me to a lifelong condition requiring lifelong treatment and full surrender to its authority—and entered another, one without the pills and professionals and locked wards but still one that said I had a lifelong disease requiring lifelong treatment and full surrender to a higher power.

I left AA gradually, making no announcements. I stopped calling my sponsor every day. Decided to miss a meeting here and there. Stopped offering myself up as a sponsor and eventually stopped raising my hand to share altogether. I'd heard many in the halls call this kind of resistance "self-will run riot." "That's your disease talking," they'd say. "It's doing pushups in the parking lot. It wants you dead!" As I now saw it, just as psychiatry had turned my resistance into "noncompliance," AA called it "active alcoholism." After I stopped coming to meetings entirely, a few friends stayed in touch with me, including my sponsor, but most of the hundreds of people

I'd connected meaningfully with over the years simply disappeared from my life. The irony of AA was that it helped me become aware of how driven by fear I'd been—fear of being loved or unloved, fear of success or failure, fear of loneliness or intimacy—and it offered me liberation from that fear. But it did so by instilling in me an even deeper kind of fear: a fear of my very nature, which it called "alcoholism." All of us seek relief—whether in alcohol, drugs, sex, product consumption, food, starvation, sleep, exercise, television, newsfeed scrolling, or psychiatric drugs and therapy—but some of us end up doing so much of it that it starts to fuck our lives up royally. AA spoke this language of pain to me, and spoke it compellingly, just as psychiatry's medical model of mental illness once had. When you're isolated, terrified, and hopeless, it's hard to ignore an ideology that seems to offer both an explanation for why you feel what you feel and the solution for resolving it. I no longer think the desire for relief that fueled me to drink myself into oblivion was alcoholism. I think it was me being human.

THIRTY-FOUR

Critical Thinking

It took several years of life off meds for me to fully grasp the significance of how fast I'd come off them. I'd been so focused on educating myself about their disabling long-term effects that I'd ignored the fact that stopping them too quickly could also have catastrophically disabling results. I think part of the reason for this was stubborn pride: I wanted to be done with these harmful pills, and acknowledging that I'd likely exacerbated that harm by stopping them abruptly felt akin to letting the pharmaceutical industry win. When I did begin to understand, it was in large part through osmosis, as I absorbed increasing numbers of personal withdrawal stories: the harrowing aftermath of cold turkeys and rapid tapers, and the frequency with which people had to reinstate their medications because they couldn't handle the symptoms of too-fast withdrawal. How much better things often went once they waited to restabilize and then tried tapering again, much more slowly, calculating their monthly reductions using the 5 or 10 percent rate that had proven successful for so many of their withdrawal compatriots. (The vast majority of these success stories were of people who'd relied solely on the lay expertise of the online withdrawal community, and not on their prescribers, who were frequently described as too afraid or otherwise unwilling to participate in something so foreign to them.)

More than anything, the gravity of what I'd been through really sank in once I began to educate myself about basic biochemistry: how the drugs I'd taken had disrupted my body's various systems (digestive, nervous, immune, et cetera), the physical dependence my body had formed in response to so many years of them, and what this meant for me when those chemicals were suddenly no longer present. It felt quite relieving when it finally clicked: the constipation, diarrhea, headaches, achy joints, acne, hair loss, memory issues, inability to express myself or focus, lack of comprehension, ramped-up paranoia, panic, angst, and despair I'd been feeling for years, all of which had slowly but steadily been receding, were tied into my long-term relationship with psychiatric drugs and this complicated process I'd been in of breaking up with them. These symptoms were indicative not of my new baseline state off meds but of a pharmaceutically induced injury from which my body was still very much recovering. When would I ever actually reach a true baseline? And how would I know once I'd gotten there? These were questions I had to accept were impossible to answer.

The clearer I got about the fact that I'd been going through withdrawal, the more baffled I became by a deeper question: How had I gotten myself into this mess to begin with?

I dove into books, journal articles, and investigative journalism that looked critically at the various industries I was coming to understand had each played a part in shaping my relationship to psychiatric drugs: not just psychiatry and the pharmaceutical industry but also psychology and social work, the managed care and hospital industries, the elite education industry, even multinational food corporations. Though I'd long been aware that it was legal to lobby politicians in the United States, I'd always brushed it off as this abstract Washington, D.C., thing that didn't really have much to do with me. Now I saw how wrong I'd been—that the money the drug industry had put toward influencing the decision-making of our country's policymakers had played a central part in my psychiatrization. (According to OpenSecrets, a nonprofit organization that tracks money in American politics, drug and health product companies spent more than $382 million on lobbying efforts in 2023 alone, with nearly 60 percent of their 1,854 lobbyists listed as former government employees. For reference, the next-biggest lobby, the electronics manufacturing and equipment industry—think Oracle, Apple, Microsoft, and Intel—spent just under $244 million. And the broader health sector, which, in addition to drug companies, includes the health insurance industry, hospitals, and professional organizations like the American Psychiatric Association, spent a combined $747.5 million on lobbying in 2023, with just about half of its 3,310 lobbyists listed as former government employees.)

It wasn't just conventional medicine that I was now thinking critically about but the world of so-called alternative medicine, too—the integrative health, holistic health, and wellness industries—which I had occasionally utilized as I healed from psychiatric drugs but was now recognizing had their own profit-driven motives behind convincing me I was in need of their offerings. ("We estimate the global wellness market at more than $1.5 trillion, with annual growth of 5 to 10 percent," said McKinsey & Company in 2021.) I was even stepping back from the very concept of "self-care," recognizing that it, too, arises from a powerful industry that has ingrained in us the belief that we must focus endlessly on improving and maintaining ourselves as individuals through the purchase and use of an overwhelming number of consumer products.

I discovered the philosopher Jiddu Krishnamurti and dove into his writings. Soon thereafter, the poetry of Rainer Maria Rilke and David Whyte. The words of these men ignited a fire in me to *feel*, to just *sit and feel*, for how beautifully they articulated the art of leaning into the darkness of being alive, instead of denying it.

I eventually found the work of community organizer and educator John L. McKnight, whose book *The Careless Society: Community and Its Counterfeits* helped me unpack the many years I'd spent relying on professionalized services as my primary source of "care," in turn disconnecting me from the authentic, freely given kind. I read other books that got me reflecting on all the ways that our societal embrace of the medicalized ideology of mental illness and mental health has shaped the very way we make sense of ourselves and one another—and how the quick-fix, relief-seeking approach to personal struggle has pathologized healthy, understandable responses to socioeconomic and political problems. In the words of psychologist Bruce E. Levine, whose 2003 book, *Commonsense Rebellion: Taking Back Your Life from Drugs, Shrinks, Corporations, and a World Gone Crazy*, was one of the first that I stumbled upon, "When we hear the words *disorder, disease,* and *illness,* we think of individuals in need of treatment, not of a troubled society in need of restructuring." I felt years away—and I was—from having anything near a meaningful grasp of this colossal machine we inarticulately call the mental health system, but I kept reading.

This process of educating myself left me grappling with many questions. Where would we be, I now wondered, if the nineteenth- and early-twentieth-century women of the suffrage movement had concluded their despair and anger were signs they should admit themselves to an insane asylum? Or if, beginning in the 1960s, the gay people who courageously led the fight for equal rights had instead taken themselves to psychiatrists to be diagnosed and treated with pills and electroshock? (At the time, the *DSM-II* listed homosexuality as a mental disorder. The American Psychiatric Association didn't eliminate it as a diagnosis until the release of the seventh printing of the second *DSM*, in 1973, though it continued to pathologize gay people who were "either disturbed by, in conflict with, or wish[ed] to change their sexual orientation" with a new diagnosis, "Sexual orientation disturbance [homosexuality]," variations of which would remain in the *DSM* until its revised third edition, in 1987.)

All these years later, the questions have only grown more urgent. What does it mean for our collective future that one in every three kids in foster homes is having his noncompliance controlled with tranquilizing antipsychotics and other psychiatric drugs? Or that, according to the American Psychiatric Association, a mother "still" grieving the loss of her child more than two weeks out now meets the criteria for a major depression diagnosis and antidepressant treatment? (In 2013, the American Psychiatric Association removed what was called the "bereavement exclusion" from the "major depressive disorder" diagnosis in its fifth edition of the *DSM*, and in 2022 it went so far as to add a new mental illness, "prolonged grief disorder," to the fifth *DSM*.) One in every four boys between the ages of ten and nineteen is having his floppy, fiddling classroom energy managed by a steady prescription of amphetamine. (I know, from having connected with many regretful parents of these medicated boys over the years, how much pressure or outright coercion there can be from schools to do this.) Between 2016 and 2022, the monthly rate at which antidepressants were dispensed to American children and young adults between ages twelve and twenty-five increased 66.3 percent (according to the researchers of this study, these rates were already increasing prior to the arrival of COVID-19). According to the CDC, in 2021, nearly one in three high school girls seriously considered killing herself, and 57 percent reported persistent feelings of sadness or hopelessness. A November 2023 Gallup survey found that 55 percent of adolescent girls spent at least 4 hours a day on social media, with a daily average of 5.3 hours.

What factors have led our society to the point at which it makes sense to tell these proverbial "canaries in the coal mine" that their emotions, thoughts, and behaviors are a sign that something's wrong with *them*—that their grief, their insecurities, their loneliness, their fears, their anxieties, their despair, are the problems in need of fixing? And at a deeper level, what has led so many of us "canaries" to be the driving forces behind our respective psychiatrizations—to be the ones taking ourselves to diagnosing and prescribing clinicians in pursuit of psychiatric explanations and pharmaceutical cures, convinced this is a one-stop shop for our questions' answers and our struggles' cures?

To grapple with these questions honestly is to grapple with the very legitimacy of the ideological foundations of today's mental health industry, for just as its scale, scope, and power have grown dramatically over the past seventy-five years, so too have the numbers of people who are breaking down, falling apart, and profoundly suffering—people young and old, rich and poor, people of all races and faiths and politics, ones who've grown up in sprawling cities or humming suburbs or at the end of a backcountry road, men and women who spend their days at laptops in coffee shops or on their feet on the factory floor. For decades, governmental and health authorities have promised that answers and relief are on the horizon for us if we just invest *more* money to research the inner workings of the brain, build *bigger and better* hospitals and clinics, bring *more* mental health professionals into schools and workplaces and communities, provide *easier and cheaper* access to psychiatric drugs along with *easier* pathways to diagnosis. "Fight the stigma of mental illness!" we're told by industry-funded advocacy campaigns designed to turn *more* people into lifelong consumers, as though our society hasn't already completely accepted—even encouraged and praised— the practice of thinking and talking about oneself as psychiatrically sick. Decades ago, while writing about the medical nemesis of modern, industrialized health care, Ivan Illich said that "social iatrogenesis is at work when health care is turned into a standardized item, a staple; when all suffering is 'hospitalized' and homes become inhospitable to birth, sickness, and death; when the language in which people could experience their bodies is turned into bureaucratic gobbledygook; or when suffering, mourning, and healing outside the patient role are labeled a form of deviance." All these years later, his words have never been more resonant.

What will it take for our society to begin questioning the collective assumption that the industries that have made trillions off our worsening pain—among them health, hospital, pharmaceutical, biotech, and tech—are the very ones we should trust to provide us resolution? Two things are undeniably true about our society today: we're growing ever more unwell in mind, body, and spirit, and the business of health is thriving. Industry has subjugated the natural world around us through commodification and profitization; what's left for it to conquer is the space between our ears. It is now a radical act in our medicalized, professionalized world to look in the mirror for answers and to turn to your neighbor in times of difficulty and to open your door to them in return—or, if you don't yet know the person who's living life next to you, to bring a pot of homemade soup over and introduce yourself. For thousands of years, we wrote poems and plays and made music and comedy and art out of our suffering that we shared with one another in community; today we take it to a doctor and the pharmacy under the false premise that it can and must be obliterated.

In 2013, I came across an American Psychiatric Association news release written by David Kupfer, then chair of the *DSM-5* Task Force, which said, "In the future, we hope to be able to identify disorders using biological and genetic markers that provide precise diagnoses that can be delivered with complete reliability and validity. Yet this promise, which we have anticipated since the 1970s, remains disappointingly distant. We've been telling patients for several decades that we are waiting for biomarkers. We're still waiting." By then, it had been a few years since I'd believed that my suffering was caused by a chemical imbalance, and I'd let go of a medicalized self-understanding, so this official announcement was refreshing to read. But the message seemed to go mostly unnoticed by the general public until a decade later, when a 2022 systematic umbrella review published in *Molecular Psychiatry* analyzing all relevant studies looking at links between serotonin and depression found "no convincing evidence" that low levels of the chemical are tied to depressed mood. The authors concluded, "We suggest it is time to acknowledge that the serotonin theory of depression is not empirically substantiated." The review took the internet by storm, with patients expressing outrage at having been misled into believing their suffering had a chemically imbalanced cause and prominent psychiatrists in turn claiming they had always known this and had never actually said such a thing. (Ronald W. Pies, one of those psychiatrists, attempted to clarify the "crucial difference between a *hypothesis*—essentially, an informed guess— and a full-blown scientific *theory*," claiming that it was the former— an informed guess—that academics within his profession had always considered the serotonin hypothesis of depression to be.)

Pies isn't completely wrong; it's easy to find acknowledgment of the hypothetical nature of the "low serotonin causes depression" idea peppered throughout the medical literature. But he's not right, either, according to the findings of a comprehensive analysis published that same year in *Social Science & Medicine—Mental Health* in which the authors looked at how academic psychiatry has historically represented the serotonin theory of depression. They scoured six of the most well-respected British and American textbooks, along with sixty of the most influential and cited journal articles, that had been published between 1990 and 2010 in order to determine how exactly the low-serotonin story of depression had been represented in the literature. Of those sixty papers, they found, twenty-seven expressed "unequivocal support for serotonin having a direct role in the aetiology [cause] of depression," fifteen discussed "serotonin as part of the causal pathway of depression," and five showed "suggestive support for the serotonin hypothesis." While all six textbooks acknowledged that the low serotonin model of depression lacked evidence, each nonetheless "devoted considerable space to describing the serotonin system, how it might be involved in the aetiology of depression, the action of antidepressant drugs on serotonin, and evidence that supports the role of serotonin in depression." The authors conclude, "In the light of the interests the theory subserves, the attempt by leading psychiatrists to deny that it was ever influential can be understood as a tactic whereby criticism can be deflected, and the theory, in some marginally modified version, can continue to be accepted." In the decade since that APA press release, nothing has changed: as of 2024, not a single biomarker of any kind—no measurable substance in the body, chemical, genetic, or otherwise—has ever been validated scientifically as the cause of any mental illness, including diagnoses like bipolar disorder and schizophrenia. In the words of prominent neuroscientist Raymond Dolan and coauthors in a 2022 review of the history of neurobiological research into psychiatric diagnoses, "It is sobering to acknowledge that functional neuroimaging . . . plays no role in clinical psychiatric decision making, nor has it defined a neurobiological basis for any psychiatric condition or symptom dimension. Thus, it remains difficult to refute a critique that psychiatry's most fundamental characteristic is its ignorance, that it cannot successfully define the object of its attention, while its attempts to lay bare the etiology of its disorders have been a litany of failures."

I know I'm not the only one who missed the memo on the mythological nature of chemical imbalances and mental illness biomarkers. In one American survey, 92 percent of people interviewed said that they "had previously seen or heard depression described as being caused by a 'chemical imbalance' or 'imbalance of chemicals in the brain'" and 85 percent "viewed chemical imbalance as a potential cause of depression." This message was heard most often through television, which makes sense, as the United States is one of only two countries in the world that allow direct-to-consumer advertising of prescribed drugs. (Who can forget that sweet, sad, sighing Zoloft blob from the 2000s, with the gentle voice in the background explaining that "while the cause is not known, depression may be related to an imbalance of natural chemicals between nerve cells in the brain" and that Zoloft "works to correct this imbalance.") In 2022, drug companies spent almost $8.1 billion targeting Americans through advertisements.

By the time that news release was published, I'd learned that the American Psychiatric Association's *Diagnostic and Statistical Manual of Mental Disorders* is not the scientifically legitimate medical textbook I'd always assumed it was. In 2013, *The New York Times* ran an article titled "Psychiatry's Guide Is Out of Touch with Science, Experts Say," after the then head of the U.S. National Institute of Mental Health, Thomas Insel, announced, "While *DSM* has been described as a 'Bible' for the field, it is, at best, a dictionary, creating a set of labels and defining each," and its "weakness is its lack of validity." He even went so far as to acknowledge that its diagnoses are based on subjective consensus, "not any objective laboratory measure." (Indeed, the process by which a psychiatric diagnosis is added or removed from the *DSM* is a simple committee vote.) Further, I learned that of the 170 *DSM-IV* Work Group members, who together were tasked with defining the criteria for each psychiatric diagnosis in the manual (which was used to diagnose me with bipolar disorder in the mid-1990s), more than half had ties to pharmaceutical companies through research funding, consultancies, and paid speakers' bureaus, including 100 percent of the *DSM-IV* Work Group members for the "Schizophrenia and Other Psychotic Disorders" and "Mood Disorders" categories. Little has changed since then: nearly 70 percent of the Work Group members of *DSM-5*, the current edition as of 2024, have financial ties to pharmaceutical companies.

I began to question the very language we use to think and talk about psychiatric drugs—that they are "medications" that "treat" "illnesses." University College London professor Joanna Moncrieff calls this the disease-centered model, in which drugs are conceptualized "through the prism of the disease, disorder or constellation of symptoms [they] are thought to treat." In other words, if you are told that Prozac is an "antidepressant," you naturally might assume it "works" by targeting, and acting against, underlying "symptoms" of an "illness" called "depression." The problem is that in the case of psychiatric diagnoses, there are no actual underlying pathologies. "Psychiatry adopted the disease-centred model of drug action because it bolstered the idea that psychiatric disorders were the same as other medical conditions, and could be managed and treated in the same sort of way," Moncrieff explains. "The model was never tested . . . [and] simply came to be assumed to be the case. People stopped considering that there could be an alternative."

In reality, all classes of psychiatric drugs are psychoactive chemicals that cross the blood-brain barrier and have direct effects on human emotions, thoughts, and behaviors, just as alcohol, cocaine, nicotine, and other psychoactive chemicals do. This explanatory framework is what Moncrieff calls a drug-centered model, in which a drug is understood to work not by fixing an abnormal state in the body but rather by creating one. "In psychiatry, an accepted example of a drug-centred treatment is the recognized benefits of alcohol in social phobia," says Moncrieff. "Alcohol can help people with social anxiety because a state of mild intoxication, feeling merry in other words, is associated with a lessening of social inhibitions. No one suggests that alcohol works by reversing an underlying biochemical imbalance or correcting an insufficiency of alcohol in the brain. Alcohol works because it substitutes the alcohol-induced brain state, with its characteristic weakening of inhibitions, for the normal anxious state." In other words, a more accurate way to understand a psychiatric drug is as a psychoactive substance that disrupts bodily functions, which in turn can sometimes yield effects that feel helpful, at least in the short term. This more straightforward, drug-centered understanding of any psychiatric prescription, whether it's an SSRI, a benzodiazepine, lithium, or Ritalin, is essential to making a truly informed choice about whether and for how long to take it.

The more I read, the more I could see that the personal mess I'd gotten myself into with psychiatric drug dependence and withdrawal was actually a complex, politicized, society-wide mess in which many millions of people had gotten lost. How could this have happened on such a massive scale? When I dove into learning about the process by which psychiatric drugs are researched and brought to market, I began to understand a big part of the answer.

More than 80 percent of the nearly 59 million U.S. adults currently taking psychiatric drugs have been on them long term; of the nearly 6 million American children prescribed these drugs, what percentage has taken them for months or years is hard to say, but my hunch is that the number is similarly high. With years of pharmaceutical treatment as the standard of care in today's mental health system, one might assume these meds have been studied for years before being approved as safe and effective by the FDA in the United States, the EMA (European Medicines Agency) in the EU, and the MHRA (Medicines and Healthcare Products Regulatory Agency) in the UK. In actuality, the length of a psychiatric drug efficacy trial is typically about six to eight weeks.

I have yet to meet a long-term taker of these drugs who knew this prior to starting them; I certainly didn't. In fact, most often I hear that people were told, as I was, they'd likely need them for the rest of their lives due to the incurable nature of their conditions.

I couldn't fathom how it was possible that so many of us could be prescribed psychiatric drugs for so many years based on essentially zero scientific evidence for long-term use. At first, I assumed that pharmaceutical companies must have hidden the fact that their trials typically lasted several weeks; what else could explain our collective oblivion? But after I sat down to read the lengthy FDA labels for each of the drugs I'd once been on, I was shocked to see I was wrong. Take Effexor, an antidepressant I was put on after my overdose in 2008; its label clearly explains that the drug's efficacy was established on the basis of four six-week trials and one four-week trial, and yet I took it for two years. Or Lexapro, another antidepressant that I took for many years; its approval was on the basis of three eight-week trials. I was outraged to learn that Lamictal, which I'd diligently taken for six years after being told it was an effective bipolar medication, had never even been approved as effective for any length of time as a bipolar treatment. (Its sole approved psychiatric use is to "delay the time to occurrence of mood episodes," and this was given on the basis of two flawed trials in which researchers first started all patients on Lamictal while simultaneously stopping any other psychiatric drugs they were taking, then removed any patients who didn't respond positively to Lamictal, then finally randomized remaining patients into a

Lamictal arm or a placebo arm, the latter of which involved abruptly stopping the Lamictal those patients had previously been taking.) And the label for the benzodiazepine Klonopin says, "There is no body of evidence available to answer the question of how long the patient treated with clonazepam should remain on it." I took this drug daily, exactly as prescribed by my doctor, for upwards of seven years. (A decade after I came off Klonopin, the FDA announced it would require all benzodiazepines to include a "black box warning" in their drug labels. Klonopin's label now clearly states that "the continued use of benzodiazepines, including Klonopin, may lead to clinically significant physical dependence" and that "abrupt discontinuation or rapid dosage reduction . . . after continued use may precipitate acute withdrawal reactions, which can be life-threatening.")

There are profound public health consequences to this glaring disconnect between the short-term evidence base for psychiatric drugs and the long-term relationships most of us go on to have with them. Besides the risk of long-term, disabling withdrawal symptoms caused by physiological dependence, there are the many possible adverse effects induced by all classes of these drugs, some of which might occur after short-term use and others after taking these drugs for months or years. These include (and are certainly not limited to) metabolic syndrome, diabetes, weight gain and obesity, fatty liver disease, parkinsonism, glaucoma, kidney disease, dementia, autoimmune conditions such as lupus, ventricular arrhythmias and other major adverse cardiovascular events, and sudden cardiac death.

Governmental and nonprofit mental health organizations often share the concerning statistic that people diagnosed with serious mental illness die an average of ten to twenty-five years early. The World Health Organization explains that these early deaths are often caused in part by "low motivation (e.g., treatment seeking, adherence)," "poor diet," "low health literacy," and "severity of disorder." Pharma-funded consumer organizations like the National Alliance on Mental Illness declare that stigma and discrimination are a big part of why the psychiatrically diagnosed die so relatively young, because they aren't taken seriously by medical professionals when they seek help for physical ailments. This high rate of premature mortality is often used by consumer advocates and lobbyists to push an agenda of more and better access to psychiatric treatment. But what percentage of these deaths—the majority of which are cardiovascular in nature—are caused directly or indirectly by long-term treatment itself? No one has ever conducted the important clinical research needed to determine an answer.

This information had been freely available to me and my doctors over the entire course of my time as a psychiatric patient, but I do not recall ever once discussing any of it with any of them. In fact, as I got progressively worse with each passing year, the explanation always seemed to be that we just hadn't yet found the right treatment regimen. Had any of my former prescribers ever taken the time to understand how briefly the meds they were doling out to me had actually been studied in humans, or to look closely at the actual outcomes upon which these drugs were declared effective in the first place? Had they even read the drug labels at all? At first, overwhelmed by bitterness and rage, I read bad intentions into all of them, but as time passed, I realized that the explanation was quite simple: my former prescribers, along with so many of the other mental health professionals I'd turned to through the years, had been misled and indoctrinated into these faulty belief systems, just as I had.

Plagued with regret, I considered the questions I'd never thought to ask the many doctors I'd seen over the years: *How would you define a chemically balanced brain versus a chemically imbalanced brain? Can you present me with a brain scan or lab result showing proof of my alleged pathology? How can you be so sure that I'll be mentally ill for the rest of my life after spending only an hour with me? Have you ever met with a drug representative or received gifts or income from pharmaceutical companies? Upon what specific data are you basing your decision to put me on this particular med? Does this combination of meds you have me on have any evidence base? Would you put your daughter on this drug you're telling me I need—and would you take it yourself?*

And then it hit me: Of course I hadn't been able to ask these questions, or to even think critically about any of it. For nearly half my life, I'd been under the influence of drugs that had impaired the parts of my brain needed to process, comprehend, retain, and recall information, the parts that fueled logic and reason and forethought. The parts of my brain that housed my consciousness, that made me a thinking being, that made me *me.*

THIRTY-FIVE

Recovering from Psychiatry

When I started my peer specialist job, I imagined I'd be spending my days helping people stand up against psychiatric coercion, spring themselves from locked wards, and successfully get themselves off meds they'd decided they no longer wanted to take. Within a short time, I realized that this wasn't the kind of support that most people wanted. Often they wanted my help finding new therapy groups they might sign up for, or a different doctor. Some simply wanted a weekly ride to the convenience store to stock up on scratch cards and cigarettes that their mental health workers wouldn't drive them to get. A few wanted absolutely nothing to do with a peer specialist in the first place. More than anything, people wanted to feel seen and heard. To be treated with respect. They wanted, at the most basic level, human companionship.

I quickly recognized how naive I'd been to assume that all clients of my employer should come off psychopharmaceuticals simply because these drugs are known to cause harm—I saw that I'd come into the job lacking a sense of the complexity of people's lives. Most of the people I supported (some of whom lived in group homes, others in government-subsidized apartments) had negligible family support, zero financial resources beyond their disability payments, and serious health considerations. Some had spent decades interacting almost solely with people paid to be with them—people who often also managed their disability checks, doled out their meds, drove them to appointments, and, in group homes, did most of the grocery shopping, meal preparation, and laundry. Had these mental health professionals been introduced to the possibility that their clients might one day be able to live without clinical services—let alone without meds—they understandably would have considered such a proposition absurd. And even if they *had* gained an understanding of the harmful effects of long-term psychiatric treatment—or even further, of the possibility that it had been largely the long-term treatment itself, along with the "medical nemesis" of institutionalized care, that disabled their clients in the first place—what would this new awareness actually have done for their clients? Without a radical transformation of the funding mechanisms, organizational incentives, bureaucratic bloat, regulatory capture, and corporate interests that fuel the American mental health system, as I now saw it, I couldn't fathom how the people I'd been supporting could ever gain access to the information, support, and resources they might need to build a life beyond professionalized, pharmaceuticalized help.

Coming off psychiatric drugs had been the hardest thing I'd ever done—and this was the case even with all the moral and material support I'd been given. To say that it had been the right decision for me to come off psych drugs, I now saw, was just half the story. It was right for me in large part because the conditions of my life had made the decision possible at all. I'd had access to financial security; all the time I'd needed to recover; a safe, secure home; nutritious food; a supportive family; and an undrugged mind, I'd been pleasantly surprised to discover, that was naturally predisposed to absorbing, analyzing, and unpacking rather dense pharmacological information along with the history of science, technology, and industry. For the majority of the people I'd met as a peer specialist, life circumstances would have made coming off meds unfeasible. I resolved to set aside my perspectives on psychiatric drugs and diagnoses at work; the purpose of my job, after all, was to amplify the desires of the people I supported, *not* to change them. With what I'd learned about the inner workings of the public mental health system, this task felt relatively easy to do—easy, with the exception of Clara.

Clara lived in a group home with three cantankerous, loosely dentured sixty-year-old women who'd been on heavy doses of old-school neuroleptics for decades. Unlike her housemates and most of the other people I supported in different group homes, Clara was young, twenty-two. I couldn't shake the notion that her whole life lay ahead of her—that a life of treatment-resistant mental illness didn't have to be her fate. Clara's favorite thing to do when I came to visit was search the woods behind her group home for BB gun pellets. She had a jar full of them in various colors and would finger them delicately like they were precious jewels (besides her pet ferret and Mariah Carey CD collection, they were her most treasured possessions). I'd ask how she was doing, and she'd share how much she hated being there, how much she hated her meds, but that she had no other choice: she was too far gone, she was evil, this was all that was in store for her. I tried countless times to gently challenge this, sharing about the hopelessness that I had once felt about my own situation, that I too had once been convinced of my brokenness. She'd nod as though taking it in, then switch the topic: How was I? Had I seen any good movies lately? What music was I listening to these days? When I'd turn the conversation back to her, she'd share about how much she liked her boyfriend, who lived in a different group home; because neither of them had a driver's license or reliable access to transportation, they didn't get to see each other often.

A year into my job, the circumstances of Clara's life hadn't changed.

The only way she got a break from the misery of group home life with curmudgeonly old women and largely checked-out staff was by getting herself locked up on a psych ward, which was also the only visible place she saw to make meaningful connections with other young people. I knew that part of why she never seemed to absorb my hopeful encouragements was that she saw no way out of the isolation and meaninglessness. (After trying and failing to help her switch to a different group home with younger residents, I had a hard time seeing a way out for Clara myself, though I refused to believe this meant there wasn't one.) I now wondered if part of it, as well, was that she saw me—quite understandably—as just another person paid to be there. This began to keep me up at night, until I couldn't deny it any longer: far from helping to spark the possibility of a life beyond the confines of the mental health industry for Clara, I'd unwittingly expanded its power and size around her by joining its ranks as just another person providing a service called "care." This painful realization forced me up against another one in short order: I was just as dependent on the mental health system as before, only this time as its employee instead of as its patient.

In the spring of 2013, about a year and a half into the job, I gave my notice. It was a bittersweet decision, for I knew, no matter how hard I tried to convince myself otherwise, that I'd lose touch with Clara and the other people I'd grown especially close to through my work, which I did. A month or so later, at the end of May, Clara killed herself. On my way to her funeral, with tears streaming down my cheeks, I felt complicit in her death, having earned a paycheck from the very system that had taught her to believe she had a hopeless life sentence of incurable mental illness.

By the time I'd left my job as a peer specialist, I was working part time for Bob Whitaker editing personal story submissions that he'd begun to publish on his growing Mad in America website. Enough people were reaching out for help through my blog that I was also spending about twenty-five hours a week talking to them. I saw the demand for what I had to offer and made the difficult decision to stop giving my time away for free. I started my own psychiatric drug withdrawal consulting business and called it Recovering from Psychiatry, LLC.

Sometimes I advised people who needed help preparing for the safest possible medication taper, but most often people found me after they'd come off their meds too fast. Terrified, they sought validation that the difficulties they were going through could actually be withdrawal, not the relapse of mental illness that everyone around them was insisting it was. I coordinated family calls in which I explained psychiatric drug dependence and withdrawal to overwhelmed, exhausted partners and parents. I provided people with hope that withdrawal symptoms would lessen over time, along with practical tips for enduring them while they lasted. I helped people better advocate for themselves with their doctors about their desire to come off medications; sometimes people asked me to get on the phone with their prescribers to explain the technical aspects of tapering, along with the unconventional prescription writing that might be necessary to enable small enough reductions in dose (it's nearly impossible to taper safely by simply dropping down to the next-smallest pill size available from the manufacturer, as this usually forces a person to reduce far too quickly). Nearly every person who contacted me for help wanted to be told what to do to find relief—an impulse to which I could very much relate but that I had to consistently work to dismantle. "I won't tell you what to do," I invariably responded, "because there is no one who knows you better than you know yourself. But I'm here by your side as you sort out your next steps." I'd go on to explain that my job was to provide them with the information they needed to make better informed decisions about whether and how to stay in relationship to psychiatric diagnoses and drugs—information that we'd never been given at the outset of our respective psychiatrizations. I shared about how liberating it had been for me to shift my faith off outside experts and onto myself—and to discover, as well, that the quest for solutions to my pain had been my biggest prison.

I'd spent most of my life assuming that discomfort was a problem to be fixed, numbed, or run away from—that I needed to *do something* whenever I felt sad or anxious or angry or headachy or otherwise uncomfortable: seek out some kind of professional help or service, take pills, eat something, buy something, get drunk, scroll through a newsfeed, distract myself with television. Now I was focusing on *not doing something* when I hurt. I tried out a mindfulness class but soon realized this was unnecessary: Why had I assumed I needed to purchase a training from a certified someone in order to just sit? And so I began to do so, every day, for just a few minutes at the start. And then I pushed it to fifteen, thirty, forty-five, sometimes sixty minutes at a time. No longer compelled to hide in a hunch, I'd sit straight-backed on the couch or floor and close my eyes. In the stillness, I'd listen to my breath, in and out, as waves of pain coursed through me. There were the despairing thoughts about all the children across the country who, that day, had been started on their first psychiatric medication. The cramps in my stomach, the aching in my joints. There was the anger, all that anger: for Clara, and for all of us who'd been so desperate for relief that we'd lost ourselves in the mental health system. It seemed impossible, at first, to remain still while my thoughts careened around to dark places, but right there with the discomfort was an even more compelling determination. *Just sit with yourself, Laura. Just be here, with all of it.* The very act that I'd believed for so many years I was too sick to practice.

My consulting business kept growing, along with requests for me to speak at conferences around the United States and eventually beyond it. I kept plugging away at work, waking up at sunrise each morning to sit silently for an hour before making coffee and sitting down to write the inklings of what would eventually become this book. The emotional pain didn't lessen with time—in fact, the more I came back into my body in the wake of pharmaceuticals, the more it hurt to be alive, for how in touch I felt with my surroundings: the toddler on the subway platform being told to stop crying by a clearly exhausted, stressed-out mother trying to juggle three cumbersome grocery bags; the ancient tree slowly dying in the cement sidewalk; the mascaraed high school girl scanning my items at the register with shaky hands and thin white lines of scar on her forearm. And the more my brain healed from pharmaceutical trauma, the more clearly I recognized all that I'd lost, all that I'd missed out on, all the possible pathways that a psychiatrized young adulthood had prevented me from entertaining. I insisted on letting this grief envelop me, and at the same time, I insisted on living. Before long, a new sensation began to expand within me alongside that pain, directly in proportion to how much I put myself out there into the world each day, not in spite of my exquisite agony but because of it. At first, this sensation felt like the absence of pain, a nonhurt, but soon it morphed into the presence of something else, a capacity that had, for so many years, been forgotten to me: a sense of belonging. I belonged here, and the more I could trust this, the easier it got to open myself up to the fullness of life: to the cutting fear and the ache of yearning, to joy and to overwhelm, to cold aloneness and the warmth of solitude, to all the fuckups and triumphs and embarrassments and struggles, to the never-ending chance at redemption.

I began to reflect a lot on my early childhood, remembering what it felt like to wake up to the wonder and terror of the world: traversing the woods around my house until I knew each rock, rotting log, and rabbit hole like the back of my hand; lying down to feel the sun on my face as blades of grass slipped over my bare limbs like tickling fingernails; picking up shiny, sun-dried worms from the slate walkway in summer to bury them ceremoniously in my mother's garden, considering that I, too, would one day be dead and buried, forever mixed with the earth beneath my feet. I was coming to understand that I was still her. That little girl who believed in the possibility of anything was me.

THIRTY-SIX

Goodbye, Dr. Weinberg

There I was, in November 2015, on the edge of my couch with my jaw dropped, watching *Going Clear: Scientology and the Prison of Belief*, a film by Alex Gibney, and utterly transfixed by a woman on the screen named Spanky.

"It's such a hard thing when you do wake up," she said, "to go, *Oh my God*, because you have this wave of regret. I just started to think that maybe my entire life has been a lie."

I rewound, replayed, and repeated what she said, and then I recorded her words, and transcribed them, and read them over and over until they'd sunk in. I thought about how, in spite of the many obvious differences between the institutions of Scientology and psychiatry—and ironically, considering how often I saw anyone critical of psychiatry labeled as a Scientologist, given the church's historically antipsychiatry stance—the potent tenets underpinning each were eerily similar: *Turn yourself over to these people who say they have answers to your pain and struggle. Unquestioningly accept whatever they tell you to do, because they know you better than you know yourself. Salvation can be yours, but only if you comply.*

For years, I'd been devouring mental illness memoirs in the hope that, in at least one of them, I'd see my story. But I hadn't yet, which was baffling, because I knew there were thousands of others who'd rejected their diagnoses and come off their meds as I had. The stories I'd found in bookstores were most often about accepting a diagnosis, finding the right treatment, fighting the stigma of being sick, figuring out how to manage life with mental illness. Where did the experiences of those of us who'd decided to head in the opposite direction fit?

Gibney's documentary was what I'd been looking for. My experiences had never been about illness, health, or recovery. I, like so many fellow ex-patients, had surrendered my personal agency, misplaced my faith, and been indoctrinated into a compelling ideology. I could see myself so clearly in Spanky's testimony: the regret that comes from realizing your fear and self-doubt led you to comply with an institutional authority that took you far away from who you truly were. She was struggling to understand how she ever could have had such unquestioning trust in Scientology's false promises. I was struggling to understand how I'd ever grown so distrustful of myself that I was willing to turn my identity, my biochemistry, and my life over to the mental health industry.

• ● •

December 10, 2015

Julia Weinberg, MD
XXXXXXXXX
Cambridge, MA XXXXX

Dear Dr. Weinberg,
*   I hope all is well, and that your family is happy and healthy. I've tried reaching out a couple of times—by email,*

by voicemail, and by a letter I'm not sure you received—so I figured I'd drop this by your mailbox in the chance that it might reach you.

As you might now know from my previous messages, I'm writing to ask for a complete copy of my records from you during the years we worked together, including therapy notes and medication records. I want to assure you that this request arises from only good will, and that, to this day, I hold the same respect and gratitude for our time together that I've always held.

The primary reason I'm seeking my medical records—I should say that I'm doing this for all of my past treatment beginning at the age of thirteen—is to try to piece together and make sense of what happened to me during all those years I was a patient. It also feels symbolically important to have a copy of all of my records, like I'm finally fully "owning" myself and my past.

I hope you understand and will be supportive and in alignment with this request. I'd be happy to talk further with you, as well, if that would be helpful. Please do reply to me by e-mail or letter within thirty days of receiving this, and let me know when and how I can obtain my records.

Kindest regards,
Laura

It was cold and dark out when I walked down Weinberg's private lane to hand-deliver my letter. Ahead of me, a bundled-up figure walking what looked like a springer spaniel.

"Dr. Weinberg?"

"Yes?" A hesitant reply.

"It's Laura . . . Laura Delano."

She instantly knew why I was there. "Oh, hi, yes, hi, I know you've been trying to reach me." Her anxiety was palpable.

"Can I give you a hug?" I blurted the question out before I had the chance to stop myself. We held each other for a moment as the dog pulled at her arm. I told her that I wasn't angry or out for vengeance. "The letter explains everything," I said. "I'd really appreciate it if you'd have a read and let me know when we can meet."

"Yes, I will. We'll of course meet. Can you call me in mid-January? It's quite busy right now with the holidays. We'll schedule a time then, okay?" I nodded. "You're doing well, I take it?" She hesitated before continuing in a confessional tone, "You know, I've read some of your blog."

I had suspected as much, given her avoidance of me. We chatted for a few more minutes as I stroked her dog's coat. "How's your son's hockey?" I inquired.

"Oh, it's going very well. He's playing D3 next fall." I nodded, said how great it was to hear. "Well, I should get back inside."

"Great. Please do read the letter when you can—really, it'll put you at ease. And I'll call you in January. Have a nice holiday with your family."

It wasn't until I was back in the driver's seat of my car that I realized I'd been holding my breath.

It took several more voicemails plus a strongly worded letter sent on my behalf by a lawyer friend before Weinberg finally set a time for us to meet. Four months after I hand-delivered that letter, and five years since I'd last been her patient, I sat in her waiting room. There was the sound of her heels on the slate sidewalk, the twist of the door handle, the suck of air, the pad of feet up the stairs. The second I saw her, I got teary-eyed, which I hadn't been expecting.

Weinberg sat in a different chair than she used to, one next to me rather than across the room. The face of the clock on the table between us was carefully angled toward her. As soon as I settled into my seat, she dove right into a monologue about our work together: what our goals had been, the big topics and themes we'd focused on over the years, the main challenges of mine that we'd grappled with together, the frequency of our meetings, the time surrounding my suicide. She left no space for me to chime in.

I had intended to ask if I could record our conversation—in preparation for the meeting, I'd discovered that Massachusetts has a two-party consent law—but she'd launched so quickly into talking that I'd had no chance. I didn't even look down at the list of questions I'd brought, especially the one I'd starred and boxed: *I've been off my meds for nearly six years now and I've never felt more alive, more connected to myself, more capable. What do you make of this, given that I met the criteria for bipolar disorder, that I wasn't misdiagnosed?*

For the entire hour, she dominated the room. Words gushed from her. She'd clearly gone to great lengths preparing this case she was now making that during our time together, she had worked hard, so hard, to help me.

I was irritated at first but took some slow breaths, felt my feet on the floor, my body in the seat. I lifted my chin, closed my eyes for a moment, and was next overtaken by an unexpected compassion. I looked into her eyes, which only occasionally looked back at me, and sensed it wasn't the content of her rambling that was important to focus on but what sat beneath it: *I didn't mean to hurt you,* she was really saying. *I was doing the best I could. We did the best we could, together. Please don't be angry with me.* I suddenly felt compelled to understand her, to step into her shoes and see myself through her eyes, with all her years of education and training and career building shaping her perceptions. It dawned on me that I didn't need her to understand me, or even see me at all in the life I was now living.

What she thought about me and my history was no longer relevant for me.

Before we said goodbye, she presented me with a thin manila envelope. "This is a summary of our work together," she said. "Thanks for being patient." She offered to meet again once I'd had a chance to take a look. I thanked her and said I'd be in touch.

At home, I slipped the envelope into a storage box, where it would sit, unopened, for many years.

THIRTY-SEVEN

Here

With each passing year, my body slowly and steadily healed from pharmaceuticals, including oral contraception, which I'd come off a few years after stopping psychiatric drugs. (This felt like an obvious decision to make after I finally took the time to read up on all I'd never been told about the so-called Pill; subsequently, I taught myself about the female reproductive system for the first time, reading books like *Taking Charge of Your Fertility*.)

After years spent believing that my lithium-induced autoimmune thyroid condition was incurable, I decided to taper off my synthetic thyroid replacement drug to see what would happen—a complex process that took several years. (I wouldn't have my thyroid function tested for a few more years, at which point I was pleased but not surprised to discover that it was working completely normally and that I no longer had an autoimmune condition.)

Over time, the skin boils and acne disappeared, my hair thickened and grew shiny, my nails stopped flaking off, and my metabolism sorted itself out: I stopped craving sugar, the sensations of hunger and satiation returned, and I stopped gorging myself. The achy joints and headaches and burning explosions in my neck subsided, along with the excessive sweating and hypersensitivity to loud or sudden stimuli. My sleep grew ever deeper and more satisfying. My memory and focus reignited and grew increasingly potent. The constant onslaught of angst that had once tortured me quieted to a manageable hum, and the terrifying paranoia that had long ago etched itself into thought grooves became increasingly easy to disregard, sometimes even laugh at. When I'd first gotten off my meds, I felt buffeted about in a sea of uncertainty, struggling to trust that my brain and body would ever recover. Once I began to see and feel these changes, it became easy to have faith.

I started to pay closer attention to how I felt after eating and realized, very quickly, how clearly my body was communicating to me about what felt vitalizing and what felt detrimental. Eventually my excess flesh dissipated, aided not by any kind of intentional effort at weight loss but rather by my new orientation toward avoiding, wherever possible, foods that came from a factory or ingredients invented by scientists. I read up on the backstories of the goods and products that I'd been unquestioningly purchasing for most of my life: everything from shampoos, antiperspirants, moisturizing lotions, and sunscreens to household cleaners and laundry detergents and bug sprays to the materials in my clothing and kitchen. I taught myself about what was in them, how they were made, and the regulations (or lack thereof) that shaped the decision-making of the corporations that profited from my consumer loyalty. And then I took what I'd learned, considered the ramifications of what it all might mean for me and my well-being, and acted commonsensically: I chose to stop putting toxins in, on, or around my body wherever possible, referring to organizations like the nonprofit Environmental Working Group to help me inform myself about the carcinogenic, endocrine- and reproduction-disrupting, autoimmune-inducing, and otherwise disabling chemicals in things like pesticides, nonpsychiatric pharmaceuticals, artificial colors and sweeteners, stabilizers, and preservatives.

After so many years of self-destruction, I steadily extricated myself from the compelling impulse to ignore my own needs and instead began to pay them better attention: *Your day starts out pretty poorly when the first thing you do upon waking is pick up your phone; why don't you start leaving it in the kitchen at bedtime? You've been at your desk for five hours straight; get outside for some fresh air. You're getting a little wrapped up in your own problems; why don't you reach out to someone you know is having a hard time and make plans to get together? You've been zoned out on Twitter for the past thirty minutes; please get back into your body, remember yourself.* This was a wholly organic, commonsensical process: I bought no self-help books and sought no practitioners, protocols, supplements, products, or formulaic practices to teach me. Instead, I looked inward and listened.

In the spring of 2017, slightly under the weather, I made my way to Hartford, Connecticut, where I was scheduled to present on psychiatric drug withdrawal to a conference largely composed of peer specialists.

Soon after arriving, I was standing with the event organizer as she yelled, "Cooper! Cooper, over here!" Turning to me, she said, "You're probably hungry. I'm going to set you up with Cooper so he can make sure you get everything you need."

"Oh, don't worr—" I started to say, before cutting myself off as a man around my age approached. He had lichen green eyes and thick salt-and-pepper hair.

"This is Cooper," she said. "He's going to make sure you eat before your presentation. Just skip right to the front of the line, okay?"

"Nice to meet you." Cooper put out his hand. I introduced myself and apologized for how out of it I was. "Yeah, I heard you're feeling sick? Your lips do look a little blue. Are you cold? Can I get you some tea?"

We spent the entire lunch ignoring everyone else at our table and, after my presentation, found each other again. Sitting side by side on a bench, we watched the crowds wax and wane, growing increasingly consumed in conversation. We discussed many things: music, politics, our favorite journalists, our families and upbringings, our favorite places in the world, writing, the Atlantic Ocean. I asked what had brought him there, and he gave me a brief history: After getting diagnosed with ADD as a kid, he was eventually prescribed stimulants in high school. A few years in, a doctor offered him a benzodiazepine to help him better "tolerate" the high dose of amphetamine he was on, the side effects of which eventually necessitated an antidepressant. ("Prescription cascade" is one term used to describe this very common progression.) By the end of his thirteen-year relationship to psychopharmaceuticals, like me, Cooper had tried every major class of psychiatric drug; also like me, he no longer took them, and had started a job as a peer specialist. He asked about my psychiatric backstory, as he'd never read it before. (This was a relief; seven years after starting my blog, which had been read by many people who attended conferences like this one, I'd begun to feel a bit boxed in by it.) The sun was setting by the time the cleaning crew politely interrupted us and asked if we could leave. We stumbled out into the parking lot, rubbing our eyes as if jolted from a dream. We exchanged phone numbers and said our goodbyes.

Cooper and I began dating the next fall, just before I was scheduled to fly to Berlin, where I'd been invited to present at the annual conference of the World Psychiatric Association on the safest known psychiatric drug tapering protocols devised by laypeople—the very information that I'd never had when I'd come off my meds back in 2010. (To my understanding, a presentation like this is not typical for a psychiatric association event; I've been told this particular panel took place mostly because a prominent German ex-patient activist I knew happened to have a solid professional relationship with the head of the German Psychiatric Association, which was organizing the conference.) On the day of my talk, there I was, squinting in the hot glare of overhead lights as I stood onstage in front of two hundred seated psychiatrists. As my eyes adjusted, the crowd began to undulate before me, waves of navy blue and black, herringbone, houndstooth, twill, and tartan. Among the many bow ties and fancy leather men's shoes, a smattering of women.

I wondered, for the briefest of moments, if I was hallucinating, and then I thought about everything that had led me here: all those years I'd spent enmeshed with the mental health system and the many more I'd spent breaking up with it; the thousands of connections I'd made with other human beings in the midst of reclaiming themselves from their psychiatrized pasts; the years I'd spent supporting struggling people inside and outside the mental health system; the many talks and workshops I'd delivered; and Inner Compass Initiative, the nonprofit organization I'd spent the previous two years building, which would launch in January 2018 to help people make more informed choices about taking and coming off psychiatric drugs.

I knew my presentation like the back of my hand, just as well as I suspected that not even one of these psychiatrists to whom I was about to speak had any understanding of what it looked like to bring a patient off psychiatric drugs safely. (As of 2024, I can count on one hand the number of psychiatrists I've been made aware of in the world who really understand just how slow "slow" tapering is.) The other presenters in my session (one of them the German ex-patient I knew, the other three medical doctors) would also be covering psychiatric drugs and diagnoses from a critical perspective, so I expected defensiveness and pushback from the crowd—in fact, I welcomed it. When it was my turn, I brought my slides up on the giant screen behind me, took a deep breath, felt the life in my lungs, my feet on the ground. I lifted my chin, gazed out over the audience, and began to speak.

After our presentations, one psychiatrist declared that it was irresponsible to suggest that mental illness isn't a medical condition. We are biological beings, he said, and therefore, when we have problems with our thoughts or emotions, their cause must also be biological! Another suggested I'd been misdiagnosed with bipolar disorder. Next, a psychiatrist stood up to defend the benefits of lithium, especially for relapse prevention, outraged that this gold-standard drug would be called into question. One speaker responded that the evidence base supporting lithium as a means of preventing relapse of mania is unreliable, since it's largely based on trials in which the placebo group was actually a group of participants who had been abruptly withdrawn from existing medications. Another psychiatrist said he disagreed strongly with my claim that it's impossible to distinguish a person's "baseline condition" from withdrawal symptoms, and that you certainly could tell when someone was relapsing, though he offered no explanation as to how.

For all the resistance we received, I had to trust that at least one psychiatrist out there had heard us. That at least one would go home wondering if his treatment wasn't as safe and effective as he'd been led to believe. That at least one would rethink how he approached the next struggling young girl who sat herself down before him and, before pulling a prescription pad from his drawer, consider that there might be an alternative way to help her make sense of her pain.

On the plane ride back, I thought about that night in the mirror, all those years earlier, when I was thirteen and saw that stranger looking back at me. I thought about how, if I could go back there, I'd say to me, "There is nothing wrong with you for feeling so afraid and confused, for feeling so damn angry, for not knowing who you are." Such wisdom I had then—such wisdom all struggling children have as they wake up to the tyranny of self.

It had taken me all these years to realize the objective isn't to find an answer to "Who am I?" but rather to let go of needing to ask the question at all.

As soon as I got back to the United States, I headed straight to Massachusetts to meet Cooper's family for the first time. It was his father's sixty-fifth birthday, and his many aunts, uncles, and cousins had traveled from near and far to be together to celebrate.

None of his family had any knowledge about me or my history. "So, what do you do?" I was asked over and over, and each time I was struck by how pleasant it felt to be asked this, how simple it felt to be there as me. Not as a psychiatric patient, or a survivor of psychiatry, or an ex–psychiatric patient, or an advocate, or an activist. Just me, freed from all of it.

Late in the evening, after the cake and singing, a live band played in the packed barn. It was hot and loud and sweaty, and I was in Cooper's arms, spinning fast, everything around us a blur, banjo and violin and drum through the amps as I heard a song I'd dreamed of before. I remember wondering how this could be real, this moment, how *here* I felt, how free from the past I was, Cooper's hands on the base of my back, pulling me in close, my face buried in his neck, smelling his still-new smell of wood and barbecue smoke, sweat and grease, us slowing to sway and nestle into each other, after all the minutes and hours and days and months and years of all that anger and terror and loneliness and shame and emptiness and yearning and grief and despair, all of it having brought me here, to this second chance at savoring this *here*, the two of us clinging to each other for dear life, for how not afraid we were now.

Epilogue

Today I am a wife, stepmother, and mother to a toddler. My neighbors, with whom I organize potluck dinners and carpools and lawn mower shares, have no idea that I've been on a locked psych ward four times, not because I feel any shame but because my past simply isn't relevant. When I'm out of bed at 3:00 a.m. these days, it's not because I'm spun out in a self-destructive spiral but because I've taken my toddler to the potty. And while I can still hum the CVS pharmacy's hold music on cue, it's been fourteen years since I called it up to fill a prescription. When I drive my car decorated with partnerless kid socks, chewed-up board books, LEGO pieces, and dehydrated apple cores, it's to tae kwon do practice or the park or the grocery store, not to the driveway outside the office of a shrink.

So many of my difficulties are delightfully pedestrian: my frustration that Cooper has, *yet again*, put my favorite ceramic mug in the dishwasher; my upset about the kids shooting Nerf guns too close to each other's heads; my annoyance at having to wipe up obscene amounts of boy pee from the vicinity of the toilet. And when the difficulties feel more substantive, they are always meaningful, and for good reason: How overwhelmed I feel running Inner Compass Initiative, along with the withdrawal consulting business that Cooper and I have operated together for years. How hard it is to raise children and keep a household going while working full time, and the complex feelings I have whenever I grapple with my reality that "having it all" as a working mother has meant I've inevitably lost some important things along the way. How exhausted I am after more than three beautiful years of nursing a squirmy, sleeping toddler next to me, and the understandable frustration that Cooper feels about the situation. The grief and rage that overtake me when I hear that another person in debilitating psychiatric drug withdrawal has killed herself. All the feelings that sweep in each time I hear parents say that they finally took their anxious or sad or distractible twelve-year-old to a psychiatrist. And if I pause long enough to feel the ubiquitous consequences of modern, industrialized living—the screen-lit faces sitting silently across from one another at the restaurant table, the unsustainable levels of distracting stimuli that we are simply not designed for, or the millions of children who spend their days trapped at tiny desks beneath glaring fluorescent lights while being told to sit still—the reservoir of despair that lives deep in me will surge up: *How far we are from our primal nature, how much our current way of life has disconnected us from ourselves.*

People often reach out to me assuming that I'm now happy and high functioning—that I've "recovered" or climbed atop some "mentally healthy" pedestal. My first instinct when I hear this, ironically, is to clarify that I'm by no means what psychiatry would consider "well"—though this doesn't mean anything to me. Instead, I explain how I've come to view the paradigm of "mental illness" and "mental health" as a false binary, and that I have found, in shedding this medicalized framework of self-understanding, that no state of being is permanent or anything to be attached to or worried about. And when I *do* seem to be falling into some kind of particularly unhelpful emotional or thinking "pattern," I typically don't need to sleuth around too long to figure out what's going on. Inevitably, it's rooted in my relationship to life around me: there is unresolved conflict between me and someone I care about; I have deprioritized social connection because I feel exhausted; I'm powerless about a difficult circumstance but haven't yet let go of needing it to change; I'm placing too much attention on matters that really have no relevance for me. Much of the time, it's because I've slipped back into my old habit of ignoring my intuition: I've spoken yes when my instincts said no. I haven't had restful time to myself. Too many hours in front of a computer and not enough put toward the things and people that really matter—the things that, when I'm at death's door one day, I'll wish I'd done more of: expansive conversations at the reservoir with Cooper with scootering kids in tow, despite all those emails beckoning me to catch up on them; letting the boys blow up the living room to build that pillow fort even though it means more tidying; calling up the people who ignite me to catch up on life instead of just working more.

My life looks completely different now than it once did, but I'm very much the same. I am extremely sensitive and primed to jump right to extreme distrust, even paranoia, when I feel vulnerable. I can still get sucked into the people-pleasing tendencies that have plagued me since youth, and wrack myself with worry if I think I've caused disappointment. I often struggle to have difficult conversations with people I rely on. I generally operate from worst-case assumptions. I can be brutally stubborn when I am determined to do something. Intense outrage is a frequent companion of mine—along with intense grief.

Since giving birth to my son in our bedroom at the end of 2020, I have almost never rigorously exercised, sat with myself in extended silence, or even taken so much as twenty minutes to stretch my ridiculously tight shoulders and hips. I haven't had a single night of uninterrupted sleep in four years—not one. If you asked for an estimate of how full my tank has been, I'd say, on my best day, 20 percent. I've made many choices over these past few years that I've known full well would lead me away from vitality and toward tension, anxiety, depletion. Much of this has been beyond my control, of course, part and parcel of mothering two young children while working and helping to manage a household; much of it, however, has been wholly within my reach to do differently, and I've just chosen not to. In the past, I would have freaked out about this, pathologizing myself in a futile effort at gaining control through definition. I would have desperately tried to analyze my behaviors through redundant conversations with someone whose degrees I was convinced meant *exclusive knowledge about people like me*, which I was sure I needed. I'd have been convinced I'd dug myself into a massive hole that needed months if not years of "hard work" to get out of. I know none of this is true today. None of these struggles causes me concern. I've lived long enough in the wake of my psychiatrization to have cultivated the presence of mind to bear with my wounded, still-learning self. To be patient with me. To show myself grace, at least some of the time. I am doing my best. There is nothing wrong with me. This is simply the current chapter of this brutal and wondrous life, and with time, I'll turn its last page, where a more vital, attuned, energized chapter awaits me. I don't need to "figure myself out" to force a change in my day-to-day reality. I trust fully in my own process—in this intelligence within me, within each and every one of us, I believe, that sits deeper than thought, that knows where to take us each from here.

AUTHOR'S NOTE

This story is based primarily on my own recollections, supported by old journal entries, emails, and other personal writing. I used my medical records to confirm details like which drugs were prescribed when, how long hospitalizations lasted, and when diagnoses were made. Any records excerpted here are included purely as artifacts: those reams of pages written about me by others are best understood as imaginative works of historical fiction.

What happened to me did not occur in a vacuum; it unfolded within the broader context of the American mental health industry over the past century. As such, I have traced the contours of that bigger story through the aperture of my own experience. But this book is not a comprehensive history or analysis of the psychiatric enterprise, nor is it meant to be. I focused my attention on the specific drugs, diagnoses, and institutions that played significant parts in my story, relying wherever possible on primary sources such as conference transcripts, journal articles, press releases, court documents, industry materials, and FDA drug approval packages. I owe a huge debt of gratitude to the many researchers, historians, and journalists whose work both inspired and informed the writing of this book.

I found the courage to question my faith in the mental health industry by learning from the people who'd done so before me; reading their stories inspired me to grapple with what I'd intuitively sensed but had not let myself see. If you recognize some part of your own experience in these pages, I want you to know: what you've been through means something and might one day be the best medicine for a fellow struggling human.

ADDITIONAL RESOURCES

If you are taking psychiatric medications—or if someone you care about is on them—you might be at a crossroads. Perhaps your meds once afforded you relief that's since dissipated, or you're now experiencing adverse drug effects that outweigh any benefits. Maybe you've begun to wonder whether the issues you'd previously assumed were symptoms of mental illness might not be—or that lifelong, pharmaceutically managed mental illness isn't necessarily inevitable.

The good news is that there are countless pathways forward from the place you're in. Only *you* can and should choose where to go from here—what's right for you, given your personal circumstances and needs—but meaningful choices are possible only if you have all the information required to make them.

Figuring out where to turn for trustworthy resources and support can feel overwhelming. When it comes to caring for ourselves—and caring for one another as families, and in workplaces, schools, places of faith, and broader neighborhoods and communities—we owe it to ourselves to reclaim personal and collective power by connecting with reliable information.

If you're ready to take your next step—whether that means learning more, asking new questions, exploring safer ways to taper off psychiatric drugs, or simply opening yourself up to the idea that a more vital, connected life awaits you or the person you care about—you can find free resources at lauradelano.com/unshrunk-resources.

ACKNOWLEDGMENTS

I've cried gratitude so many times while writing this book, but nowhere more than in the writing of this section. I'll start with my agent, Liz Parker: thank you for seeing the story I had to tell, encouraging me to write it, and remaining by my side through all the ups and downs over the many years it's taken me to do so. I am very lucky to be on this wild ride with you. To Allison Lorentzen and Camille LeBlanc, my patient, steadfast editors: it's still hard to believe that this book is *actually here.* You guided me with such care through the exquisitely terrifying and wondrous experience of first-time book writing; without your faith in me and this project, I'm not sure I could have navigated all the uncertainty. And to Viking: it is an honor to be one of your authors. Thank you for taking a chance on me.

Peter, I am deeply appreciative that you provided me with a second set of eyes on this book's facts: your sharp attention to detail, your rigorous commitment to accuracy, your flexibility. I'd also like to thank Periscope Foundation for providing generous support during my early stages of book writing, and John C., our "Fake Uncle John," for being such a loyal, supportive friend to us through the years. Wendy, our friendship has meant more to me than you could possibly know. Cindy, without you I wouldn't be where I am today; thank you for believing in me and for your years of heartfelt support and encouragement. To the people who helped me find my way to this story, including Rob W. and my teachers at Grub-Street all those years ago in Boston, James S. for your caring feedback, and the friends and family who provided me cover design feedback, my deep thanks. Kelsey Osgood and Jessica Nordell, I am blessed to be friends with you, and beyond grateful that you were each there for me in such big ways as I wrote this book, including but certainly not limited to those reassuring pep talks as I brought it over the finish line.

I'd be remiss without thanking the places that let me camp out over empty mugs and plates for hours on end through the years, especially Small State Provisions, GastroPark, and Artisan, along with the artists whose music helped me access tucked-away parts of myself, in particular Hannah Epperson, Andrew Bird, Justin Vernon, Thom Yorke, Jónsi, Amelia Meath, and Nick Sanborn.

To all the beautiful strangers I'll never know who cared for me in the ambulance, the helicopter, the emergency room, and the intensive care unit back in November 2008: thank you for saving my life. And if you happen to be the brown-haired male ICU nurse who pulled my parents aside to tell them God had a plan for me: I am eternally grateful to you for nourishing them with hope in those dark hours.

So many people have believed in me through the various stages of my life when I struggled to believe in myself. Thank you for serving as mentors, friends, and mirrors when I needed to be reminded that I belong here: Mr. and Mrs. Hammond; Mr. and Mrs. Heise; Nate G.; Mary-Jo and Byron; Mandela, Lee, Scott, Mia, Grant, and Graham; Amrit, Ali F., Nabil, Jon, and Monica; Kenji F.; David and Meredith K.; Keith S.; Justin C., Jim, Robin, and Sarah H. There are so many more of you whom I could and should be including here.

To all the beautiful souls who loved me in the halls of AA just as I was, right when I most needed it: I'll always hold a tender place in my heart for every one of you.

Judi Chamberlin and Leonard Roy Frank, you forged the path for us. Judi, though you died before we had a chance to meet, you've long been my hero. Leonard, I'll treasure those precious days we had together in San Francisco; I often feel your spirit by my side.

To my brothers and sisters around the world who've reached out to me through my writing over the years to share heartfelt stories of struggle and triumph (and the many whom I've been lucky enough to break bread and cry and laugh and rage and grieve and organize with): I am so grateful to you for helping me find my way back to connection, to what it feels like to be meaningfully here.

My thanks to David Cohen, Bruce and Bonnie Levine, and David Edward Walker for your friendship and mentorship; back when I felt like a deer in headlights every day, you put your arms around my shoulders, saw my potential, believed in me, and provided endless encouragement.

Joanna Moncrieff, I'll never forget the day in upstate New York when I sat down by the lake to read *The Myth of the Chemical Cure* for the first time. Your years of tireless courage have helped to enable so many of us to make more meaningfully informed choices for ourselves about the mental health industry.

Robert Whitaker, what a journey we've been on together. I don't know if I'd be here without you, and that's not hyperbole: thank you for your writing, your enterprising spirit, your generous heart, your patience, your guidance, your friendship. Though a heavily medicated me highlighted *Mad in America* for a Harvard class a lifetime ago, I wasn't then ready to absorb what you'd written. I thank my lucky stars that I crossed paths with *Anatomy of an Epidemic* years later, at the very moment when my desperation had made it such that I could truly read it. The impact your work has had on me and countless friends and fellows around the world is immeasurable. You took a leap of faith and gave me a platform upon which I could find and use my voice. May every struggling person seeking to make sense of herself be so fortunate as to have an opportunity like the one you offered me.

Sara and Bill, you opened your house and your hearts to me when I needed respite from the storms, and sat patiently by my side through all the tumult and uncertainty. I remain forever grateful for all that you've so freely given.

To my kids: how lucky I am to be your stepmother and mother. My sweet stepson, meeting you on that warm early fall afternoon when you showed me your Play-Doh solar system was one of my life's biggest blessings; you've taught me how to be a parent, and been so patient and understanding each time I've had to lock myself away in the office these past few years.

Cooper, my beloved husband, how do I begin to put words to the appreciation I feel for your endless patience, your nourishing meals, the sacrifices you've made, your unrelenting capacity to not take the by-products of my anxiety personally. For embracing me exactly as I am, flaws and wounds and fears and all. For giving me the privilege of getting to live on both sides of unconditional love. You've hung in with me month after month, year after year, as I've told you, like a broken record, "It's going to feel so much less stressful when this book is done," which we both know is pure delusion. The Universe certainly conspired in our favor the day it crossed our paths at that conference. I can't imagine where I'd be without you beyond knowing I'd still be searching. Without you, this book would not exist.

And finally, to my dear parents and sisters: the last time I sat down to write to you like this was on those rocks that November late afternoon in 2008. Then, my gratitude was fueled by the recognition that I'd never see you again; all these years later, it's fueled by the second chance we've been given to find our way together: through the failures and successes, the wounding and the healing, the letting down and the letting go and the embracing, the forgetting, the remembering, the frustrations and disappointment, the forgiveness, the endless opportunity that all families have to keep evolving together. I am grateful that you never gave up on me, no matter how exhausting it must have been, and I'm grateful for the days that lie ahead. As Virginia Woolf once wrote, "What is the meaning of life? That was all—a simple question; one that tended to close in on one with years. The great revelation had never come. The great revelation perhaps never did come. Instead there were little daily miracles, illuminations, matches struck unexpectedly in the dark; here was one."

NOTES

Chapter 4: Ask Your Doctor If Depakote and Prozac Are Right for You(r Child)

27 **fifty-seven-page label:** AbbVie Inc., Depakote (divalproex sodium) package insert, revised October 2017, accessdata.fda.gov/drugsatfda_docs/label/2018/018723s060lbl.pdf.

28 **sixty-point Young Mania Rating Scale:** MEASURE (Modeling Effective Antipsychotic Therapeutic Success by Utilizing Real Evidence), "Young Mania Rating Scale," n.d., dcf .psychiatry.ufl.edu/files/2011/05/Young-Mania-Rating-Scale-Measure-with-background .pdf, adapted from R. C. Young et al., "A Rating Scale for Mania: Reliability, Validity and Sensitivity," *British Journal of Psychiatry* 133, no. 5 (November 1978): 429–35, doi.org/10.1192 /bjp.133.5.429.

28 **This was the sole basis:** AbbVie Inc., Depakote.

29 **The most used assessment tool:** Max Hamilton, "A Rating Scale for Depression," *Journal of Neurology, Neurosurgery, and Psychiatry* 23, no. 1 (February 1960): 56–62, doi:10.1136 /jnnp.23.1.56.

29 **scale between 0 and 2:** Glaxo Wellcome Inc., "The Hamilton Rating Scale for Depression," 1997, theinnercompass.org/sites/default/files/2017-05/Hamilton-Rating-Scale-for-Depression .pdf, adapted from J. L. Hedlung and B. W. Vieweg, "The Hamilton Rating Scale for Depression," *Journal of Operational Psychiatry* 10, no. 2 (1979): 149–65.

29 **placebo run-in phase:** Irving Kirsch, "Antidepressants and the Placebo Effect," *Zeitschrift für Psychologie* 222, no. 3 (2014): 128–34, doi.org/10.1027/2151-2604/a000176.

29 **In a 2012 *60 Minutes* segment:** CBS News, "*Treating Depression: Is There a Placebo Effect?*," February 19, 2012, YouTube video, 13:43, at 5:20, youtube.com/watch?v=Zihdr36WVi4.

30 **well-established benefits:** Kirsch, "Antidepressants and the Placebo Effect."

30 **Freedom of Information Act:** CBS News, "*Treating Depression*," at 4:09.

30 **The 2002 study:** Kirsch, "Antidepressants and the Placebo Effect."

30 **"For all but one sample":** Irving Kirsch et al., "Initial Severity and Antidepressant Benefits: A Meta-analysis of Data Submitted to the Food and Drug Administration," *PLoS Medicine* 5, no. 2 (February 2008): e45, doi.org/10.1371/journal.pmed.0050045.

31 **"Even among those patients":** Kirsch, "Antidepressants and the Placebo Effect."

32 **While it's legal for doctors:** Gail A. Van Norman, "Off-Label Use vs Off-Label Marketing: Part 2: Off-Label Marketing—Consequences for Patients, Clinicians, and Researchers," *JACC: Basic to Translational Science* 8, no. 3 (March 27, 2023): 359–70, doi.org/10.1016 /j.jacbts.2022.12.012.

32 **Abbott Laboratories pleaded guilty:** U.S. Department of Justice (Office of Public Affairs), "Abbott Labs to Pay $1.5 Billion to Resolve Criminal & Civil Investigations of Off-Label Promotion of Depakote," press release, May 7, 2012, justice.gov/opa/pr/abbott-labs-pay-15 -billion-resolve-criminal-civil-investigations-label-promotion-depakote.

32 **GlaxoSmithKline pleaded guilty:** U.S. Department of Justice (Office of Public Affairs), "GlaxoSmithKline to Plead Guilty and Pay $3 Billion to Resolve Fraud Allegations and Failure to Report Safety Data," press release, July 2, 2012, justice.gov/opa/pr/glaxosmithkline-plead -guilty-and-pay-3-billion-resolve-fraud-allegations-and-failure-report.

32 **"One major source of diagnostic confusion":** Janet Wozniak and Joseph Biederman, "Childhood Mania: Insights into Diagnostic and Treatment Issues," *Journal of the Association for Academic Minority Physicians* 8, no. 4 (1997): 78–84, pubmed.ncbi.nlm.nih.gov/9494329/.

33 **"Unlike adult bipolar patients":** Wozniak and Biederman, "Childhood Mania."

33 **Between 1994 and 2003:** Gardiner Harris and Benedict Carey, "Researchers Fail to Reveal Full Drug Pay," *New York Times*, June 8, 2008, nytimes.com/2008/06/08/us/08conflict.html.

33 **a decade after Anuja:** 154 Cong. Rec. S5029 (daily ed. June 4, 2008) (statement of Sen. Grassley), govinfo.gov/content/pkg/CREC-2008-06-04/pdf/CREC-2008-06-04-pt1-PgS5029-2.pdf#page=1.

33 **$4.2 million from various:** Jeanne Lenzer, "Review Launched after Harvard Psychiatrist Failed to Disclose Industry Funding," *BMJ* 336, no. 7657 (June 14, 2008): 1327, doi.org/10.1136/bmj.39609.364688.DB.

33 **Internal emails revealed:** Georges Garabawi, email to Janet Vergis, February 5, 2002, s.wsj.net/public/resources/documents/WSJ_Risperdal46-47-112408.pdf. This email between Johnson & Johnson employees was included among several internal Johnson & Johnson documents posted on *The Wall Street Journal*'s website in 2008.

Chapter 7: Asylum for the Insane

53 **"We . . . profess to do little":** Samuel Tuke, *Description of the Retreat: An Institution Near York for Insane Persons of the Society of Friends* (York, UK: W. Alexander, 1813), 216–17, books.google.com/books?hl=en&lr=&id=k3cCtMOrFJwC&oi=fnd&pg=PA21&dq=samu el+tuke+description+of+the+retreat&ots=MpEESJiu5J&sig=3IYcM0XvNeN8cShhop1bdi5sFZI#v=onepage&q=samuel%20tuke%20description%20of%20the%20retreat&f=false.

53 **These patients' elite status:** Jack David Pressman, *Last Resort: Psychosurgery and the Limits of Medicine* (Cambridge, UK: Cambridge University Press, 1998), 246.

53 **"Nurses and attendants were instructed":** Pressman, *Last Resort*, 246.

54 **"If it had been your fate":** Pressman, *Last Resort*, 242–43.

54 **Well-to-do clientele:** In addition to Pressman's *Last Resort*, you can learn about McLean Hospital and its history in the following books: Alex Beam, *Gracefully Insane: Life and Death inside America's Premier Mental Hospital* (New York: PublicAffairs, 2001); Lisa Berger and Alexander Vuckovic, *Under Observation: Life inside the McLean Psychiatric Hospital* (New York: Penguin Books, 1995); S. B. Sutton, *Crossroads in Psychiatry: A History of the McLean Hospital* (Washington, D.C.: American Psychiatric Press, 1986); and Edward Shorter, *A History of Psychiatry: From the Era of the Asylum to the Age of Prozac* (New York: John Wiley & Sons, 1997).

54 **nudity, visible urine and feces:** Pressman, *Last Resort*, 247.

54 **freezing water from a fire hose:** Beam, *Gracefully Insane*, 12.

55 **These included pulling teeth:** Beam, *Gracefully Insane*, 74.

55 **McLean administrators were initially:** See Sutton, *Crossroads in Psychiatry*, chapter 8.

55 **insulin coma therapy:** For a personal account of surviving insulin coma therapy at McLean Hospital, see Don Weitz, "Insulin Shock—a Survivor's Account of Psychiatric Torture," 2004, available on the website of Law Project for Psychiatric Rights, psychrights.org/Stories/InsulinShock-A-Survivor-Account.pdf.

55 **Causing seizures by injecting:** Charles F. Read, "Consequences of Metrazol Shock Therapy," *American Journal of Psychiatry* 97, no. 3 (November 1940): 667–76, doi.org/10.1176/ajp.97.3.667.

55 **A primary difference between electroshock:** See Linda Andre, *Doctors of Deception: What They Don't Want You to Know about Shock Treatment* (New Brunswick, NJ: Rutgers University Press, 2009), chapter 9.

56 **Between 1938 and 1954:** Pressman, *Last Resort*, 443.

56 **In 1947 alone:** Beam, *Gracefully Insane*, 87.

56 **about a million people a year:** Kari Ann Leiknes, Lindy Jarosh-von Schweder, and Bjørg Høie, "Contemporary Use and Practice of Electroconvulsive Therapy Worldwide," *Brain and Behavior* 2, no. 3 (May 2012): 283–344, doi.org/10.1002/brb3.37.

56 **100,000 of them:** Vabren Watts, "Psychiatrists Discuss Benefits, Risks of ECT," *Psychiatrics News*, June 15, 2015, doi.org/10.1176/appi.pn.2015.6b16.

56 **In 2016, McLean proudly:** McLean Hospital, "Transcranial Magnetic Stimulation (TMS) Service," n.d., mcleanhospital.org/news/fighting-depression-tms-and-ect-are-sought-after-treatments, accessed May 24, 2024.

56 **"We only perform the surgery":** G. Rees Cosgrove, "Neuroscience, Brain, and Behavior V: Deep Brain Stimulation" (presentation, Meeting of the President's Council on Bioethics, Washington, D.C., June 25, 2004), bioethicsarchive.georgetown.edu/pcbe/transcripts/june04/session6.html.

57 **"So you must look":** Cosgrove, "Neuroscience, Brain, and Behavior."

57 **Besides MGH, other U.S.:** Massachusetts General Hospital, "Neurotherapeutics Program," n.d., massgeneral.org/psychiatry/research/neurotherapeutics-program, accessed May 23, 2024.

57 **Brigham and Women's Hospital:** Brigham and Women's Hospital, "Functional Brain Disorders: Experts in Treating Functional Brain Disorders," n.d., brighamandwomens.org/neuro surgery/functional-brain-disorders, accessed May 23, 2024.

57 **Butler and Rhode Island hospitals:** Butler Hospital, "Psychiatric Neurosurgery Program," n.d., butler.org/psychiatric-neurosurgery-program, accessed May 23, 2024.

57 **Columbia University Irving Medical Center:** Columbia University Irving Medical Center, "Cingulotomy," n.d., neurosurgery.columbia.edu/patient-care/treatments/cingulotomy, accessed May 23, 2024.

57 **In the wake of ice picks:** Juho Joutsa et al., "The Return of the Lesion for Localization and Therapy," *Brain* 146, no. 8 (August 1, 2023): 3146–55, doi.org/10.1093/brain/awad123.

57 **drilling of one or more holes:** See the section on capsulotomy in Butler Hospital, "Psychiatric Neurosurgery Program."

57 **ten-millimeter exposed-tip electrode:** G. Rees Cosgrove, "Surgery for Psychiatric Disorders," *CNS Spectrums* 5, no. 10 (October 2000): 43–52, doi.org/10.1017/S1092852900007665.

57 **"there are notable obstacles":** Jhin Goo Chang, Se Joo Kim, and Chan-Hyung Kim, "Neuroablative Intervention for Refractory Obsessive-Compulsive Disorder," *Psychiatry Investigation* 20, no. 11 (November 25, 2023): 997–1006, doi.org/10.30773/pi.2023.0214.

58 **"focal electrically administered seizure therapy":** Harold A. Sackeim, Therapy device with current adjustment, U.S. Patent 10583288B2, filed September 6, 2017, and issued March 10, 2020, patents.google.com/patent/US10583288B2.

58 **has received decades of funding:** For a 2019 list of Sackeim's reported conflicts of interest, see the "Declaration of Interest" section in Harold A. Sackeim et al., "The Assessment of Resistance to Antidepressant Treatment: Rationale for the Antidepressant Treatment History Form: Short Form (ATHF-SF)," *Journal of Psychiatric Research* 113 (June 2019): 125–36, doi.org/10.1016/j.jpsychires.2019.03.021.

58 **"Our study indicates":** Harold. A. Sackeim et al., "Continuation Pharmacotherapy in the Prevention of Relapse Following Electroconvulsive Therapy: A Randomized Controlled Trial," *JAMA* 285, no. 10 (March 14, 2001): 1299–307, doi.org/10.1001/jama.285.10.1299.

58 **The two medicated groups:** Sackeim et al., "Continuation Pharmacotherapy."

58 **A 2013 meta-analysis:** Ana Jelovac, Erik Kolshus, and Declan M. McLoughlin, "Relapse Following Successful Electroconvulsive Therapy for Major Depression: A Meta-analysis," *Neuropsychopharmacology* 38, no. 12 (November 2013): 2467–74, doi.org/10.1038/npp.2013.149.

59 **Only eleven placebo-controlled trials:** John Read, Irving Kirsch, and Laura McGrath, "Electroconvulsive Therapy for Depression: A Review of the Quality of ECT versus Sham ECT Trials and Meta-analyses," *Ethical Human Psychology and Psychiatry* 21, no. 2 (October 1, 2019): 64–103, doi.org/10.1891/EHPP-D-19-00014.

59 **"Five of these studies":** John Read, "A Response to Yet Another Defence of ECT in the Absence of Robust Efficacy and Safety Evidence," *Epidemiology and Psychiatric Sciences* 31 (February 15, 2022): e13, doi.org/10.1017/S2045796021000846.

59 **"The quality of most SECT-ECT studies":** Read, Kirsch, and McGrath, "Electroconvulsive Therapy for Depression."

60 **Insofar as ECT's safety is concerned:** Andreas Duma et al., "Major Adverse Cardiac Events and Mortality Associated with Electroconvulsive Therapy: A Systematic Review and Meta-analysis," *Anesthesiology* 130, no. 1 (January 2019): 83–91, doi.org/10.1097/ALN.0000000000002488.

60 **"Although clinical trials concluded that":** Diana Rose et al., "Patients' Perspectives on Electroconvulsive Therapy: Systematic Review," *BMJ* 326, no. 7403 (June 19, 2003): 1363, doi.org/10.1136/bmj.326.7403.1363.

60 **Even ECT proponent:** Harold A. Sackeim, "Memory and ECT: From Polarization to Reconciliation," *Journal of ECT* 16, no. 2 (June 2000): 87–96, doi.org/10.1097/00124509-200006000-00001.

60 **He then goes on, however:** Sackeim, "Memory and ECT."

60 **"Some critics would ask":** The American Foundation (chaired by Curtis Bok and led by Esther Everett Lape), *Medical Research: A Midcentury Survey, vol. 2, Unsolved Clinical Problems: In Biological Perspective* (Cambridge, MA: Riverside Press, 1955), 668.

61 **It went on to state that:** The American Foundation, *Medical Research*, 669.

61 **One prominent Columbia University:** The American Foundation, *Medical Research*, 667.

61 **"Things obviously were possible":** Joel Elkes, "Psychopharmacology: On Beginning in a New Science," in *Discoveries in Biological Psychiatry*, ed. Frank J. Ayd Jr. and Barry Blackwell (Philadelphia: J. B. Lippincott, 1970), 33.

61 **In "our own new science":** Elkes, "Psychopharmacology," 48.

61 **"it would seem we are":** Elkes, "Psychopharmacology," 49.

62 **As one founding biological psychiatrist:** Barry Blackwell, "The Process of Discovery," in *Discoveries in Biological Psychiatry*, ed. Frank J. Ayd Jr. and Barry Blackwell (Philadelphia: J. B. Lippincott, 1970), 16.

62 **McLean nearly sold itself:** John F. Baughman, "McLean May Be Leased to For-Profit Company," *Harvard Crimson,* June 5, 1984, thecrimson.com/article/1984/6/5/mclean-may-be -leased-to-for-profit/.

62 **Researchers saw the apathy-inducing:** For more on the birth of biological psychiatry, see Edward Shorter, *A History of Psychiatry: From the Era of the Asylum to the Age of Prozac* (New York: John Wiley & Sons, 1997), and Robert Whitaker, *Mad in America: Bad Science, Bad Medicine, and the Enduring Mistreatment of the Mentally Ill* (Cambridge, MA: Perseus, 2002).

62 **is often credited with bringing:** According to historian Edward Shorter, it was actually a French surgeon named Henri Laborit who first noted a level of "désintéressement," or indifference, in patients on the drug. For more, see Shorter, *History of Psychiatry*, chapter 7.

63 **"after initial trials, specialists":** Pierre Deniker, "Introduction of Neuroleptic Chemotherapy into Psychiatry," in *Discoveries in Biological Psychiatry*, ed. Frank J. Ayd Jr. and Barry Blackwell (Philadelphia: J. B. Lippincott, 1970), 158–59.

63 **"It was found that neuroleptics":** Deniker, "Introduction of Neuroleptic Chemotherapy," 160.

63 **Deniker goes on to say:** Deniker, "Introduction of Neuroleptic Chemotherapy," 161.

63 **"pharmacological substitute for lobotomy":** Heinz E. Lehmann, "Therapeutic Results with Chlorpromazine (Largactil) in Psychiatric Conditions," *Canadian Medical Association Journal* 72 (January 15, 1955): 91–99, ncbi.nlm.nih.gov/pmc/articles/PMC1825483/pdf /canmedaj00701-0018.pdf.

63 **"The most noticeable effect":** Joint Commission on Mental Illness and Health, *Action for Mental Health: Final Report* (New York: John Wiley & Sons, 1961), 39.

63 **1973 passage of the Health Maintenance:** To find the original act, see Human Resources Division of the United States Department of Health, Education, and Welfare, "Implementation of the Health Maintenance Organization Act of 1973, as Amended," March 3, 1978, gao .gov/products/105122#:~:text=The%20Health%20Maintenance%20Organization% 20(HMO,establishment%20and%20expansion%20of%20HMOs.

64 **Whether this has been a successful:** The Commonwealth Fund, "Mirror, Mirror 2021: Reflecting Poorly," August 4, 2021, doi.org/10.26099/01dv-h208.

Chapter 8: Ambien

70 **Of note, Lorex actually included:** See Section 5.1.1 of the November 19, 1991, memorandum from Thomas P. Laughren, MD, included in the "Medical Review(s)" portion of U.S. Food and Drug Administration, "Drug Approval Package: Ambien (zolpidem tartrate) NDA 19908," accessdata.fda.gov/drugsatfda_docs/nda/pre96/019908_s000_ambientoc.cfm.

71 **according to a 2016 paper:** David L. Reed and William P. Sacco, "Measuring Sleep Efficiency: What Should the Denominator Be?," *Journal of Clinical Sleep Medicine* 12, no. 2 (February 15, 2016): 263–66, doi.org/10.5664/jcsm.5498.

71 **The second and third trials:** For more about the single-blind run-in phase, see Howard Mann, "Deception in the Single-Blind Run-in Phase of Clinical Trials," The Hastings Center, February 13, 2016, thehastingscenter.org/irb_article/deception-in-the-single-blind-run-in -phase-of-clinical-trials/.

72 **Researchers in the third trial:** See Section 5.1.2.3.4 of the Laughren memorandum included in the "Medical Review(s)" portion of U.S. Food and Drug Administration, "Drug Approval Package: Ambien."

72 **"Sleep medicines can cause dependence":** See the "Information for Patients Taking Ambien" section in the "Approval Letter(s) & Printed Labeling" portion of U.S. Food and Drug Administration, "Drug Approval Package: Ambien."

72 **When I began Ambien:** Associated Press, "Sleep Pill War Means Late Nights for Ad Makers," *Los Angeles Times*, March 31, 2006, latimes.com/archives/la-xpm-2006-mar-31-fi-ambien31 -story.html.

72 **By 2005, Sanofi-Aventis was making:** Anne Underwood, "Wake-up Call," *Newsweek,* March 15, 2006, newsweek.com/ambien-cost-bad-publicity-106209.

75 **"Patients, their families, and their caregivers":** Eli Lilly and Company, Prozac (fluoxetine capsules) package insert, revised August 2023, accessdata.fda.gov/drugsatfda_docs/label /2023/018936%20s112lbl.pdf.

78 **daytime drowsiness had been:** Sanofi-Aventis, Ambien (zolpidem tartrate) package insert, revised February 2022, accessdata.fda.gov/drugsatfda_docs/label/2022/019908s40s044s047l bl.pdf.

Chapter 9: Provigil

79 **Similar to cocaine and methamphetamine:** Nora D. Volkow et al., "Effects of Modafinil on Dopamine and Dopamine Transporters in the Male Human Brain: Clinical Implications," *JAMA* 301, no. 11 (March 18, 2009): 1148–54, doi.org/10.1001/jama.2009.351.

79 **"improv[ing] wakefulness in patients":** Cephalon Inc., Provigil (modafinil) [FDA-approved draft labeling], December 1998, accessdata.fda.gov/drugsatfda_docs/label/1998/20717lbl.pdf.

79 **two to three minutes longer:** See table 14 in the "Medical Review(s), Part 1" portion of U.S. Food and Drug Administration, "Drug Approval Package: Provigil," accessdata.fda.gov /drugsatfda_docs/nda/98/020717A_Provigil.cfm.

79 **In the one study that tracked:** See the "Total Sleep Time" section in the "Medical Review(s), Part 2" portion of U.S. Food and Drug Administration, "Drug Approval Package: Provigil."

80 **Among the significant percentage:** See Table 2.1-2 in Cephalon Inc., Provigil.

85 **she ate "raw eggs":** Civil Complaint Class-Action, *Makinen v. Sanofi-Synthelabo*, case no. 06civ1762, U.S. District Court, Southern District of New York, filed March 6, 2006, web .archive.org/web/20080907094953/http://www.appellate-brief.com/Ambien/Compl -AmbienClass.pdf. Accessed May 24, 2024.

86 **"A variety of abnormal thinking":** See Section 5.3 of Sanofi-Aventis, Ambien package insert, revised March 2007, accessdata.fda.gov/drugsatfda_docs/label/2007/019908s022lbl .pdf, accessed May 24, 2024.

Chapter 11: The Haven

101 **its own golf course:** Betsy Brown, "Plans for Hospital's Land Stir Debate," *New York Times,* November 27, 1983, nytimes.com/1983/11/27/nyregion/plans-for-hospital-s-land-stir-debate.html.

Chapter 12: Panopticon

110 **"full lighting and the eye":** Michel Foucault, *Discipline and Punish: The Birth of the Prison,* trans. Alan Sheridan, 2nd Vintage Books ed. (1975; repr., New York: Vintage Books, 1995), 200.

111 **the "tranquil prison":** Erick Fabris, *Tranquil Prisons: Mad Peoples Experiences of Chemical Incarceration under Community Treatment Orders* (Toronto: University of Toronto Press, 2011), doi.org/10.3138/9781442696884.

Chapter 13: Medical Nemesis

118 **"the negative feedback":** Ivan Illich, *Limits to Medicine: Medical Nemesis, the Expropriation of Health,* updated ed. (London and New York: Marion Boyars, 2002), 275.

Chapter 14: The Motions of Living

125 **around 70 percent of electroshock recipients:** Samuel T. Wilkinson et al., "Identifying Recipients of Electroconvulsive Therapy: Data from Privately Insured Americans," *Psychiatric Services* 69, no. 5 (May 1, 2018): 542–48, doi.org/10.1176/appi.ps.201700364.

Chapter 15: The Anatomy of Treatment Resistance

129 **"There is now no doubt":** Beverly T. Mead, Robert B. Ellsworth, and John O. Grimmett, "The Treatment of Drug-Resistive Chronic Schizophrenics," *Journal of Nervous and Mental Disease* 127, no. 4 (October 1958): 351–58, journals.lww.com/jonmd/Citation/1958/10000 /THE_TREATMENT_OF_DRUG_RESISTIVE_CHRONIC.6.aspx.

129 **"one of the founders":** "Harold Sackeim, PhD," Columbia University Department of Psychiatry, n.d., web.archive.org/web/20220123212837/https://www.columbiapsychiatry.org/profile /harold-sackeim-phd, accessed May 24, 2024.

129 **"Treatment-resistant depression is a major":** H. A. Sackeim, "The Definition and Meaning of Treatment-Resistant Depression," *Journal of Clinical Psychiatry* 62, no. S16 (2001): 10–17, pubmed.ncbi.nlm.nih.gov/11480879/.

129 **nearly 39 million American:** To make this calculation, I looked at the U.S. Medical Expenditure Panel Survey for 2020, which I located in the following post on X (formerly Twitter) by clinical psychologist Martin Plöderl: Martin Plöderl (@PloederlM), "Antidepressant prescription by age, US, data from the Medical Expenditure Panel Survey, year 2020 (just released). Plateauing among adults and adolescents, record levels for young adults. Nearly 15% of adults are on antidepressants, drugs with poor efficacy for most," Twitter, September 6, 2022, 12:55 p.m., twitter .com/PloederlM/status/1567239996980994048/photo/1. I then tracked down U.S. Census Bureau 2020 data here: U.S. Census Bureau, "Population under Age 18 Declined Last Decade," August 21, 2021, census.gov/library/stories/2021/08/united-states-adult-population-grew-faster -than-nations-total-population-from-2010-to-2020.html. Finally, I calculated 15 percent of the total number of U.S. adults in 2020 through that census and arrived at 38,751,492.2.

130 **"only between 20% and 40% of patients":** Sackeim, "Definition and Meaning of Treatment-Resistant Depression."

130 **Sackeim received over $5 million:** To calculate this total, I tallied up the monetary amounts of all listed NIMH grants that Sackeim received beginning in 2000 (no monetary amounts were provided for the previous grants going back to 1986) by visiting Grantome and searching "@author Harold Sackeim" (grantome.com/search?q=@author%20%20Harold%20Sackeim, accessed May 24, 2024).

130 **in the conflicts of interest section:** Harold A. Sackeim, "Modern Electroconvulsive Therapy: Vastly Improved Yet Greatly Underused," *JAMA Psychiatry* 74, no. 8 (August 1, 2017): 779–80, doi.org/10.1001/jamapsychiatry.2017.1670.

130 **"Even though a plethora":** Lucie Bartova et al., "Combining Psychopharmacotherapy and Psychotherapy Is Not Associated with Better Treatment Outcome in Major Depressive Disorder—Evidence from the European Group for the Study of Resistant Depression," *Journal of Psychiatric Research* 141 (September 1, 2021): 167–75, doi.org/10.1016/j.jpsychires.2021.06.028.

132 **the many reported adverse effects:** John Read and James Williams, "Adverse Effects of Antidepressants Reported by a Large International Cohort: Emotional Blunting, Suicidality, and Withdrawal Effects," *Current Drug Safety* 13, no. 3 (2018): 176–86, doi.org/10.2174/157488 6313666180605095130.

Chapter 18: Lithium

153 **"Those who have experimented with guinea pigs":** John F. J. Cade, "The Story of Lithium," in *Discoveries in Biological Psychiatry*, ed. Frank J. Ayd Jr. and Barry Blackwell (Philadelphia: J. B. Lippincott, 1970), 223.

153 **"mischievous and interfering":** J. F. Cade, "Lithium Salts in the Treatment of Psychotic Excitement. 1949," *Bulletin of the World Health Organization* 78, no. 4 (2000): 519, ncbi.nlm .nih.gov/pmc/articles/PMC2560740/.

153 **"There is no doubt that":** Cade, "Lithium Salts," 520.

153 **But this declaration was just part:** Walter Armin Brown, *Lithium: A Doctor, a Drug, and a Breakthrough* (New York: Liveright, 2019), 77–79.

154 **Half a year before Cade:** Robert Whitaker, *Anatomy of an Epidemic: Magic Bullets, Psychiatric Drugs, and the Astonishing Rise of Mental Illness in America* (New York: Crown, 2010), 183.

154 **"One can hardly imagine":** Cade, "Story of Lithium," 219.

154 **"Stop using this dangerous poison":** "Salt Substitute Kills 4, AMA Says; Food and Drug Administration Warns Lithium Chloride Is a 'Dangerous Poison,'" *New York Times*, February 19, 1949, timesmachine.nytimes.com/timesmachine/1949/02/19/86767583.html.

154 **"The lithium level necessary":** C. H. Noack and E. M. Trautner, "The Lithium Treatment of Maniacal Psychosis," *Medical Journal of Australia* 2, no. 7 (August 1951): 220, doi.org/10.5694 /j.1326-5377.1951.tb68249.x.

154 **"Most . . . resemble those of Addison's":** Noack and Trautner, "Lithium Treatment of Maniacal Psychosis," 220.

155 **the "mischievous" WB had died:** Brown, *Lithium*, 79–80.

155 **In 1952, when Cade took over:** Brown, *Lithium*, 95.

155 **"We will never know":** Brown, *Lithium*, 80–81.

155 **"early detection of toxicity":** P. K. Newman and M. Saunders, "Lithium Neurotoxicity," *Postgraduate Medical Journal* 55 (October 1979): 701–3, ncbi.nlm.nih.gov/pmc/articles/PMC24 25735/pdf/postmedj00250-0004.pdf.

155 **The International Society for Bipolar Disorders:** Felicity Ng et al., "The International Society for Bipolar Disorders (ISBD) Consensus Guidelines for the Safety Monitoring of Bipolar

Disorder Treatments," *Bipolar Disorders* 11, no. 6 (September 2009): 559–95, doi.org/10.11
11/j.1399-5618.2009.00737.x.

156 **growing pressure from lobbyists:** For more on the history of lithium in the United States, see Edward Shorter, "The History of Lithium Therapy," *Bipolar Disorders* 11, no. S2 (June 2009): 4–9, doi.org/10.1111/j.1399-5618.2009.00706.x.

156 **Ward staff tracked mania levels:** M. Schou et al., "The Treatment of Manic Psychoses by the Administration of Lithium Salts," *Journal of Neurology, Neurosurgery, and Psychiatry* 17, no. 4 (November 1954): 250–60, doi.org/10.1136/jnnp.17.4.250.

156 **FDA expanded lithium's approved uses:** Brown, *Lithium*, 145.

156 **One study split fifty patients:** P. C. Baastrup et al., "Prophylactic Lithium: Double Blind Discontinuation in Manic-Depressive and Recurrent-Depressive Disorders," *Lancet* 296, no. 7668 (August 1970): 326–30, doi.org/10.1016/S0140-6736(70)92870-9.

157 **"there was no indication":** Baastrup et al., "Prophylactic Lithium," 329.

157 **financial ties to more than fifteen:** See the "Conflict of Interest" section of Mark J. Millan et al., "Learning from the Past and Looking to the Future: Emerging Perspectives for Improving the Treatment of Psychiatric Disorders," *European Neuropsychopharmacology* 25, no. 5 (May 1, 2015): 599–656, doi.org/10.1016/j.euroneuro.2015.01.016.

157 **"Frank manic symptoms":** Guy M. Goodwin, "Recurrence of Mania after Lithium Withdrawal: Implications for the Use of Lithium in the Treatment of Bipolar Affective Disorder," *British Journal of Psychiatry* 164, no. 2 (February 1994): 149–52, doi.org/10.1192/bjp.164.2.149.

157 **That same Oxford bipolar researcher:** Goodwin, "Recurrence of Mania after Lithium Withdrawal," 149.

157 **American Psychiatric Association's current Practice Guideline:** American Psychiatric Association, "Practice Guideline for the Treatment of Patients with Bipolar Disorder," 2nd ed., originally published April 2002, updated 2010, psychiatryonline.org/pb/assets/raw /sitewide/practice_guidelines/guidelines/bipolar.pdf, psychiatry.org/psychiatrists/practice /clinical-practice-guidelines.

158 **"offer lithium as a first-line":** See Section 1.7.5 of National Institute for Health and Care Excellence, "Bipolar Disorder: Assessment and Management," published September 24, 2014, updated December 21, 2023, nice.org.uk/guidance/cg185/resources/bipolar-disorder-assessment -and-management-pdf-35109814379461.

158 **"I will be riding on top":** Jaime Lowe, "'I Don't Believe in God, but I Believe in Lithium,'" *New York Times Magazine*, June 25, 2015, nytimes.com/2015/06/28/magazine/i-dont-believe -in-god-but-i-believe-in-lithium.html.

158 **After seven years of doing well:** Lowe, "'I Don't Believe in God.'"

158 **"In my view":** Joanna Moncrieff, "Reasons Not to Believe in Lithium," *Joanna Moncrieff* (blog), July 1, 2015, joannamoncrieff.com/2015/07/01/reasons-not-to-believe-in-lithium/.

Chapter 22: The Father of BPD

190 **"Borderline personality disorder has long been":** This quote comes from a book endorsement by Glen O. Gabbard, MD, on the description page for Lois W. Choi-Kain, John G. Gunderson, and American Psychiatric Association Publishing, eds., *Applications of Good Psychiatric Management for Borderline Personality Disorder: A Practical Guide* (Washington, D.C.: American Psychiatric Association Publishing, 2019), appi.org/Products/Personality -Disorders/Applications-of-Good-Psychiatric-Management-for-Bo?sku=37225&filters =814f13cb-de43-4409-be03-8b899792c48e.

190 **borderline referrals as a "no-no":** Jacqueline Simon Gunn and Brent Potter, "The Scarlet Label: Close Encounters with 'Borderline Personality Disorder,'" *Mad in America*, October 22, 2014, madinamerica.com/2014/10/scarlet-label-close-encounters-borderline-personality-disorder/.

190 **"borderline has become the most pejorative":** Dana Becker, "When She Was Bad: Borderline Personality Disorder in a Posttraumatic Age," *American Journal of Orthopsychiatry* 70, no. 4 (2000): 422–32, doi.org/10.1037/h0087769.

191 **"With few exceptions, most researchers":** Randy A. Sansone and Lori A. Sansone, "Responses of Mental Health Clinicians to Patients with Borderline Personality Disorder," *Innovations in Clinical Neuroscience* 10, no. 5–6 (2013): 39–43, ncbi.nlm.nih.gov/pmc/articles /PMC3719460/pdf/icns_10_5-6_39.pdf.

192 **Gunderson and a colleague were the first:** Benedict Carey, "Dr. John Gunderson, 76, Dies; Defined Borderline Personality Disorder," *New York Times*, February 8, 2019, nytimes.com /2019/02/08/obituaries/dr-john-gunderson-dead.html.

193 **"After a woman has conscientiously"**: Paula J. Caplan, "Gender Issues in the Diagnosis of Mental Disorder," *Women & Therapy* 12, no. 4 (December 1992): 71–82, doi.org/10.1300 /J015v12n04_07.

193 **In ancient Egypt and Greece**: Cecilia Tasca et al., "Women and Hysteria in the History of Mental Health," *Clinical Practice and Epidemiology in Mental Health* 8 (October 19, 2012): 110–19, doi.org/10.2174/1745017901208010110.

193 **Aretaeus of Cappadocia**: Aretaeus, *De causis et signis acutorum morborum (lib. 1)*, in *The Extant Works of Aretaeus, the Cappadocian*, ed. Francis Adams, LLD (1856; repr., Boston: Milford House, 1972), book 2, chapter 11, "On Hysterical Suffocation," data.perseus.org /citations/urn:cts:greekLit:tlg0719.tlg001.perseus-eng1:2.11.

193 **"sent me home with solemn advice"**: Charlotte Perkins Gilman, "Why I Wrote *The Yellow Wallpaper*," *The Forerunner*, October 1913, available at ic.media.mit.edu/people/davet/yp /whyiwrote.html.

194 **"chronic anger/frequent angry acts"**: M. C. Zanarini et al., "Discriminating Borderline Personality Disorder from Other Axis II Disorders," *American Journal of Psychiatry* 147, no. 2 (1990): 161–67, doi:10.1176/ajp.147.2.161.

194 **Today, 75 percent of borderline diagnoses**: Andrew E. Skodol and Donna S. Bender, "Why Are Women Diagnosed Borderline More Than Men?," *Psychiatric Quarterly* 74, no. 4 (2003): 349–60, doi.org/10.1023/a:1026087410516.

194 **It's been reported that up to 90 percent**: Paola Bozzatello et al., "The Role of Trauma in Early Onset Borderline Personality Disorder: A Biopsychosocial Perspective," *Frontiers in Psychiatry* 12 (September 23, 2021): 721361, doi.org/10.3389/fpsyt.2021.721361.

Chapter 24: Iatrogenic Process

208 **The 2007 psychiatric disability rate**: Robert Whitaker, *Anatomy of an Epidemic: Magic Bullets, Psychiatric Drugs, and the Astonishing Rise of Mental Illness in America* (New York: Crown, 2010), 6. In a November 2021 email exchange, Robert Whitaker informed me that by 2019, almost a decade after *Anatomy of an Epidemic's* publication, the psychiatric disability rate was up to 1 in every 70 Americans, or 4.67 million American adults. As for children, in 1987, there were 16,600 on disability due to a psychiatric diagnosis; in 2020, there were 717,907. Of the total of all kids on government disability, the percentage of those receiving payments for psychiatric reasons increased from 5 percent in 1987 to 65 percent in 2020.

210 **"It was fabulous"**: Whitaker, *Anatomy of an Epidemic*, 30.

210 **"If you expand the boundaries"**: Whitaker, *Anatomy of an Epidemic*, 30.

211 **I looked it up and saw**: *New Oxford American Dictionary*, 3rd ed. (2010), s.v. "iatrogenic."

Chapter 26: Wellness Check

221 **One study published**: Randy A. Sansone, R. Jordan Bohinc, and Michael W. Wiederman, "Borderline Personality Symptomatology and Compliance with General Health Care among Internal Medicine Outpatients," *International Journal of Psychiatry in Clinical Practice* 19, no. 2 (June 2015): 132–36, doi.org/10.3109/13651501.2014.988269.

Chapter 28: Pharmaceutical Trauma

238 **Serotonin also plays a crucial role**: Miles Berger, John A. Gray, and Bryan L. Roth, "The Expanded Biology of Serotonin," *Annual Review of Medicine* 60 (2009): 355–66, doi.org /10.1146/annurev.med.60.042307.110802.

238 **In other words, repeated use**: For further reading on antidepressants and withdrawal, please see Emilia G. Palmer et al., "Withdrawing from SSRI Antidepressants: Advice for Primary Care," *British Journal of General Practice* 73, no. 728 (March 1, 2023): 138–40, doi.org /10.3399/bjgp23X732273; Mark Abie Horowitz et al., "Estimating Risk of Antidepressant Withdrawal from a Review of Published Data," *CNS Drugs* 37, no. 2 (February 1, 2023): 143–57, doi.org/10.1007/s40263-022-00960-y; Jim Van Os and Peter C. Groot, "Outcomes of Hyperbolic Tapering of Antidepressants," *Therapeutic Advances in Psychopharmacology* 13 (January 2023): 204512532311715, doi.org/10.1177/20451253231171518.

239 **A 2022 survey of nearly**: John Read, "The Experiences of 585 People When They Tried to Withdraw from Antipsychotic Drugs," *Addictive Behaviors Reports* 15 (March 17, 2022): 100421, doi.org/10.1016/j.abrep.2022.100421.

239 **studies relevant to antidepressant withdrawal:** Researchers have also observed antidepressant withdrawal symptoms in a significant percentage of babies born to SSRI-taking mothers. For more, see C. Gastaldon et al., "Neonatal Withdrawal Syndrome Following In Utero Exposure to Antidepressants: A Disproportionality Analysis of VigiBase, the WHO Spontaneous Reporting Database," *Psychological Medicine* 53, no. 12 (2023): 5645–53, doi .org/10.1017/S0033291722002859; Rachel Levinson-Castiel et al., "Neonatal Abstinence Syndrome after In Utero Exposure to Selective Serotonin Reuptake Inhibitors in Term Infants," *Archives of Pediatrics & Adolescent Medicine* 160, no. 2 (February 1, 2006): 173, doi.org /10.1001/archpedi.160.2.173; Silvia Corti et al., "Neonatal Outcomes in Maternal Depression in Relation to Intrauterine Drug Exposure," *Frontiers in Pediatrics* 7 (July 26, 2019): 309, doi .org/10.3389/fped.2019.00309.

239 **"We recommend that U.K.":** James Davies and John Read, "A Systematic Review into the Incidence, Severity and Duration of Antidepressant Withdrawal Effects: Are Guidelines Evidence-Based?," *Addictive Behaviors* 97 (October 2019): 111–21, doi.org/10.1016/j .addbeh.2018.08.027.

242 **If you imagine the gentle downward slope:** To learn more about tapering off psychiatric drugs, please visit Inner Compass Initiative at www.theinnercompass.org.

243 **2022 paper in *Molecular Psychiatry*:** Anders Sørensen, Henricus G. Ruhé, and Klaus Munkholm, "The Relationship between Dose and Serotonin Transporter Occupancy of Antidepressants—a Systematic Review," *Molecular Psychiatry* 27, no. 1 (January 2022): 192–201, doi.org/10.1038/s41380-021-01285-w.

243 **the UK's professional psychiatric guild organization:** Royal College of Psychiatrists, "Stopping Antidepressants," March 2024, www.rcpsych.ac.uk/mental-health/treatments -and-wellbeing/stopping-antidepressants.

244 **On r/AskReddit, over six hundred:** LightyearKissthesky9, "How bad was your SSRI withdrawal?," 2023, Reddit, reddit.com/r/AskReddit/comments/14y6zzt/how_bad_was_your _ssri_withdrawal/.

245 **After scanning the literature:** Mark Abie Horowitz et al., "Estimating Risk of Antidepressant Withdrawal from a Review of Published Data," *CNS Drugs* 37, no. 2 (February 2023): 143–57, doi.org/10.1007/s40263-022-00960-y.

246 **withdrawal is called "discontinuation syndrome":** Ivana Massabki and Elia Abi-Jaoude, "Selective Serotonin Reuptake Inhibitor 'Discontinuation Syndrome' or Withdrawal," *British Journal of Psychiatry* 218, no. 3 (March 2021): 168–71, doi.org/10.1192/bjp.2019.269.

Chapter 29: Dear Mr. Whitaker

254 **what those pills had taken:** Not a day goes by in which I don't count my blessings that I regained sexual function so quickly. Many people aren't so lucky, and a growing body of research indicates that for a small but significant percentage of people, post-SSRI sexual dysfunction (PSSD) may be irreversible. To learn more, visit PSSD Network here: pssdnetwork.org.

Chapter 30: My Healing

259 **sued its manufacturer, Johnson & Johnson:** Jonathan Stempel, "Judge Slashes $8 Billion Risperdal Award against Johnson & Johnson to $6.8 Million," Reuters, January 17, 2020, reuters.com/article/idUSKBN1ZG292/; *Murray v. Janssen Pharmaceuticals*, 180 A.3d 1235 (Pa. Super. 2018), caselaw.findlaw.com/court/pa-superior-court/1889831.html.

259 **J&J had settled nearly nine thousand:** Reuters, "J&J Settles Most Risperdal Lawsuits, with $800 Million in Expenses," November 1, 2021, reuters.com/business/healthcare -pharmaceuticals/jj-settles-most-risperdal-lawsuits-with-800-million-expenses-2021-10-30/.

259 **"If there is a meaning":** Viktor E. Frankl, *Man's Search for Meaning* (1946; repr., New York: Washington Square Press/Pocket Books, 1985), 88.

260 **"The true meaning of life":** Frankl, *Man's Search for Meaning*, 133.

Chapter 31: Peer Support

261 **"puts wealth, property, and power":** Judi Chamberlin, *On Our Own: Patient-Controlled Alternatives to the Mental Health System* (New York: McGraw-Hill, 1979), 7.

261 **"When the emphasis is on":** Chamberlin, *On Our Own*, 7.

263 **activist named Leonard Roy Frank:** A comprehensive archive of Leonard Roy Frank's writing is available at psychiatrized.org/LeonardRoyFrank/FromTheFilesOfLeonardRoyFrank.htm.

263 **"When you lock someone up":** Terry Messman, "Electroconvulsive Brainwashing: The Odyssey of Leonard Roy Frank," *Street Spirit*, July 2003, freedom-center.org/pdf/leonardroy frankstreetspirit.pdf.

264 **Around 1.2 million Americans:** Rob Wipond, "Opinion: California Wants More Psychiatric Detentions. That's Unlikely to Improve Anyone's Mental Health," *Los Angeles Times*, May 1, 2023, latimes.com/opinion/story/2023-05-01/mental-health-california-us-homelessness-psychiatric -detentions.

264 **"It must be stressed":** "Report of the Special Rapporteur on Torture and Other Cruel, Inhuman or Degrading Treatment of Punishment" (A/HRC/43/49, Human Rights Council, 43rd session, February 14, 2020), paragraph 37, ohchr.org/EN/HRBodies/HRC/RegularSessions /Session43/Documents/A_HRC_43_49_AUV.docx.

Chapter 34: Critical Thinking

280 **According to OpenSecrets:** "Industry Profile: Pharmaceuticals/Health Products, 2023," OpenSecrets, n.d., opensecrets.org/federal-lobbying/industries/summary?cycle=2023&id=H04, accessed May 25, 2024.

280 **For reference, the next-biggest:** OpenSecrets, "Industry Profile: Electronics Mfg & Equip, 2023," n.d., opensecrets.org/federal-lobbying/industries/summary?cycle=2023&id=B12, accessed May 25, 2024.

280 **And the broader health sector:** OpenSecrets, "Industry Profile: Electronics Mfg & Equip, 2023," n.d., opensecrets.org/federal-lobbying/sectors/summary?cycle=2023&id=H, accessed May 25, 2024.

280 **"We estimate the global":** McKinsey & Company, "Feeling Good: The Future of the $1.5 Trillion Wellness Market," April 8, 2021, mckinsey.com/industries/consumer-packaged -goods/our-insights/feeling-good-the-future-of-the-1-5-trillion-wellness-market.

281 **"When we hear the words":** Bruce E. Levine, *Commonsense Rebellion: Taking Back Your Life from Drugs, Shrinks, Corporations, and a World Gone Crazy* (New York and London: Continuum, 2003), 3.

281 **The American Psychiatric Association didn't eliminate:** American Psychiatric Association, "Homosexuality and Sexual Orientation Disturbance: Proposed Change in DSM-II, 6th Printing, Page 44, Position Statement (Retired)," 1973, APA Document Reference No. 730008, pages.uoregon.edu/eherman/teaching/texts/DSM-II_Homosexuality_Revision.pdf.

282 **"Sexual orientation disturbance (homosexuality)":** Jack Drescher, "Out of DSM: Depathologizing Homosexuality," *Behavioral Sciences* 5, no. 4 (December 4, 2015): 565–75, doi .org/10.3390/bs5040565.

282 **one in every three kids:** American Academy of Pediatrics, "Children in Foster Care Much More Likely to Be Prescribed Psychotropic Medications Compared with Non-foster Children in Medicaid Program," news release, October 7, 2021, aap.org/en/news-room/news-releases /aap/2021/children-in-foster-care-much-more-likely-to-be-prescribed-psychotropic -medications-compared-with-non-foster-children-in-medicaid-program/.

282 **In 2013, the American Psychiatric Association:** Ronald Pies, "The Bereavement Exclusion and DSM-5: An Update and Commentary," *Innovations in Clinical Neuroscience* 11, no. 7–8 (2014): 19–22, ncbi.nlm.nih.gov/pmc/articles/PMC4204469/.

282 **"prolonged grief disorder":** American Psychiatric Association, "Prolonged Grief Disorder," May 2022, psychiatry.org/patients-families/prolonged-grief-disorder.

282 **One in every four boys:** Amy R. Board et al., "Trends in Stimulant Dispensing by Age, Sex, State of Residence, and Prescriber Specialty—United States, 2014–2019," *Drug and Alcohol Dependence* 217 (December 1, 2020): 108297, doi.org/10.1016/j.drugalcdep.2020.108297.

282 **Between 2016 and 2022:** Kao-Ping Chua et al., "Antidepressant Dispensing to US Adolescents and Young Adults: 2016–2022," *Pediatrics* 153, no. 3 (March 1, 2024): e2023064245, doi.org/10.1542/peds.2023-064245.

282 **According to the CDC:** Centers for Disease Control and Prevention, "U.S. Teen Girls Experiencing Increased Sadness and Violence," press release, February 13, 2023, cdc.gov/media /releases/2023/p0213-yrbs.html. The survey can be directly accessed here: cdc.gov/healthy youth/data/yrbs/pdf/YRBS_Data-Summary-Trends_Report2023_508.pdf.

282 **A November 2023 Gallup survey:** Jonathan Rothwell, "Teens Spend Average of 4.8 Hours on Social Media per Day," *Gallup*, October 13, 2023, news.gallup.com/poll/512576/teens -spend-average-hours-social-media-per-day.aspx.

NOTES 336

284 **"social iatrogenesis is at work":** Ivan Illich, *Limits to Medicine: Medical Nemesis, the Expropriation of Health,* updated ed. (London and New York: Marion Boyars, 2002), 41.

284 **American Psychiatric Association news release:** American Psychiatric Association, "Statement by David Kupfer, MD, Chair of DSM-5 Task Force Discusses Future of Mental Health Research," Release No. 13-33, May 3, 2013, available at theinnercompass.org /sites/default/files/2017-01/Statement%20on%20the%20Lack%20of%20Biological %20Markers%20for%20Diagnoses%20from%20DSM-5%20Chair%20David%20 Kupfer.pdf.

285 **"We suggest it is time":** Joanna Moncrieff et al., "The Serotonin Theory of Depression: A Systematic Umbrella Review of the Evidence," *Molecular Psychiatry* 28, no. 8 (August 2023): 3243–56, doi.org/10.1038/s41380-022-01661-0.

285 **Ronald W. Pies:** George Dawson and Ronald W. Pies, "An 'Urban Legend' Remains an 'Urban Legend,'" *SSM—Mental Health* 2 (December 1, 2022): 100133, doi.org /10.1016/j.ssmmh.2022.100133.

285 **the findings of a comprehensive analysis:** Benjamin Ang, Mark Horowitz, and Joanna Moncrieff, "Is the Chemical Imbalance an 'Urban Legend'? An Exploration of the Status of the Serotonin Theory of Depression in the Scientific Literature," *SSM—Mental Health* 2 (December 1, 2022): 100098, doi.org/10.1016/j.ssmmh.2022.100098.

286 **"In the light of the interests":** Ang, Horowitz, and Moncrieff, "Is the Chemical Imbalance an 'Urban Legend'?"

286 **as of 2024, not a single:** For a thorough examination of the scientific validity of the genetic explanation for psychiatric diagnoses, see Jay Joseph, *The Gene Illusion: Genetic Research in Psychiatry and Psychology under the Microscope* (New York: Algora, 2004).

286 **"It is sobering to acknowledge":** Matthew M. Nour, Yunzhe Liu, and Raymond J. Dolan, "Functional Neuroimaging in Psychiatry and the Case for Failing Better," *Neuron* 110, no. 16 (August 2022): 2524–44, doi.org/10.1016/j.neuron.2022.07.005.

287 **In one American survey, 92 percent:** Christopher M. France, Paul H. Lysaker, and Ryan P. Robinson, "The 'Chemical Imbalance' Explanation for Depression: Origins, Lay Endorsement, and Clinical Implications," *Professional Psychology: Research and Practice* 38, no. 4 (August 2007): 411–20, doi.org/10.1037/0735-7028.38.4.411.

287 **Who can forget:** Pfizer, Zoloft advertisement (Burbank, CA: NBC 2004), quoted in Ang, Horowitz, and Moncrieff, "Is the Chemical Imbalance an 'Urban Legend'?"

287 **In 2022, drug companies spent:** Ben Adams, "The Top 10 Pharma Drug Ad Spenders for 2022," *Fierce Pharma,* May 1, 2023, fiercepharma.com/special-reports/top-10-pharma-drug -brand-ad-spenders-2022.

287 **In 2013, *The New York Times*:** Pam Belluck and Benedict Carey, "Psychiatry's Guide Is Out of Touch with Science, Experts Say," *New York Times,* May 7, 2013, nytimes.com/2013/05/07 /health/psychiatrys-new-guide-falls-short-experts-say.html.

287 **"While DSM has been described":** Thomas Insel, "Transforming Diagnosis," National Institute of Mental Health, April 29, 2013, web.archive.org/web/20210509074446/https://www .nimh.nih.gov/about/directors/thomas-insel/blog/2013/transforming-diagnosis.

288 **the 170 DSM-IV Work Group members:** Lisa Cosgrove et al., "Financial Ties between DSM-IV Panel Members and the Pharmaceutical Industry," *Psychotherapy and Psychosomatics* 75, no. 3 (2006): 154–60, doi.org/10.1159/000091772.

288 **Little has changed since then:** Lisa Cosgrove and Sheldon Krimsky, "A Comparison of DSM-IV and DSM-5 Panel Members' Financial Associations with Industry: A Pernicious Problem Persists," *PLoS Medicine* 9, no. 3 (March 13, 2012): e1001190, doi.org/10.1371 /journal.pmed.1001190.

288 **calls this the disease-centered model:** Joanna Moncrieff, "Models of Drug Action," *Joanna Moncrieff* (blog), November 21, 2013, joannamoncrieff.com/2013/11/21/models-of-drug -action/.

288 **"Psychiatry adopted the disease-centred":** Joanna Moncrieff, *A Straight Talking Introduction to Psychiatric Drugs,* Straight Talking Introductions to Mental Health Problems (Rosson-Wye, UK: PCCS Books, 2009), 14.

289 **"In psychiatry, an accepted example":** Moncrieff, *A Straight Talking Introduction,* 13.

289 **In other words, a more accurate:** For a comprehensive explanation of the drug-centered versus disease-centered models for understanding psychiatric drugs, and for a broader overview of the scientific validity of psychiatry's medical model of mental illness, see Joanna Moncrieff, *The Myth of the Chemical Cure: A Critique of Psychiatric Drug Treatment,* rev. ed. (Basingstoke, UK: Palgrave Macmillan, 2009).

289 **More than 80 percent:** Thomas J. Moore and Donald R. Mattison, "Adult Utilization of Psychiatric Drugs and Differences by Sex, Age, and Race," *JAMA Internal Medicine* 177, no. 2 (February 1, 2017): 274–75, doi.org/10.1001/jamainternmed.2016.7507.

289 **nearly 59 million U.S. adults:** I came to this total by referring to the U.S. Centers for Disease Control and Prevention (CDC) and National Center for Health Statistics (NCHS) Household Pulse Survey conducted between 2020 and 2022, which calculated that 23.1 percent of U.S. adults were on psychiatric medications as of April 27–May 9, 2022. (According to the U.S. Census Bureau, the adult population in 2022 was 255.3 million; 23.1 percent of 259.6 million is nearly 59 million.) Next I referred to the NCHS Data Brief on the number of U.S. children on psychiatric medications as of 2021, according to a CDC and NCHS National Health Interview Survey, which found that 8.2 percent of children aged five through seventeen had received medication in the previous twelve months. (According to the U.S. Census Bureau, the youth population—ages zero through seventeen—in 2021 was 72.8 million; 8.2 percent of 72.8 million is nearly 6 million.) Combining the figures for adults and children equals nearly 65 million Americans taking psychiatric drugs. My CDC/NCHS sources for these calculations: National Center for Health Statistics and U.S. Census Bureau, "Household Pulse Survey, 2020–2022, Mental Health Care," generated interactively on May 25, 2024, cdc.gov /nchs/covid19/pulse/mental-health-care.htm; Brian Zablotsky and Amanda Ng, "Mental Health Treatment among Children Aged 5–17 Years: United States, 2021," *NCHS Data Brief* 472 (2023):1–8, pubmed.ncbi.nlm.nih.gov/37314377/.

290 **In actuality, the length:** Center for Drug Evaluation and Research, "Major Depressive Disorder: Developing Drugs for Treatment, Guidance for Industry," draft guidance, June 2018, fda.gov/media/113988/download; Center for Drug Evaluation and Research, "Improving the Design of Clinical Trials of Drugs to Treat Schizophrenia," *U.S. Food and Drug Administration*, November 10, 2020, fda.gov/drugs/regulatory-science-action/improving -design-clinical-trials-drugs-treat-schizophrenia; Andrea Cipriani et al., "Comparative Efficacy and Acceptability of 21 Antidepressant Drugs for the Acute Treatment of Adults with Major Depressive Disorder: A Systematic Review and Network Meta-analysis," *Lancet* 391, no. 10128 (April 2018): 1357–66, doi.org/10.1016/S0140-6736(17)32802-7.

290 **Take Effexor, an antidepressant:** Wyeth Pharmaceuticals, Effexor (venlafaxine hydrochloride) package insert, December 2012, accessdata.fda.gov/drugsatfda_docs/label/2008 /020151s051lbl.pdf.

290 **Or Lexapro, another antidepressant:** AbbVie, Lexapro (escitalopram) package insert, revised October 2023, accessdata.fda.gov/drugsatfda_docs/label/2024/021323s058lbl.pdf.

290 **Its sole approved psychiatric use:** GlaxoSmithKline, Lamictal (lamotrigine) package insert, revised March 2015, accessdata.fda.gov/drugsatfda_docs/label/2015/020241s045s051lbl.pdf.

291 **"There is no body of evidence":** Cheplapharm, Klonopin (clonazepam) package insert, revised January 21, 2023, accessdata.fda.gov/drugsatfda_docs/label/2023/017533s062lbl.pdf.

291 **"the continued use of benzodiazepines":** Cheplapharm, Klonopin (clonazepam) package insert, 1.

291 **The World Health Organization explains:** Nancy H. Liu et al., "Excess Mortality in Persons with Severe Mental Disorders: A Multilevel Intervention Framework and Priorities for Clinical Practice, Policy and Research Agendas," *World Psychiatry* 16, no. 1 (February 2017): 30–40, doi.org/10.1002/wps.20384; Liselotte D. De Mooij et al., "Dying Too Soon: Excess Mortality in Severe Mental Illness," *Frontiers in Psychiatry* 10 (December 6, 2019): 855, doi .org/10.3389/fpsyt.2019.00855.

292 **consumer organizations like:** Senator Charles E. Grassley to Michael J. Fitzpatrick, executive director of the National Alliance on Mental Illness, and Anand Pandya, board president of the National Alliance on Mental Illness, April 6, 2009, grassley.senate.gov/imo/media/doc /NAMI.pdf. In the letter, Grassley requests an "accounting of industry funding that pharmaceutical companies or foundations established by these companies have provided to the National Alliance on Mental Illness (NAMI)."

292 **stigma and discrimination are a big part:** Katherine Ponte, "The Many Forms of Mental Illness Discrimination," National Alliance on Mental Illness, March 11, 2020, nami.org/Blogs /NAMI-Blog/March-2020/The-Many-Forms-of-Mental-Illness-Discrimination.

Chapter 36: Goodbye, Dr. Weinberg

302 **"It's such a hard thing":** *Going Clear: Scientology and the Prison of Belief*, directed by Alex Gibney, written by Alex Gibney and Lawrence Wright, aired March 29, 2015, on HBO, at 1:50:12.

100 YEARS of PUBLISHING

———◇———

Harold K. Guinzburg and George S. Oppenheimer founded Viking in 1925 with the intention of publishing books "with some claim to permanent importance rather than ephemeral popular interest." After merging with B. W. Huebsch, a small publisher with a distinguished catalog, Viking enjoyed almost fifty years of literary and commercial success before merging with Penguin Books in 1975.

Now an imprint of Penguin Random House, Viking specializes in bringing extraordinary works of fiction and nonfiction to a vast readership. In 2025, we celebrate one hundred years of excellence in publishing. Our centennial colophon will feature the original logo for Viking, created by the renowned American illustrator Rockwell Kent: a Viking ship that evokes enterprise, adventure, and exploration, ideas that inspired the imprint's name at its founding and continue to inspire us.

———◇———

For more information on Viking's history, authors, and books, please visit penguin.com/viking.